Lecture Notes in Artificial Intelligence   2581

Subseries of Lecture Notes in Computer Science
Edited by J. G. Carbonell and J. Siekmann

Lecture Notes in Computer Science
Edited by G. Goos, J. Hartmanis, and J. van Leeuwen

T0233028

Springer
Berlin
Heidelberg
New York
Hong Kong
London
Milan
Paris
Tokyo

Jaime Simão Sichman   François Bousquet
Paul Davidsson (Eds.)

Multi-Agent-Based Simulation II

Third International Workshop, MABS 2002
Bologna, Italy, July 15-16, 2002
Revised Papers

 Springer

Series Editors

Jaime G. Carbonell, Carnegie Mellon University, Pittsburgh, PA, USA
Jörg Siekmann, University of Saarland, Saarbrücken, Germany

Volume Editors

Jaime Simão Sichman
University of São Paulo, Polytechnical School
Computer Engineering Department, Intelligent Techniques Laboratory
Av. Prof. Luciano Gualberto, 158, travessa 3, 05424-970, São Paulo, Brazil
E-mail: jaime.sichman@poli.usp.br

François Bousquet
IRRI-Cirad
P.O. Box 9-159, Chatuchak 10900 Bangkok, Thailand
E-mail: bousquet@cirad.fr

Paul Davidsson
Blekinge Institute of Technology
Department of Software Engineering and Computer Science
P.O. Box 520, 372 25 Ronneby, Sweden
E-mail: paul.davidsson@bth.se

Cataloging-in-Publication Data applied for

A catalog record for this book is available from the Library of Congress.

Bibliographic information published by Die Deutsche Bibliothek.
Die Deutsche Bibliothek lists this publication in the Deutsche Nationalbibliografie;
detailed bibliographic data is available in the Internet at <http://dnb.ddb.de>.

CR Subject Classification (1998): I.2.11, I.2, I.6, C.2.4, J.4, H.5

ISSN 0302-9743
ISBN 3-540-00607-9 Springer-Verlag Berlin Heidelberg New York

Springer-Verlag Berlin Heidelberg New York
a member of BertelsmannSpringer Science+Business Media GmbH

http://www.springer.de

© Springer-Verlag Berlin Heidelberg 2003
Printed in Germany

Typesetting: Camera-ready by author, data conversion by PTP-Berlin, Stefan Sossna e.K.
Printed on acid-free paper   SPIN: 10872386   06/3142   5 4 3 2 1 0

Preface

This volume presents extended and revised versions of the papers presented at the Third International Workshop on Multi-Agent Based Simulation (MABS 2002), a workshop federated with the First International Joint Conference on Autonomous Agents and Multi-Agent Systems (AAMAS 2002), which was held in Bologna, Italy, in July, 2002.

This workshop was the third in the MABS series. The earlier two were organized as workshops of the two most recent ICMAS conferences (ICMAS 1998, Paris, France and ICMAS 2000, Boston, USA). Revised versions of the papers presented at these workshops were published as volumes 1534 and 1979 in the Lecture Notes in Artificial Intelligence series.

One aim of the workshop was to develop stronger links between those working in the social sciences and those involved with multi-agent systems. We are pleased to note that many important conferences in various disciplines such as geography, economics, ecology, sociology, and physics have hosted workshops on MABS-related topics and that many respected journals publish papers that include elements of MABS. But although MABS is gradually acquiring legitimacy in many disciplinary fields, much remains to be done to clarify the potential use of MABS in these disciplines. Researchers from these disciplines have different points of view on issues such as time-frame, space, geographical scales, organizational levels, etc. Moreover, the interest in MABS goes beyond the scientific community, as MABS models have been developed and used interactively with other communities as well. For instance, research is being done on the interactions between societies of robots and groups of people, and simulation models are being developed with stakeholders for environmental issues in a participatory way, through the Internet or directly in the field. These new approaches lead to new research questions regarding the use of MABS for collective decision making, but also regarding the conceptual and technical aspects of MABS.

Within this framework of interactions between artificial and human societies, special attention was given to the conceptual and technical aspects (agent architecture, interaction protocols, simulation platforms, modeling protocols, time and space representation, presentation of simulation results) resulting from these interactions and favoring them.

A total of 26 papers were submitted to the workshop. After having been reviewed by at least two referees, 12 were accepted for presentation. After the workshop, all papers were extended and revised, and reviewed a second time. At the workshop Alexis Drogoul gave an invited talk and an article by him and his colleagues has been added to those accepted for the workshop proceedings.

We are very grateful to the participants who engaged enthusiastically in the discussions about both individual papers and the general issues facing the MABS community. We are also grateful to the authors for their punctuality and the grace with which they received and responded to the second round reviews. We would like to thank Keith Decker, the AAMAS 2002 workshop chair, for having selected the Multi-Agent Based Simulation workshop among a large number of interesting proposals. We are also grateful to Maria Gini and Toru Ishida, the AAMAS 2002 general chairs, and to Cristiano Castelfranchi and Lewis Johnson, the AAMAS 2002 program chairs, for having organized such an excellent conference. Particularly, we would like to express our gratitude to Andrea Omicini and Franco Zambonelli, the AAMAS 2002 local organization chairs, for arranging the infrastructure for the workshop.

Finally, we thank Alfred Hofmann and his team at Springer-Verlag for giving us the opportunity to continue to disseminate the results of the multi-agent based simulation research agenda to a broader audience.

São Paulo, November 2002   Jaime Simão Sichman
                                                        François Bousquet
                                                        Paul Davidsson

Workshop Chairs

Jaime Simão Sichman (University of São Paulo, Brazil)
François Bousquet (IRRI-Cirad, Thailand)
Paul Davidsson (Blekinge Institute of Technology, Sweden)

Program Committee

Innocent Bakam (University of Douala, Cameroon)
Rafael Bordini (Federal University of Rio Grande do Sul, Brazil)
François Bousquet (CIRAD/IRRI, Thailand)
Helder Coelho (University of Lisbon, Portugal)
Rosaria Conte (IP/CNR, Italy)
Paul Davidsson (Blekinge Institute of Technology, Sweden)
Jim Doran (University of Essex, UK)
Alexis Drogoul (University Paris VI, France)
Nigel Gilbert (University of Surrey, UK)
Mat Hare (University of Zurich, Switzerland)
Wander Jager (University of Groningen, The Netherlands)
Marco Janssen (Indiana University, USA)
Scott Moss (University of Manchester, UK)
Christof le Page (CIRAD, France)
Jouliette Rouchier (GREQAM/CNRS, France)
Keith Sawyer (Washington University in St. Louis, USA)
Jaime Simão Sichman (University of São Paulo, Brazil) **(Chair)**
Klaus Troitzsch (University of Koblenz, Germany)
John Tyler (MITRE Corporation, USA)
Harko Verhagen (University of Stockholm, Sweden)

Table of Contents

Invited Paper

Emergence, Alliances, and Groups

MABS Platforms and Languages

MABS Applications

Multi-agent Based Simulation: Where Are the Agents?

Alexis Drogoul, Diane Vanbergue, and Thomas Meurisse

LIP6 – Université Paris 6 – 4 Place Jussieu 75252 PARIS CEDEX 05
{Alexis.Drogoul, Diane.Vanbergue, Thomas.Meurisse}@lip6.fr

Abstract. This paper is devoted to exploring the relationships between computational agents, as they can be found in multi-agent systems (MAS) or Distributed Artificial Intelligence (DAI), and the different techniques regrouped under the generic name "multi-agent based simulation" (MABS). Its main purpose is to show that MABS, despite its name, is in fact rarely based on computational agents. We base our demonstration on an innovative presentation of the methodological process used in the development of current MABS systems. This presentation relies on the definition of the different roles involved in the design process, and we are able to show that the notion of "agent", although shared at a conceptual level by the different participants, does not imply a systematic use of computational agents in the systems deployed. We then conclude by discussing what the use of computational agents, based on the most interesting research trends in DAI or MAS, might provide MABS with.

1 Introduction

1.1 Multi-agent Based Simulation

Multi-agent based simulation is nowadays used in a growing number of areas, where it progressively replaces the various micro-simulation [1], object-oriented [2] or individual-based simulation techniques [3] previously used. It is due, for the most part, to its ability to cope with very different models of "individuals", ranging from simple entities (usually called "reactive" agents [4]) to more complex ones ("cognitive" agents [5]). The easiness with which modelers can also handle different levels of representation (e.g., "individuals" and "groups", for instance) within an unified conceptual framework is also particularly appreciated, with respect, for instance, to cellular automata [6].

This versatility makes MABS emerge as the support of choice for the simulation of complex systems, and, if we are to trust the proceedings of the various events dedicated to it (i.e., MABS, Simulating Societies, ABS, etc.) since the last ten years, it is appealing to more and more scientific domains : sociology [7,10,11,13], biology [8,14], physics [15], chemistry [8], ecology [9], economy [12] etc.

J.S. Sichman, F. Bousquet, P. Davidsson (Eds.): MABS 2002, LNAI 2581, pp. 1-15, 2003.

1.2 Syntax and Semantics

This success is, however, ambiguous. While most of the researchers seem to agree on a common terminology for designating the core multi-agent concepts used in MABS, it appears that this agreement is, at best, syntactic. The semantics associated differ considerably from one model to another, or from one implementation to another. What do the agents described in MANTA [14] have in common with the ones used in Sichman's work [16] ? Nothing beside the label. How come that it is usually impossible to compare two different implementations of the same "specifications" (see, e.g., these papers about Sugarscape [17,18,19]) ? What are the differences between the various platforms available, like Swarm, MadKit, StarLogo, CORMAS, etc. and which one should be chosen given a particular project ? This fuzziness, at the computational level, about *what an agent really is* can be found in all the other levels required for the design of a simulation. Domain experts (*thematicians*, as we will call them later) have, at best, a sketchy idea about what is really allowed or not for defining their models. Contrary to numerical simulation, where their knowledge can only be represented by variables and relationships between variables, MABS allows, in theory, for a much wider range of representations : formulae, rules, heuristics, procedures, etc. This wealth is source of confusion for many thematicians and, eventually, disillusion during the course of a project, since only a few of them really know *how* this knowledge is to be computationally translated and interpreted (it may depend on the platform, the architecture of the MAS, even the language used).

As a matter of fact, in most MABS researches, the languages used by thematicians, modelers and computer scientists, while syntactically coherent, often hide important semantic disparities [10,20]. As long as these discrepancies remain implicit, and do not end up in strong incompatibilities, they can be "masked" with the — unfortunately traditional — help of little "compromises" at the computational level. But the negative side-effect is that there is absolutely no guarantee that what is being designed and implemented corresponds to what has been desired and modeled by the thematician [45]. Furthermore, as far as multi-agent systems are concerned, another consequence of these discrepancies is that, in order to agree upon a shared notion of "agent", the researchers have to make it "weak", i.e. as consensual as possible given their different backgrounds. An "agent" is then described as an "autonomous", "proactive", "interacting" entity, but we will show in this paper that these features, defined at a metaphorical level, do not translate into computational properties. Computational agents as they are defined in MAS [5] are simply not used in today's MABS.

To illustrate this opinion, we will review, in section 2, the main methodological proposals for multi-agent simulation found in the recent literature. We will show that they underestimate most of the difficulties found in building the computational model, which leads us to propose, in section 3, our own methodological framework (more details may also be found in [21]). We use this framework, in section 4, to detail the models in which the concept of agent is being used and conclude, in section 5, on the benefits that agent-based computational models could provide to MABS. The assumptions found in this paper are based on our experience in MABS, which we used, for instance, for simulating biological [14], physical [22], social [23] or economic systems [12].

2 Designing MABS: Methodologies

2.1 Fishwick [24,25]

Fishwick, in [24], defines computer simulation as the discipline of designing a model of an actual or theoretical physical system, executing the model on a digital computer, and analysing the execution output. The *model design* associates the real system with a representation of this system (*the model*). The data gathered to build this model may be 'real observations' (numerical values), or knowledge (a more subjective point of view on the system) and are usually formalized using formal semantics or mathematical logic to reduce ambiguities as much as possible. It is then converted to algorithms, which will run on a computer in the *model execution* phases to produce numerical outputs. The third stage, called *execution analysis*, deals with the analysis and confrontation of the results of the program with the behaviours observed in the model.

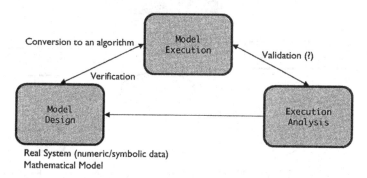

Fig. 1. Fishwick's succession of tasks (taken from [24])

Generally, researchers are more interested in *model design* [24]. The *model execution* (the execution on a digital computer of a particular program) and the *execution analysis* (analysis of results of this program) are viewed as a less scientific work, more relevant to specialized techniques (executing the program and analysing the results can be automated in particular cases). Thus, *model design* reflects *"how we should design and engineer models from concepts to something that can be executed on a computer"* [25].

Each of these stages (model design, model execution, execution analysis) is tightly coupled with the others, and the whole process of simulation consists in a finite number of iterations between them.

The problem in this proposal is that the translation of the initial model to a computational model seems to be "natural". There seems to be no additional steps between designing a model and implementing it, although, as pointed out by [26]: "[any] *implementation of a model (…) will again likely raise major problems because of the many ways in which particular specified abilities may be refined into computational detail."*

2.2 Gilbert and Troitzsch [27,11,2]

Gilbert and Troitzsch [27] somehow refine this diagram (see figure 2) by adding the *model building* step: once the model is designed, its translation into something usable on a computer involves writing a special program. As they show it in [27], no programming language can provide the designer with all the prerequisites for simulation (well structured, efficient, allowing incremental refinement and an easy and rapid debugging, with good graphics libraries, portable and familiar for both the modelers and the computer engineers). Therefore, the conversion of the model to an algorithm is not as trivial as suggested by Fishwick, whatever the formal aspect of the model, and can be source of problems of non-replicability, as pointed out by Axelrod [28]. The transformation of the formal model into a computer program is not a straightforward operation, but they do not detail other steps between the two representations.

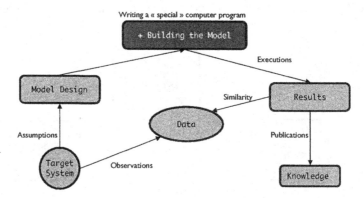

Fig. 2. Gilbert's and Troitzsch's methodological proposal (the diagram has been drawn by us and does not appear in [27])

3   Design as a "Role-Playing Game"

These two proposals, although useful when it comes to understand how to design a simulation, have two major drawbacks for our purpose : (1) they do not specifically address *multi-agent* based simulation, but rather *computer* simulation in general; (2) they are mainly task-oriented, rather than model-oriented, and make it difficult to understand the difficulties found in translating conceptual to computational models.

If we want, first, to carefully express these difficulties and, second, to offer some solutions for them, we have to focus on *what* is being produced by *whom* during the life cycle of a simulation before detailing, like in the previous diagrams, *how* or *when* it should be produced [29].

Let us, then, begin to describe the roles that are involved in the design process, i.e. the different actors who will interact to produce a running simulation and their contributions. This notion of "roles" has been implicitly used by Edmonds and others (see for example [29]), but not really explained.

We can define them intuitively as follows : on the one hand, we have a target system (see Figure 2), which characterizes the phenomenon to predict or the theory that needs explanations. This part involves experts in a particular domain or in a specific theme: we shall call them *thematicians*. On the other hand, since the simulation is being run on computers, we need experts in computer science to actually build the programs: the *computer scientists*. Yet, as shown in a discussion in [ref Fishwhick], the conceptual gap between those two communities (thematicians and computer scientists) can be very important. A third community is then usually involved in the process of *building simulations* (design, building, execution, analysis): the *modelers*.

3.1 The Thematician

The thematician defines the intention of the simulation process, i.e. the association between the target system and the application of the simulation. He manipulates three kinds of data about the target system [46]:

- ☐ theories and assumptions (what he knows or estimates), which define a set of precepts associated with the specified domain.
- ☐ observations (what he sees or analyzes), which are data relative to the phenomena; they can be required to provide the parameters and initial conditions to the simulation tool, but they can also describe qualitative aspects of the phenomenon.
- ☐ questions (what he wants to understand). They can be classified into three categories : predictive ("What will happen in xx years?"), speculative ("What if we change this parameter ?"), or theoretical questions ("Which of these assumptions may explain the phenomenon ?").

Although this classification is valid for any kind of simulation, we have observed (in previous work, see, e.g. [14,12,23,22,6]) that all the thematicians interested in *multi-agent* simulations share the same profile : they usually handle two levels of knowledge at the same time, which we shall call their micro- and macro-knowledge. The latter being a set of "global" knowledge about the target system, mostly obtained from the observations, while the former is "local" knowledge about the "individuals" without which the target system would not exist; it is composed of both observations (behaviors, etc.) and assumptions. Most of these thematicians enter the design of MABS precisely because they are interested in linking these two levels, i.e. in understanding and making the contributions of the "individuals'" behaviors to the global system explicit, in situations where they cannot explain them neither deductively nor analytically.

In an agent-based formalism, be it intuitive, the micro-knowledge is translated into what we call a *domain model*, which contains "agents" provided with the behaviors and data taken from the relevant observations, assumptions or theories (see figure 3). It is usually defined using a domain-specific language (the semantics associated with the target system), which is often little formalized. The macro-knowledge is used later on, to provide scenarios and measures for the simulation. In this domain model, the thematician handles "real" agents, i.e. agents that can be observed and analyzed in the target system.

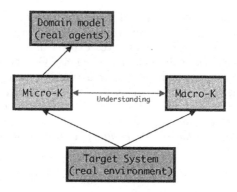

Fig. 3. Data manipulated by the thematician in the design of a simulation

Of course, in most cases, the theories associated with the target system do not define a consistent set of hypotheses. For example, in social science, as pointed out by [26], theories remain controversial in many respects and, from a computational point of view, typically ambiguous. This is why, usually, other intermediary models are necessary before building the actual simulation program [29].

3.2 The Modeler

Since the specifications of the thematician do not allow for a direct transcription to an operational solution, because the two fields have different semantics, the *domain model* has to be translated into something more formal that can be, eventually, implemented by a computer scientist. This is the duty of the *modeler*. His role is to clear the concepts and remove the ambiguities by specifying what we call a *design model*. To understand its position in the simulation process, one might say that this model is to an agent-based implementation what an UML diagram is to an object-oriented program.

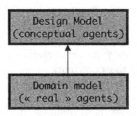

Fig. 4. Models managed by the modeler

The modeler handles *conceptual agents*, i.e. agents that constitute a formal refinement of the previous ones. Their properties are expressed using concepts taken from multi-agent systems [5] : behavioral model, interactions, communications, type of environment, etc. (see figure 5).

The design model is probably the most difficult model to define, since it depends on the information provided by the thematician and on some constraints inherent to the implementation chosen (which may, or not, be known at the time of design). His construction is rarely straightforward but results from several iterations between the two levels [47]. As such, it constitutes an ideal meeting and discussion point for the three roles we are defining.

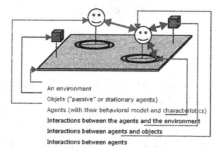

An environment
Objets ("passive" or stationary agents)
Agents (with their behavioral model and characteristics)
Interactions between the agents and the environment
Interactions between agents and objects
Interactions between agents

Fig. 5. An example of the information found in a *design model*

3.3 The Computer Scientist

The aim of the computer scientist is not only to write a computer program (although it is his main duty), but also to propose a model that could allow for a discussion with the modeler. Without this model, his propositions and choices may not receive any feedback from the two other roles.

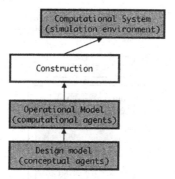

Fig. 6. Models taken in charge by the computer scientist

Shaping the *operational model* is an operation that immediately precedes the actual construction of the *computational system*. In this model, the computer scientist ought to handle *computational agents*, i.e. agents as an implementation technique (like objects). The semantics associated with the *operational model* is thus constrained by the possibilities of the implementation. This model is often overridden and directly replaced by the implementation, since the computer scientist, in many institutions, is still considered as a simple "technician" [39]. But it is important to understand that his point of view on the global simulation, expressed through this operational model, allows the two other roles to understand, and even change, what is going to be implemented. In particular, by specifying technical properties such as the distribution of the agents, the time scheduling techniques used, etc., and by giving them an existence in the global model, he may facilitate the comparison between different models or help understanding the role of computational-specific features in the emergence of structures in a simulation [41].

3.4 Summary

In this description of, we associate each model (domain, design and operational ones) with a specific role. It is important to note that people involved in simulation design are not usually aware of the implication (or existence) of these three roles. As a matter of fact, this decomposition is seldom made according to an association <role, actor>. It frequently happens that one and the same person takes on two different roles. For example, a domain expert can incarnate both the role of the thematician and that of the modeler if the domain lends itself to a quasi-formal transcription (not ambiguous; see for instance [15]). In the same way, the computer scientist may take on the role of modeler if his knowledge allows him to correctly apprehend the domain of the target system (it is the case in MANTA [14]). For fairly simple target systems, an actor can even take on the three roles, for instance when a thematician comes to implement obvious operational solutions (in the case of analytical models like simple systems of differential equations or for testing ideas in an ad-hoc environment like StarLogo [8]). However, it is advisable not to rely on this kind of solution, especially for complex target systems, since the modeler and the computer scientist usually bring useful know-how in terms of conceptual and operational models.

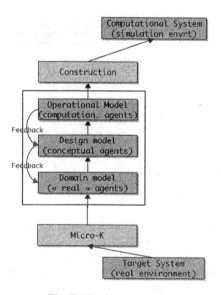

Fig. 7. The design process

If we correctly connect the models taken in charge by the three roles, we obtain the framework depicted on figure 7, which describes only a part of the simulation design process. The whole process is described on figure 8 below (a detailed explanation can be found in [21]), the horizontal layers of which correspond to the different roles. It consists in a succession of models that proceed from the real environment to the simulation environment. Every iteration is of course possible between these models, although, for clarity reasons, only the most obvious ones have been drawn on the figure.

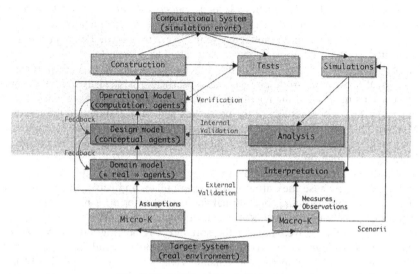

Fig. 8. The whole methodological process

These diagrams are intended to serve as guidelines for designers of multi-agent simulations, but they can also be used as an evaluation framework for existing MABS. In particular, they may help researchers to understand where their work fits within a simulation. As far as we are concerned, they will help us to review the use of "agents" in agent-based simulations.

4   (Computational) Agents?

4.1 Where Can "Agents" Be Found?

Theoretically, all the roles described before should play with a notion of agent, be it formalized or not. However, as we have shown in Section 1, this is merely a syntactic agreement that makes different communities believe they have found a *lingua franca* which can override the frontiers between the different domains of research. The "agents" used to shape each model (domain, design and operational one) ought to be defined differently (because of the difference between the semantics, and, therefore, the languages, used by the different roles) : for instance, although the agents described in the domain model will serve as a basis for the ones that will populate the operational model, they will probably be less formalized. Ideally, a parallel could be drawn between the use of "agents" in MABS and the use of "objects" in object-oriented programming [5]. The latter are used in analysis, as a support for reification, in design, as a support for the various diagrams found for example in UML, and in programming, with a strong operational semantics and languages that offer a direct manipulation of the necessary abstractions (inheritance, instantiation, etc.).

Similarly, agents can be found in the domain model, as *metaphors* of autonomous, proactive, communicating and interacting "individuals" of the target system. They can also be found in the design model, as a *conceptual support* used to formalize the definition of these individuals in terms of behaviors, communication models, etc. But, as far as we know, they cannot be found, yet, in any of the operational models presented so far in the conferences dedicated to MABS. Instead of using agent-oriented languages, people tend to use either object-oriented or logical, procedural or functional languages to implement the specifications described in the conceptual agents. This means that the resulting "computational agents" (if we can still call them this way) do not possess any of the properties generally assigned to the agents used in MAS or DAI [5]: they do not have any structural nor decisional autonomy, are not proactive, and cannot, for instance, modify their knowledge and behaviors through learning or adaptation.

We do not use agents to implement agent-based simulations, but only to design them, mainly because they are easier to manipulate, and (given the resulting lack of any associated constricting operational semantics) offer a lot more expressivity than objects or functions for the thematician or even the modeler[1]. The reason is to be found in the relative weakness of the software engineering side of MAS: there are many methodologies or agent-oriented languages available, but no strong commitment to a given operational semantics (this point is developed in [48]).

The bottom line is that *agents nowadays constitute a convenient model for representing autonomous entities, but they are not themselves autonomous in the resulting implementation of these models.*

4.2 Why Use Computational Agents in MABS?

The question immediately raised by this statement is : since no one seems to use computational agents to implement conceptual agents, would the former be of any help in multi-agent based simulations ? We believe so, just because there are absolutely no reasons why designing simulations would be different from designing other applications. Beyond today's mainstream techniques, mainly based on objects and components, computational agents represent the future of computation (see, for example, [49]). To be more concrete, we can break their potential usefulness down into four possible applications (chosen because of their generality: they might be used in any MABS): participatory design, agent-aided interpretation, system-level adaptation and agent-aided calibration.

4.2.1   Participatory Design of Simulations
One of the most difficult parts, when designing MABS, is the formalization of the behaviors of the agents after they have been defined (not formally) by the

---

[1]Which, by the way, explains the popularity of MABS, but does not clarify its position.

thematician. This extraction of knowledge may require several iterations before it satisfies all the actors involved. The recent rise of *participatory simulations* has opened a whole new field of research in this area, by allowing experts and non-experts to interactively define these behaviors, through role-playing games or by being immersed as "human agents" in a running simulation [50]. The resulting behaviors, however, are still hand-coded by computer scientists.

Fig. 9. Participatory design, involving experts and autonomous computational agents

Autonomous agents can be advantageously used in this process. They may, for example, play a twofold role (see figure 9): that of computational abstractions for implementing the simulation and that of "assistant-like" or "profiling" agents [30] dedicated to an user or an expert. If they are provided with adequate learning capabilities, they may then autonomously adjust or acquire their behavior through repeated interactions with (or observations of) their "user". This kind of learning procedures are being actively investigated in many subfields of AI under different names: Adjustable Autonomy [31], Learning by Imitation [32], Learning by Demonstration [33], Social Learning [34], Interactive Situated Learning [35], etc. One of their main advantages is that the agent may learn its behavior "in situation" and in a progressive way, and that the expert is really involved in this process [37]. The downside is that it requires, until now, domain-dependant formalisms for representing actions and contexts, which means that generic architectures will not be available before long. However, researches on this subject have already been launched in several simulation projects, and we are confident that machine learning, through agent-based simulation, will be part of any modelers' toolkit in a few years.

4.2.2   Agent-Aided Interpretation
In large-scale systems that involve thousands or millions of agents, understanding the dynamics of a simulation can be, surprisingly, as difficult as in the real world [38]. The complexity due to the number of agents, especially when they are probabilistically interacting, is absolutely similar to that of a natural system (see [22] for an example of such a system in the hydrological domain).

To ease the analysis of the results, one solution could be to provide the agents, beside their factual behavior, with local interpretation capabilities. In this way, the agents could serve as a computational support for both the domain/conceptual models and the interpretation mechanisms described in figure 8. It is a way to distribute the macro-knowledge of the thematician among the agents. It requires that the agents have access to different levels of abstractions [36], similar to the ones used by the thematician, in order for them, for example, to automatically instantiate, within the simulation, "macro" agents that could represent a specific emergent phenomenon.

Servat's work [22] is a good example of such an approach, as it has shown the accuracy and the usefulness of such agent-aided interpretations in the case of very complex simulations of hydrological networks. Following the conclusion of his paper, we strongly believe that there is a place of choice for self-monitoring, reflective architectures of agents within the future MABS.

4.2.3   System-Level Adaptation

As the complexity of the systems targeted by multi-agent based simulation increase [40], it is also necessary to consider that the computational environment be physically distributed among several networked machines. This kind of distribution raises a lot of problems (see, for instance [42]) among which the most critical are the necessity to maintain a coherent global state and to reduce the disparities between the portions of the simulation that run on different machines, the necessity to balance the load between the nodes of the network, and the necessity to make the whole system tolerant to faults or malfunctions that may happen on individual nodes.

Due to their inherent distribution, MAS have already been proposed to address these problems at the system level, through the use of mobile agents (see, for instance, [43]). These researches allow the distribution to become transparent for the users and to be constantly revised in an adaptive way with respect to the state of the network. Coupling these agents to the agents already designed in the simulation would allow for an even more interesting property: that of making the distribution not only dynamic, but also tightly adapted to the peculiarities of the simulation. Load balancing, for instance, could be improved by regrouping agents that, given the current state, are likely to interact in a future state.

More interestingly, the levels of abstraction managed on the simulation side (agents, groups, communities) could correspond to the levels of distribution on the network side, thus allowing the development of much easier to maintain and to understand distributed simulation systems [43].

4.2.4   Agent-Aided Calibration

The last, but not the least, application in which computational agents could prove useful in multi-agent simulation is the calibration process, which is, in many cases, similar to a distributed constraint-solving problem. In fact, beside the basic calibration of parameters (which is a task shared with all the other techniques of simulation and for which dedicated tools may be employed), one of the most difficult tasks found in MABS is the generation of large realistic populations of agents when the data provided by the thematician only concerns small samples. For instance, suppose, in a social simulation project, that one has to simulate a city inhabited by 40.000 people and that the data at hand only represent a set of 100 different profiles, plus global data such as averages or distributions of the population with respect to certain parameters : the difficulty is not to generate the 40.000 agents, but to make the artificial population comply to the global constraints. It is comparable to a multi-criterion optimization process and, as such, requires advanced tools, some of which are still being the subject of active research.

Viewing the agents as autonomous computational entities can be quite useful in providing the designer with conforming populations. An example is given by [12], who uses genetic algorithms at the agents' level to generate such populations in a consumer market simulation: global and individual fitnesses are expressed in terms of compliance of the population to the global measures, and compliance of the individual agent to existing profile. The agents die, reproduce themselves, and iteratively converge to a solution. In fact, there are many problems found in MABS than can be translated quite easily into multi-agent problems, for which Distributed Problem Solving [4,44] may offer robust and efficient techniques, brought into operation by the agents themselves.

5 Conclusion

In this paper, we have presented the description of a model-based methodological framework for designing multi-agent simulations. This has helped us to demonstrate that the existing simulations, although they claim to be agent-based, only use a weak notion of "agent" at the metaphorical or conceptual level, but do not use any computational agents at the operational level. This is due, for the most part, to the lack of a clear operational semantics for the implementation of multi-agent systems. Despite this, we have identified some applications where the use of computational agents inspired by the ones investigated in Distributed AI or Multi-Agent Systems could be helpful for the modelers. Our immediate perspectives are, on one hand, to develop our methodological framework in order to propose both a modeling language and a semantics dedicated to the operational level, and, on the other hand, to experiment agent-based participatory design in two different projects (one on the simulation of the coffee market in Veracruz, Mexico, and the other on the simulation of populations of fishermen along the Mekong River).

References

[1]   Orcutt, G.H.: A new type of socio-economic system. Review of Economics and Statistics 39 (1957) 116–123
[2]   Troitzsch, K.G.: Social science simulation – origins, prospects, purposes. Simulating Social Phenomena 456 (1997) 41–54
[3]   Harding, A.: Modeling techniques for examining the impact of population ageing on social expenditure. In: Conference on the Policy implications of the Ageing of Australia's Population, Melbourne, NATSEM (1999)
[4]   Drogoul, A. When Ants Play Chess. in From reaction to cognition. C. Castelfranchi & J. P. Müller, eds. Berlin-Heidelberg, Springer-Verlag. 957: 13–27. (1995)
[5]   Jennings N., « On agent-based software engineering », AI Journal,117, 277–296, (2000).
[6]   Vanbergue, D., Treuil J-P., Drogoul A.. Modelling urban phenomena with cellular automata. In Applications of Simulation to Social Science. G. Ballot & G. Weisbuch, eds. Hermes, Paris, France. (2000)
[7]   Pietrula, M., Carley, K., Gasser, L.: Simulating Organizations. M.I.T. Press (1998)
[8]   M. Resnick, Turtles, Termites and Traffic Jams, MIT Press, Cambridge, US (1995).
[9]   Huberman, B., Glance, N.: Evolutionary games and computer simulations. In: Proceedings of the National Academy of Science USA. (1993) 7716–7718

[10] Goldspink, C.: Methodological implications of complex systems approaches to sociality: Simulation as a foundation for knowledge. Journal of Artificial Societies and Social Simulation 5 (2002) http://www.soc.surrey.ac.uk/JASSS/5/1/3.html.

[11] Gilbert, N.: Computer simulation of social processes. Social Research Update 6 (1993)

[12] Ben Said L., Bouron T., Drogoul A., Agent-based interaction analysis of consumer behavior, proceedings of the First International Joint Conference on Autonomous Agents and Multi-Agent Systems (AAMAS'02), Bologna, Italy (2002)

[13] Axtell, R.: Why agents ? on the varied motivations for agent computing in the social sciences. Technical Report 17, Center on Social and Economics Dynamics – The Brookings Institution (2000)

[14] Drogoul A., Corbara B., Fresneau D., MANTA: New Experimental Results on the Emergence of (Artificial) Ant Societies, in Artificial Societies: the computer simulation of social life, Gilbert N. & Conte R. (Eds), UCL Press, London. (1995)

[15] Schweitzer F., Zimmermann J, Communication and Self-Organization in Complex Systems: A Basic Approach, in: Knowledge, Complexity and Innovation Systems (Eds. M. M. Fischer, J. Fröhlich), Springer, Berlin (2001)

[16] Jaime Simão Sichman. DEPINT: Dependence-Based Coalition Formation in an Open Multi-Agent Scenario, Journal of Artificial Societies and Social Simulation vol. 1, no. 2, (1998) <http://www.soc.surrey.ac.uk/JASSS/1/2/3.html>

[17] Lawson, B.G., Park, S.: Asynchronous time evolution in an artificial society mode. Journal of Artificial Societies and Social Simulation 3 (2000) http://www.soc.surrey.ac.uk/JASSS/3/1/2.html.

[18] Terna, P.: Creating artificial worlds: A note on sugarscape and two comments. Journal of Artificial Societies and Social Simulation 4 (2001) http://www.soc.surrey.ac.uk/ JASSS/4/2/9.html.

[19] Epstein, J.M., Axtell, R.L.: Growing Artificial Societies : Social Science from the Bottom Up. MIT Press (1996)

[20] Hannerman, R.: Simulation modeling and theoretical analysis in sociology. Sociological Perspectives 38 (1995) 457–462

[21] Vanbergue D., Meurisse T. Drogoul A.,A methodological framework for MABS, in prep., to be submitted to JASSS.

[22] Servat, D., Perrier E., Treuil J-P. Drogoul A.,. When Agents Emerge from Agents: Introducing Multi-Scale Viewpoints in Multi-Agent Simulations. Proceedings of MABS'98, 183–198, LNAI n° 1534, Springer-Verlag, Berlin. (1998)

[23] El Hadouaj S., Drogoul A., Espié S., How to Combine Reactivity and Anticipation: the Case of Conflicts Resolution in a Simulated Road Traffic, proceedings of MABS'2000, Springer Verlag LNAI series, Boston, USA. (2000)

[24] Fishwick, P.: Computer simulation: growth through extension. IEEE Potential February/ March (1996) 24 to 27

[25] Fishwick P., Simulation Model Design and Execution, Prentice Hall, (1995)

[26] Doran, J.: From computer simulation to artificial societies. Transactions of the Society for Computer Simulation 14 (1997) Special Issue: Multi-agent systems and Simulation.

[27] Gilbert, N., Troitzsch, K.G.: Simulation for the Social Scientist. Open University Press (1999)

[28] Axelrod, R.: Advancing the art of simulation in social sciences. In Conte, R., Hegselmann, R., Terna, P., eds.: Simulating Social Phenomena. Springer, Berlin (1997) 21–40

[29] Edmonds, B.: The use of models – making MABS more informative. In Moss, S., Davidson, P., eds.: Multi-Agent Based Simulation 2000. Volume 1979 of Lecture Notes in Artificial Intelligence. (2000) 15–32

[30] Maes, P., "Social Interface Agents: Acquiring Competence by Learning from Users and other Agents." Proceedings of the 1994 AAAI Spring Symposium on Software Agents, AAAI Press, Stanford, (1994).

[31] Chalupsky, H, Gil, Y., Knoblock, C., Lerman, K., Oh, J., Pynadath, D., Russ, T., Tambe, M. « Electric Elves: Applying Agent Technology to Support Human Organizations » International Conference on Innovative Applications of AI (IAAI'01). (2001).

[32] Dautenhahn, K. Getting to know each other – artificial social intelligence for autonomous robots. Robotics and Autonomous Systems 16. (1995)

[33] Gaussier, P., Moga, S., Banquet, J., and Quoy, M. From perception-action loops to imitation processes: A bottom-up approach of learning by imitation. Applied Artificial Intelligence 1, 7. (1997)

[34] Steels, L. and Kaplan, F. AIBO's first words. The social learning of language and meaning. In: Gouzoules, H. (ed) *Evolution of Communication*, vol. 4, nr. 1, Amsterdam: John Benjamins Publishing Company. (2001)

[35] Hugues, L. Drogoul A., Grounded Representations for a Robot Team. Proceedings of IROS 2000, IEEE/RSJ intern. Conference on Intelligent Robots and Systems, Japan, aug. 2000 (2000)

[36] Fianyo, E., Treuil, J., Perrier, E., Demazeau, Y.: Multi-agent architecture integrating heterogeneous models of dynamical processes: The representation of time. In Sichman, C., Gilbert, eds.: Multi-Agent Systems and Agent-Based Simulation. Volume 1534. Springer-Verlag, Berlin (1998) 226–236

[37] Hanneman, R. and Patrick, S. ,On the Uses of Computer-Assisted Simulation Modeling in the Social Sciences, Sociological Research Online, vol. 2, no. 2, http://www. socresonline.org.uk/socresonline/2/2/5.html (1997)

[38] Buss, S.R., Papadimitriou, C.H., Tsitsiklis, J.N.: on the predictability of coupled automata: an allegory about chaos. Complex Systems 5 (1991) 525–539

[39] Davidsson, P.: Agent based social simulation : A computer science view. Journal of Artificial Societies and Social Simulation 5(2002) http://www.soc.surrey.ac.uk/ JASSS/5/1/7.html.

[40] Brassel, K., Mohring, M., Schumacher, E., Troitzsch, K.G.: Can agents cover all the world ? Simulating Social Phenomena 456 (1997) 55–72

[41] Axtell, R.: Effects of interaction topology and activation regime in several multi-agent systems. In Moss, S., Davidson, P., eds.: Multi-Agent Based Simulation 2000. Volume 1979 of Lecture Notes in Artificial Intelligence. (2000) 33–48

[42] Glazer D. W., Tropper C., On Process Migration and Load Balancing in Time Warp, IEEE Transactions on Parallel and Distributed Systems, (1993) 318–327

[43] Michel, F., Bommel P., Ferber, J., Simulation interactive distribuée de SMA par des SMA, proceedings of JFIADSMA 2002 (French workshop on Multi-Agent Systems), Hermés, Paris, France. to appear (2002) (in French)

[44] Parunak, H.V.D.. Go to the Ant: Engineering Principles from Natural Agent Systems (1/97) Annals of Operations Research 75 69–101. 1997.

[45] Richardson, K.A.: Methodological implication of complex systems approaches to sociality : Some further remarks. Journal of Artificial Societies and Social Simulation 5 (2002) http://www.soc.surrey.ac.uk/JASSS/5/2/6.html.

[46] Troitzsch, K.G.: Methods of empirical social research. In: SICSS Summer School. (2000)

[47] Rasmussen, S., Barrett, C.L.: Elements of a theory of simulation. In: European Conference on Artificial Life. (1995) 515–529

[48] Prahladavaradan S., Modeling Multi-Agent Reactive Systems, Proceedings of ICLP 2002, LNCS, Springer-Verlag, to appear.

[49] Servat, D., Drogoul A., Combining amorphous computing and reactive agent based systems: a paradigm for pervasive intelligence?, proceedings of the First International Joint Conference on Autonomous Agents and Multi-Agent Systems (AAMAS'02), Bologna, Italy, (2002).

[50] Barreteau, O., Bousquet, F., and Attonaty, J.M. Role-playing games for opening the black box of multi-agent systems: method and lessons of its application to Senegal River Valley irrigated systems. Journal of Artificial Societies and Social Simulation 4(2) (2001)

BVG Choice in Axelrod's Tribute Model

Luis Antunes[1], Leonel Nóbrega[2], and Helder Coelho[1]

[1] Faculdade de Ciências, Universidade de Lisboa
Campo Grande, 1749-016 Lisboa, Portugal
{xarax,hcoelho}@di.fc.ul.pt
[2] Departamento de Matemática, Universidade da Madeira
Campus da Penteada, 9000-390 Funchal, Portugal
lnobrega@math.uma.pt

Abstract. We consider Robert Axelrod's tribute model at the light shed by the development of a choice framework called BVG (beliefs, values and goals). BVG agents use multi-varied, situated and individual rationality to perform adaptive choices in social environments. We then take the original experiment and carry it over using this choice scheme. By explicitly representing the agents preferences and the related decisional mechanisms, we are able to easily extend the experiment to tackle issues only implicitly addressed. The outcome of these new experiments is somewhat surprising, and seems to undermine the original conclusions. The experiments were carried out in a similar way to that of the original ones. However, we sustain that a more holistic attitude towards experimentation may be preferable. We conclude by arguing that the model of multiple values may help to principle the relation between experimenter and experiment, through the strengthening of bridges between the design of the experiment and the design of the agents involved in the simulation.

Keywords: Computer-based social simulation; choice models, Axelrod's tribute model; experimental methodologies for self-motivated agents.

1 Introduction

Simulation systems can give emphasis to various aspects: economical (eg. [5]), social (for instance the prisoner's dilemma game [3]), biological [6], or political [4]. In [4], Axelrod examines how political actors can emerge from aggregations of smaller political units. Unlike in most game theoretical models, the actors involved in the simulation are not given *a priori*. Instead, Axelrod shows how groups of actors behaving as independent political entities can emerge out of interactions of basic units, during the simulation of a "tribute" model where units compete with each other for "wealth."

In our previous work [1,2], we have been concerned with agent's decision, i.e., the choice of a preferred option from among a large set of alternatives, according to the precise context where they are immersed. Such a capability defines to what extent they are autonomous. But, there is no one way of deciding, and the classical mode of taking utility functions as the sole support is not adequate for

J.S. Sichman, F. Bousquet, P. Davidsson (Eds.): MABS 2002, LNAI 2581, pp. 16–25, 2003.
© Springer-Verlag Berlin Heidelberg 2003

situations constrained by qualitative features (such as wine selection, or putting together a football team). The BVG (beliefs-values-goals) agent architecture relies on the use of values (multiple dimensions against which to evaluate a situation) to perform choice among a set of candidate goals. Values can also be used to guide the adoption of new goals from other agents. We argue that agents should base their rationalities on choice rather than search.

In this paper, we take Axelrod's example and verify the effectiveness of the application of the multiple value scheme. We start by describing the example as it is originally presented, and then rebuild it in the BVG architecture. Then we show how this new scheme allows for the easy extension of the original experiment, and enrich it: in the models adopted for the description of the societies; in the models of agent; in the evaluation measures adopted; in the terms of the experiments. The kernel of the changes to the model is done through a movement of explicitation of the values involved.

2 Choice and Evaluation

The role of value as a mental attitude towards decision is to provide a reference framework to represent agent's preference during deliberation (the pondering of options candidate to contribute to a selected goal). In the BVG choice framework, the agent's system of values evolves as a consequence of the agent's assessment of the results of previous decisions. Decisions are evaluated against certain dimensions (that could be the same previously used for the decision or not), and this assessment is fed back into the agent's mind, by adapting the mechanisms associated with choice. This is another point that escapes the traditional utilitarian view, where the world (and so the agent) is static and known. BVG agents can adapt to an environment where everything changes, including the agent's own preferences (for instance as a result of interactions). This is especially important in a multi-agent environment, since the agents are autonomous, and so potentially sources of change and novelty.

The evaluation of the results of our evaluations becomes a central issue, and this question directly points to the difficulties in assessing the results of experiments. We would need meta-values to evaluate those results. But if those "higher values" exist (and so they are the important ones) why not use them for decision?

When tackling the issue of choice, the formulation of hypotheses and experimental predictions becomes delicate. If the designer tells the agent how to choose, how can he not know exactly how the agent will choose? To formulate experimental predictions and then evaluate to what extent they are fulfilled becomes a spurious game: it amounts to perform calculations about knowledge and reasons, and not to judge to what extent those reasons are the best reasons, and correctly generate the choices. We return to technical reasons for behaviour, in detriment of the will and the preferences of the agent.

By situating the agent in an environment with other agents, autonomy becomes a key ingredient, to be used with care and balance. The duality of value sets becomes a necessity, as agents cannot access values at the macro level, made judiciously coincide with the designer values. The answer is the designer, and the problem is methodological. The update mechanism provides a way to put to test this liaison between agent and designer. The designer's model of choice cannot be the model of perfect choice against which the whole world is to be evaluated. It is our strong conviction that the perfect choice does not exist. It is a model of choice to be compared to another one, by using criteria that in turn may not be perfect.

3   The Tribute Model

The basic units of the tribute model are ten actors, organised in a ring [4]. Each actor has some initial wealth, uniformly distributed between 300 and 500. In each cycle (called year), three actors are chosen to become active. An active actor can demand tribute (250) to its neighbour, and in turn, this can choose to pay or to fight, depending on which will cause less loss of wealth. Alliances are then introduced, according to a table of "commitments" between pairs or actors. An active actor can demand tribute from another if he can form a continuous sequence of allied countries one of each is neighbour to the target.

According to Axelrod, it isn't possible to develop completely rational rules for decision taking (obviously, for a "normal" notion of rationality). So, each agent uses heuristic rules of decision to capture some of the short term consideration the player find. The active actor chooses to demand tribute from a target that maximises the product of vulnerability for possible payment. The vulnerability is defined as $\frac{W_A - W_T}{W_A}$, where W_A and W_T are respectively the wealth of the attacker and of the target.

When actors engage in alliances, the commitment of actor i towards actor j increases (by 10%, until a maximum of 100%) when i pay tribute to j (subservience), i receives tribute from j (protection), or i fights in the same alliance than j (friendship). It decreases (by 10%, until a minimum of 0) when they fight in opposite alliances.

4   Re-representing the Model

The first thing to do is to determine which are the values involved, which is not always obvious. This is evident when Axelrod claims that only one resource is involved, without noting that commitments between actors can be seen as a resource. Actually, these are the main values involved here, and the calculus used for choice shows clearly that they are displayed in a hierarchy, where commitment has top priority, i.e., it is the most important value. This fact leads to an agent always respecting its commitment to another, even if that is damaging to its own wealth. But this fact also certifies that wealth is not the only resource involved.

So, leaving commitments out for the moment, the individual decision problem is solved by using the following rules, for attacking actor (a):

Demand if $Vuln_a(i) > 0$, to actor i (i neighbour of a)

so to maximise the product $Vuln_a(i) \times PossPay_a(i)$ (1)

Do nothing otherwise (2)

and for the attacked actor:

Fight if $Losses_{agent}(other) < PossPay_{other}(agent)$ (3)

Pay otherwise (4)

Now we add the additional value, commitment. Other modifications could be considered, like taking commitment as another resource to manage, or taking new actions *IncreaseCommitment* and *DecreaseCommitment*, now relevant to the decision making. If we don't embrace these questions is because they *change the character* of the problem.

The decision rules 1 to 4 can be kept with few changes, since the active actor still bases its decision in its individual gain, and not on the interest of its coalition. Besides, those coalitions depend on who the particular attacking and defending agents are. Despite the fact that the results sometimes show the formation of groups with common interests, there are also internal fights among the weaker partners inside those groups.

So, for the attacking actor (a)[1]:

Demand if $Target_a(i) \wedge Vuln_a(i) > 0$, to actor i

so to maximise the product $Vuln_a(i) \times PossPay_a(i)$ (5)

and for the attacked actor (t):

Fight if $Losses_t(t, a) < PossPay_t(a, t)$ (6)

This case is interesting because in deliberation there is one hierarchy of values, and in choice it is inverted. When each actor performs its calculations to decide if it should attack or not (or if it should join a coalition or not), commitment overcomes self interest in terms of wealth. But when it finally decides, the actor prefers the combination that provides greater gains for itself, neverminding the interests of its supporting group. In the light of the previous sections, it seems evident that there are more values at stake, namely, the *confidence* that our allies are really our allies, the *fickleness* of those allies, the *gratitude* (and consequent will of reciprocation) for the aid given, and of course the already mentioned *collective interests* in terms of *wealth*. Some of these values become relevant for the extensions to the model we present next, which illustrate the advantages of the BVG architecture.

5   Extensions to the Tribute Model

Axelrod himself examines his model and proposes some modifications, whose results he evaluates. Some of the most interesting from the decision-making

---

[1] For conciseness sake, we don't present all the necessary definitions, see [1].

standpoint are questions involving emergence of behaviours. (In the full paper we discuss some of these issues.)

We decided to experiment with the model by relaxing some of the constraints originally imposed. The one we chose to present in this paper deals with the variability of the acquisition of commitment towards other agent. Where Axelrod sets a (negative or positive) increment of 10%, we propose to use a variable quantity, which depends on a value we called fickleness: a fickler actor has bigger commitment increments. Following the original model, there aren't big changes in the rules, or their order of application. In particular, this new value is permanently in the top of the hierarchy, establishing the commitments, so determining the variations in wealth, through the results of decisions. The rules that set the dynamics of the relations among these values are the following (":=" is the symbol for assignment and ";" means sequencing of commands, i, j, k, l are actors, and v_a if fickleness of actor a):

$$
\begin{aligned}
&\text{If } Pays(i, j) \\
&\text{Then } Comm_i(j) := \max\{0, Comm_i(j) + v_i\}; \\
&\qquad\quad Comm_j(i) := \max\{0, Comm_j(i) + v_j\}
\end{aligned}
\tag{7}
$$

$$
\begin{aligned}
&\text{If } Fight(i, j) \wedge k, l \in Coalition_i(j) \\
&\text{Then } Comm_k(l) := \min(100, Comm_k(l) + v_k)
\end{aligned}
\tag{8}
$$

$$
\begin{aligned}
&\text{If } Fight(i, j) \wedge k \in Coalition_i(j) \wedge l \in Coalition_j(i) \\
&\text{Then } Comm_k(l) := \min\{100, Comm_k(l) - v_k\}; \\
&\qquad\quad Comm_l(k) := \min\{100, Comm_l(k) - v_l\}
\end{aligned}
\tag{9}
$$

The anecdotal type of presentation of results used by Axelrod does not ease up the comparison with other experiments, even because of the important intervention of random phenomena, of impossible reproduction. Hence, it is difficult to take the model as designed by Axelrod as a starting point, and let the changes we proposed provide a more complete version of the model. How could we comparatively evaluate the performances? It seems nevertheless clear that BVG architecture can provide a more principled approach to the implementation of this model, and allow a more systematic exploration of the agent design space [7].

This model of multi-agent simulation exhibits overly orchestrated interactions among the agents. As a matter of fact, we are in a closed world, a game, in which only some randomness prevents the discovery of the easy solution, and a winning behaviour. Even so, that rationality is never taken into account in the agent's reasoning, they use their designer's heuristics to make the necessary decisions, always in the more predictable way. What is nevertheless fascinating is the way how the simplicity of individual processes leads to behaviours that are so interesting from the observer standpoint (and recognisable in real situations from the history of politics).

6   Summary of Experimental Results

The experimental work was centered around the consequences in the simulations of the use of value "Commitment." For that purpose, we have introduced previously the notion of fickleness of an actor, v_a, that is, the quantity of Commitment which is incremented or decremented as a consequence of each interaction. With this little extension to the original model, we aim at testing te applicability of the multiple values framework and of the BVG architecture. In particular, by adding new values to the model (or, better said, by making explicit a previously existing value), we emphasize a methodological added value in the value-based approach. To that end, our experimental exploration work follows closely the style of exploration conducted by Axelrod himself.

We performed series of 1000 runs of the simulation, with the following parameters. In each run, the same sequence of random numbers (and so countries become active in the same sequence) is used with fickleness set to all the agents, first at 0%, then 5%, 10% (original value), 25%, 50%, 75%, and 100%.

Table 1. Minimum, average, and maximum total wealth, obtained in 1000 runs of the simulation.

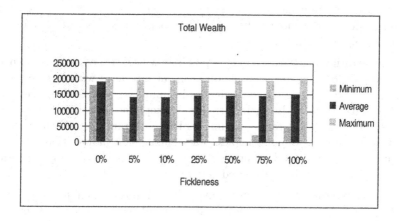

Table 1 shows the minimum, average, and maximum of the total wealth (i.e. the sum of the wealth of all the nations), obtained in 1000 runs (1000 iterations each) of the simulation. Apart from the case where all ficklenesses are zero (which in practice doesn't allow for coalitions), there is a light pattern of evolution of the medium wealth with a growth approximately linear. Actually, the zero commitment avoids many fights that are possible only in alliance (fights with distances greater than one neighbour). And a society that does not engage into fights looses less wealth (in fights there is not transfer of wealth, rather loss).

But the analysis of table 2 does not show a corresponding proportional decrease in the average number of fights. Again excluding the case when all commit-

Table 2. Minimum, average, and maximum number of fights, obtained in 1000 runs of the simulation.

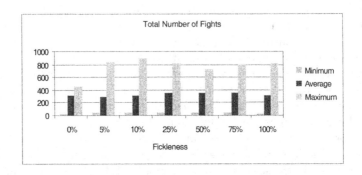

ments are zero, the maximum average number of fights is obtained with agent's fickleness equal to 50%, and the minima are at the extremes of the interval. Apparently, more fickleness, before the amount of 50%, yields an increase of the total wealth, but without reducing the number of fights. So, we have more fights, but causing less damages.

To investigate how this could be possible, we devised a battery of experiments to find out how the variation of commitment interferes with the agents interactions. Having the original experiments in mind, we preferred to keep the same order of execution of the agents (that is, we kept the experiment controlled from the standpoint of the random numbers that generate the activation sequence), and varied only the commitments. Subsequent tests showed that the activation sequences were not fundamentally important, and the conclusions of these series of experiments can be considered general.

Along several series of experiments (that cannot be included in this extended abstract due to space limitations), and control tests, we reached several interesting conclusions, summarised ahead.

In a first series of simulations, we kept $v_i = 0\%, \forall i$, and then gradually increased some of the v_i, so that the effect of the participation of actors in more and more global fights could be analysed. It resulted clear that a country doesn't have any gain in having a greater commitment towards another, it rather exposes itself to more damage. The advantage seems to reside in getting support rather then concede it. But neither is that surprising, nor do all its consequences are already visible.

Afterwards, we aim at favouring the constitution of two antagonistic blocks. We have confirmed a conjecture that a high fickleness leads to stable coalitions earlier, and so decreases the number of fights.

In table 3, we try to cause other block formations. In the first experiment, some coalitions are immediately formed to the right of 0 and 5, but with the other neighbour the relation is unstable. So, both 0 and 5 do not grow.

Table 3. Other block formations.

Fickleness $\neq 0$	Fights	Wealth (thousands)	Rich countries ($W > 1000$)	Wealth dist. (thousands)
$v_{0,5} = 25$	367	186	$(1, 3, 6, 8)$	$(51, 42, 51, 42)$
$v_{0,2,4,6,8} = 25$	49	195	$(1, 3, 5, 7, 9)$	$(40, 38, 40, 39, 38)$
$v_{i<4} = 10, v_j = 50$	293	162	$(0, 6, 8)$	$(45, 68, 48)$
$v_{i<4} = 10, v_j = 100$	399	165	$(5, 7, 9)$	$(68, 46, 56)$

A similar situation occurs in the next experiment, with a quick formation of coalitions, all to the same side, but now causing the end of fights. As expected, the five countries with zero fickleness (and so zero commitment) are the ones to grow. The demands are made to one and another sides, since commitments are not reciprocal, and this allows to make demands without risking own wealth.

In the third line simulation, the coalition (6,7,8) stabilizes quickly, whereas coalition (1,2,3) takes longer. Only when the latter coalition remains stable do fights stop. A third coalition (8,9,0,1) is formed, but it takes even longer, because $v_0 = 10$, although $v_9 = 5-$ contributes to stability. During the simulation, country 5 comes to be one of the richest, but looses all due to demands from the coalition to its left. Country 3 also has attempts of growth, but was successively attacked by 0, who, in the joint coalition with 8, have considerable force.

Finally, the last experiment of this series shows that countries with greater fickleness end up by fixing themselves easily in coalitions, especially in the company with similar partners. Neighbours to the ficklest, once obtained total adhesion, keep colligated, unless the non-neighbours, that fight a lot with their neighbours. The ones in the coalition fight from the distance, and keep in good terms with their neighbours.

In the last series of simulations (table 4), we invert the terms of the experiments, and keep few countries with zero fickleness. As always, the un-allied profit from using the others while not letting themselves be used. We confirm as well that low values of fickleness favour the existence of many fights, and not their disappearance.

An interesting experiment is that of the third line. Quickly, coalitions (2,3,4), (4,5,6,7), and (7,8,9) are formed. The bigger coalition generates wealthy countries 5 and 7, but it is noteworthy that country 1 starts off by getting wealthy first, and is then is persecuted by 0, who takes all its wealth away. Country 0 has support from 7, 8, and 9, while 1 has support from 2, 3, and 4, but only at times. Support from 7 is fundamental for the growth of 0. When this support

Table 4. Few un-allied in the colligated crowd.

Fickleness $\neq 0$	Fights	Wealth (thousands)	Rich countries ($W > 1000$)	Wealth dist. (thousands)
$v_{i \neq 0} = 10$	574	153	$(0, 4, 5)$	$(37, 33, 82)$
$v_{i>1} = 25$	303	172	$(1, 3, 6, 7)$	$(34, 40, 83, 14)$
$v_{i>1} = 60$	311	186	$(0, 5, 7)$	$(49, 70, 64)$
$v_i = 10i$	507	112	$(3, 5, 9)$	$(48, 61, 2)$

appears, 1 cannot keep demanding tribute from 0, since its supporters 2 and 3 are weak, whereas 7, 8, and 9 are very strong.

In sum, regional (local) influence is quite important, as well as specific circumstances at the time of activation. Stable coalitions favour the growth of internal collective wealth, and ease up the defense against attacks from outside the coalition. Less obvious is the fact that a high fickleness always allow to keep the stability of coalitions. However it is always possible to ensure a higher stability through the increase of fickleness. And on the other side, high fickleness offers a greater number of possibilities for the formation of stable coalitions, since it is easier to reach the commitment levels to favour that formation.

Some of our results are already dealt with in Axelrod's account, but we believe our approach carries some added value. Namely, some of the questions originally put as variations of the model can now have clearer answers. Axelrod claims that even if the runs are extended to 10000 iterations, the model doesn't settle down, and there are repeated large wars. As we have seen, this conclusion can be withdrawn by adding fickler countries, that tend to keep keen to their friends. On the other hand, Axelrod sustains that it pays to give and receive commitments, but our conclusion is quite different: what pays is to have supporting friends, and that can be achieved by having committed neighbours, while saving wealth through uncommitting.

7   Conclusions

One main conclusion is that even in the extended tribute model, coalitions have one rich country, most times only one. Only really big coalitions can allow two rich countries to develop, far from each other. More seldom it is possible to find a neighbour to a rich country with a comfortable amount of wealth, but always in a very unbalanced strength relation.

Rich countries have all interest in maintaining a support group, but giving as little support themselves as they can, in order to protect their own wealth. This unbalanced confidence relation between countries is not uncovered in the model of [4], and reveals a virtue in the methodological approach based on the analysis of relevant values for the decision situation.

During our extensive experimentation, we focussed on the issue of fight control and its consequences for wealth. The core idea of modelling of the choice process was always present in our approach, since our position is that the mentality of the agents is determinant for their behaviour. We unveiled some regularities in the global social behaviour, but sustain that more experimentation is still in need, to stress our conclusions, as well as answer new challenges in this stimulating field. However, the conduction of experiments should be more principled, and we believe that the BVG choice model can provide bridges to fill the gap between the experiment designer and the mental models of the agents involved.

Acknowledgements. The research herein reported was conducted with partial support from FCT, within research unit LabMAC. We would like to thank our colleagues at the AI Group in FC/UL, as well as the anynomous reviewers.

References

1. L. Antunes. *Agents with Value-based Decision (Agentes com Decisão baseada em Valores)*. PhD thesis, Faculdade de Ciências, Universidade de Lisboa, 2001.
2. L. Antunes, J. Faria, and H. Coelho. Improving choice mechanisms within the BVG architecture. In Y. Lésperance and C. Castelfranchi, editors, *Intelligent Agents VII, Proc. of ATAL2000*, volume 1986 of *Lecture Notes in Artificial Intelligence*. Springer-Verlag, 2000.
3. R. Axelrod. *The Evolution of Cooperation*. Basic Books, New York, 1984.
4. R. Axelrod. A model of the emergence of new political actors. In N. Gilbert and R. Conte, editors, *Artificial societies: the computer simulation of social life*. UCL Press, London, 1995.
5. J. C. Caldas and H. Coelho. Strategic interaction in oligopolistic markets – experimenting with real and artificial agents. In C. Castelfranchi and E. Werner, editors, *Artificial Social Systems, Proc. of MAAMAW'92*, volume 830 of *Lecture Notes in Artificial Intelligence*. Springer-Verlag, 1994.
6. J.-L. Deneubourg, S. Goss, N. R. Franks, A. Sendova-Franks, C. Detrain, and L. Chretien. The dynamics of collective sorting: Robot-like ant and ant-like robot. In J.-A. Meyer and S. W. Wilson, editors, *Simulation of Adaptive Behavior: From Animals to Animats*, pages 356–365. The MIT Press/Bradford Books, 1991.
7. A. Sloman. Prospects for AI as the general science of intelligence. In A. Sloman, D. Hogg, G. Humphreys, A. Ramsay, and D. Partridge, editors, *Prospects for Artificial Intelligence, Proc. of AISB'93*, Amsterdam, 1993. IOS Press.

Evolving Specialisation, Altruism, and Group-Level Optimisation Using Tags

David Hales

The Centre for Policy Modelling, The Business School, Manchester Metropolitan
University, Manchester, UK.
dave@davidhales.com

Abstract. We present a model that demonstrates the evolution of groups
composed of cooperative individuals performing specialised functions.
Specialisation and cooperation results from an evolutionary process in which
selection and reproduction is based on individual fitness. Specialists come to
help (through the donation of resources) their *non-kin* group members,
optimising their behaviour as a team and producing a fitter group. The
mechanism that promotes this benevolent, cooperative group behaviour is based
on the concept of a "tag". Tags[1] are observable markings, cues or displays.
Individuals can observe the tags of others and take alternative actions based on
those observations (e.g. to altruistically[2] help or not). We show that even
random (or *dumb*) searching for appropriate partners produces significant levels
of specialisation and cooperation. Additionally we demonstrate that non-random
(or *smart*) searching dramatically increases the effect.

1 Introduction

Recent tag models [1, 2, 8] have shown how benevolent behaviour can be evolved
between individuals in one-time interactions. However, in these models the altruistic
behaviour of individuals may be interpreted as a form of kin selection [10]. This
interpretation is possible because all the agents within a cooperative group are
identical[3] when cooperation is high.

In this paper, however, we demonstrate tag processes that are sufficient to produce
sustained altruistic behaviour towards others who are *not kin-related*. Moreover, we
show that this non-kin based altruism is a basis for the evolution of groups of
heterogeneous (specialised) individuals who, although not kin related, cooperate and
work to benefit their *group as a whole*.

---

[1] The concept of "tags" in the context of structuring social interactions among agents was first
outlined by Holland [6] and applied to *repeated* interactions by Riolo [7].

[2] By altruism, we mean that agents sacrifice fitness for others even though such donations may
not be returned (i.e. without reciprocity).

[3] In these previous models when *identical* agents are paired they *must* act altruistically.

J.S. Sichman, F. Bousquet, P. Davidsson (Eds.): MABS 2002, LNAI 2581, pp. 26-35, 2003.
© Springer-Verlag Berlin Heidelberg 2003

The tag processes presented in the model can therefore be *interpreted* as selection at a supra-individual level. Groups of specialised individuals cooperate and evolve to increase group level fitness. Specifically, we note that the model we present is constructed such that individuals cannot help kin directly and hence the cooperative behaviour *cannot* be the result of kin selection.

By *non-kin* we mean agents that do not share units of inheritance (in the natural biological world such units are called "genes"). Here we model artificial inheritable traits (numeric values) within artificial agents. By *benevolent* or *altruistic* behaviour, we mean actions by individual agents that reduce *their* fitness but enhance another agents' fitness. By fitness we mean the relative reproductive success of an agent. Biologically, the interpretation is literal reproduction of offspring. Culturally the interpretation is of imitation of the successful individuals (agents with higher fitness are more likely to reproduce their traits).

We advance the model as an example of how, even simple organisms (or artificial computational agents), can evolve to form cooperative heterogeneous groups or teams composed of individuals performing specialised tasks. The individuals within the groups work together symbiotically to produce a more efficient unit to the benefit of all – even though this requires altruistic behaviour between self-interested individuals. We therefore advance the model and results as a *minimal demonstration* of evolutionary mechanisms that can guide (boundedly rational) individual self-interested utility maximisers towards the maximisation of a social (group level) good[4].

Additionally we demonstrate that populations of agents with *smarter* partner selection strategies support higher levels of specialisation and cooperation. Finally we hypothesize that an evolutionary process would select for smart strategies.

2 The Model

The model consists of a population of 100 evolving agents. The tag matching mechanism follows that of Riolo et al [8]. The specialisation process follows Hales [3]. Here we briefly summarise the model. Each agent has three traits, a tag $\tau \in [0,1]$, a tolerance threshold $1 \leq T \geq 0$, and a skill type $S \in \{1,2\}$. Initially, tags, thresholds and skills are allocated uniformly randomly. In each generation, each agent is awarded some number P of resources. Each resource is assigned a required skill type. Resources can only be "harvested" by agents possessing the required skill type. The skill type assigned to a resource is randomly assigned from those skills that do not match the receiving agents skill[5]. An agent therefore is never awarded a resource that

---

[4] It is important to stress that such a mechanism is not advanced as an explanation of all the kinds of observed group-level adaptations that appear to occur in human societies. Rather, we present a simple mechanism that demonstrates that some apparent altruistic group-level adaptation *can* be archived bounded optimisers in a suitable environment.

[5] Results obtained from a model in which agents may be awarded resources matching their own skill types produced similar results to those presented in this paper.

matches its skill type. Since the agent cannot harvest the resource, it searches for another agent in the population with required skill and tag values.

Donation only occurs if a recipient is found with the required skill type and with a sufficiently similar tag value. A recipient tag is considered to be sufficiently similar if it is within the tolerance of the donating agent. Specifically, given a potential donor agent D and a potential recipient R a donation will only be made when $| \tau_D - \tau_R | \leq T_D$. This means that an agent with a high T value may donate to agents over a large range of tag values. A low value for T restricts donation to agents with very similar tag values to the donor. In all cases donation can only occur when the skill type of the receiving agent matches the skill type associated with the resource. If a donation is made the donating agent incurs a cost, c, and the recipient gains a benefit, b (since it can harvest the resource). In all experiments given here, the benefit b = 1 but the cost c is varied as is the size of the skill set S (see results).

In the experiments presented we compare two kinds of agent society: societies composed entirely of agents using *dumb* searching strategies and societies composed entirely of agents using *smart* searching strategies. These strategies indicate the way an agent searches for a potential recipient to donate to. Agents using a dumb strategy select an agent at random from the population, after each resource award, and make a donation if the recipient has a sufficiently similar tag and skill matching the resource skill. Agents using a smart strategy *search the entire population* for a recipient that has a sufficiently similar tag and the required skill. We assume (but do not directly model) that some efficient mechanism exists which allows agents to *find a potential recipient in the population if one exists*[6]. As discussed elsewhere [4] a number of plausible mechanisms can be hypothesised based on spatial and / or cognitive relationships (e.g. "small world" social networks [11], meeting places and central stores [9] – see the later discussion for more on this). We perhaps should make clear that the use of the term *strategy* could be misleading here because we only model the post-hoc outcomes not the actual behaviours themselves. We simply assume that more thorough searching will generally require more cognitive effort or social structure – but we don't discount the fact that agent *behaviours* (the more common use for the world strategy) could accomplish "smart" outcomes but appear to be quite dumb or irrational. After all agents have been awarded P resources and made any possible donations the entire population is reproduced. Reproduction is accomplished in the following manner – each agent is selected from the population in turn, its score is compared to another randomly chosen agent, and the one with the highest score is reproduced. Mutation is applied to each trait of each offspring. With probability 0.1 the offspring receives a new tag (uniformly randomly selected). With the same probability, gaussian noise is added to the tolerance value (mean 0, standard deviation 0.01). When T < 0 or T > 1, it is reset to 0 and 1 respectively. Also with probability 0.1 the offspring is given a new skill type (uniformly randomly selected).

---

[6] If several suitable recipients exist in the population we assume here that one of them is selected to receive the donation at random.

3 Results

The first set of results, shown in table 1 and figure 1 below, show the donation rates achieved (as a percentage of total awards made) and the average tolerance values in a 2-skill scenario (for a populations of dumb agents and populations of smart agents).

Table 1. Donation rates and tolerance levels for different numbers of awards (P) in a 2-skill scenario (i.e. when $S \; \varepsilon \; \{1,2\}$) for different search strategies and costs. Values given are averages (the values in brackets are standard deviations) over the 30 replications.

P	Donation Rate – Ave %			Tolerance – Ave		
	Dumb $c=0.1$	Smart $c=0.1$	Smart $c=0.5$	Dumb $c=0.1$	Smart $c=0.1$	Smart $c=0.5$
1	2.6 (0.000)	61.0 (0.079)	61.0 (0.076)	0.017 (0.000)	0.035 (0.157)	0.038 (0.107)
2	2.2 (0.000)	80.0 (0.011)	69.3 (0.083)	0.012 (0.000)	0.019 (0.050)	0.055 (0.182)
3	2.3 (0.000)	85.6 (0.048)	73.9 (0.052)	0.010 (0.000)	0.090 (0.216)	0.044 (0.147)
4	6.4 (0.064)	85.8 (0.031)	76.8 (0.061)	0.010 (0.000)	0.057 (0.147)	0.062 (0.172)
6	30.3 (0.007)	87.7 (0.046)	77.9 (0.008)	0.021 (0.021)	0.111 (0.217)	0.013 (0.013)
8	32.8 (0.001)	90.5 (0.062)	80.6 (0.043)	0.024 (0.024)	0.225 (0.290)	0.049 (0.136)
10	33.8 (0.015)	89.3 (0.056)	81.1 (0.039)	0.043 (0.043)	0.180 (0.279)	0.040 (0.132)
20	35.5 (0.034)	89.5 (0.057)	82.0 (0.003)	0.106 (0.078)	0.189 (0.274)	0.012 (0.005)
40	36.0 (0.047)	91.3 (0.047)	83.1 (0.015)	0.241 (0.241)	0.268 (0.305)	0.025 (0.049)

The results are over 30,000 generations with 30 replications. Each replication represents an individual run started with a different pseudo-random number seed. The standard deviations are over the 30 runs executed for each unique P value setting[7]. The column labelled "dumb" shows the results using a *dumb* random recipient search strategy. The "smart" columns show the results of the smart strategy populations. In order to make a "fair" comparison we also consider the results of the smart strategy when the cost, c, is increased from c = 0.1 to c = 0.5 (in all cases the benefit, b, is held at 1). The donation rate represents the percentage of attempted donations that resulted in an actual donation. This is averaged over the entire run to 30,000 generations and over 30 replications.

---

[7] The standard deviations are not calculated over the percentages given but over proportions.

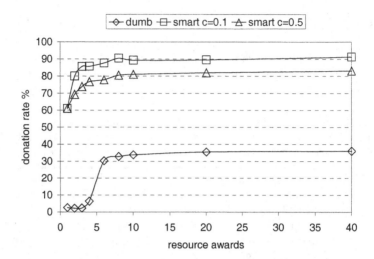

Fig. 1. A chart showing the donation rate data given in table 1 (above) for the 3 different population types in the 2-skill scenario. Note that the smart populations (with costs of 0.1 and 0.5) have much higher donation rates that the dumb population runs.

As can be seen in table 1 and figure 1, the donation rate for the *smart* strategy (when c=0.1) increases dramatically when P=2 (awards) and then increases modestly (though non-monotonically) as P is increased. In comparison with the previous results for the *dumb* searching strategy the donation rate is substantially higher (61% to 2.6% for a single award). Note also that the tolerance values are higher too and the standard deviation of tolerance (over the 30 runs) is much higher (indicating a high heterogeneity over the runs)[8]. When the cost, c, is increased to 0.5 the smart strategy does not increase as dramatically when P=2. But still shows substantially higher donation levels than the dumb strategy. The increase in donation rate as P is increased follows a more linear (monotonically increasing) path than when the cost was c=0.1 and the tolerance levels are generally reduced. The variance of the tolerance is reduced by still higher than for the dumb strategy.

In a 5-skill scenario (table 2 and figure 2) a similar (though even more dramatic) pattern is seen for the smart strategy when c = 0.1. Again a big increase in the donation rate takes place when P=2 followed by a much slower (non-monotonic rise) as P is increased. Again the variance over the 30 runs for each P value is much higher than the dumb strategy (evidenced by the standard deviation values).

When c = 0.5 the results are broadly similar to those for the 2-skill scenario. Again notice that for the smart strategy when c = 0.5 the increase when P = 2 is less dramatic, and as P increases the donation rate increases in a more linear (and monotonic) way. We note here however, that tolerance values and the variance of those values are lower than in the 2-skill scenario – almost comparable to the dumb strategy.

---

[8] This result suggests that there may not be a "single story" (i.e. evolutionary trajectory) here. This means that increases in donation and tolerance might be highly contingent on initial conditions and on-going stochasticities (this is discussed later).

4 Discussion

Let us be clear about what is being demonstrated by the model: Agents form groups, based on tag similarity, containing a diversity of skills. Agents donate resources, requiring skills (to harvest) that they do not possess, to other agents within their group *even though this causes them to incur a substantial cost*. This behaviour persists even though the agents are reproduced on the basis of individual utility. Since agents can only pass resources to others (within their group) that posses the required skill, the high-level of donation rate produced indicates that *high levels of skill diversity are being maintained within groups*. This is exactly the kind of group organisation that can best exploit the environmental scenario. So, *agents are forming into very efficient, skill diverse groups*. Since skill diversity means that agents cannot be clones, this evolved structure cannot be the result of a simple form of kin based selection.

The results presented here indicate that "smart searching" strategies, i.e. efficient methods of finding an appropriate in-group recipient for donation, substantially increase the efficiency of specialisation within groups. Since smart strategies would seem to require a higher cognitive ability within agents, can we conclude that there is strong selection pressure for such cognitive abilities? We *cannot* draw such a conclusion because *the results presented here do not pit dumb strategies against smart ones in the same evolving population*. We hypothesize, however, that smart agents would indeed out compete dumb agents – even when the cost of donating for smart agents was substantially higher. We put this hypothesis to the test in a subsequent paper [5].

As stated previously, in some of the results, very high levels of tolerance were produced. This tended to occur when P (awards) was high and a smart strategy was employed (though not when costs were high). In those cases where the tolerance was high, the variance (over the 30 replication) of tolerance was also high. This indicated heterogeneity of evolutionary trajectories taking place over replications.

To investigate this we examine the average tolerances and donation rates of the individual replication runs when P=40 in the 5-skill scenario for the smart strategy when cost c=0.1. Table 3 shows the results of the first 15 individual runs. Note that the runs fall into two categories: a) runs with low average tolerances and b) runs with very high average tolerances. The b-type runs produce almost 100% donation rates (the results are rounded to 4 significant figures in the table - the actual results are slightly less than 100%).

The a-type runs have lower (yet still high) donation rates. The column labelled "Tag Clone Donations" shows the proportion of awards that resulted in a donation to a recipient agent with an *identical tag* value to the donor. As would be expected, runs that average high tolerances result in high donation to non tag-clones, even though donation rates are almost at maximum. Such results indicate that all agents donate to all others and maintain the required skill diversity to exploit each resource type.

Table 2. Donation rates and tolerance levels for different numbers of awards (P) in a 5-skill scenario (i.e. there are 5 skill types, such that each agent has a skill S ε {1,2,3,4,5}) for different search strategies and costs. Values given are averages (the values in brackets are standard deviations) over the 30 replications.

P	Donation Rate – Ave %			Tolerance – Ave		
	Dumb c=0.1	Smart c=0.1	Smart c=0.5	Dumb c=0.1	Smart c=0.1	Smart c=0.5
1	1.5 (0.001)	29.5 (0.081)	29.5 (0.081)	0.028 (0.002)	0.021 (0.118)	0.021 (0.084)
2	1.1 (0.000)	75.3 (0.016)	47.9 (0.087)	0.01 (0.001)	0.023 (0.034)	0.030 (0.111)
3	1.0 (0.000)	81.8 (0.037)	59.9 (0.035)	0.015 (0.001)	0.056 (0.110)	0.017 (0.048)
4	0.9 (0.000)	84.3 (0.060)	66.3 (0.046)	0.013 (0.000)	0.104 (0.222)	0.028 (0.105)
6	0.9 (0.000)	84.4 (0.051)	70.9 (0.010)	0.011 (0.001)	0.099 (0.210)	0.011 (0.014)
8	0.9 (0.000)	88.5 (0.077)	73.1 (0.002)	0.010 (0.000)	0.250 (0.319)	0.009 (0.000)
10	2.1 (0.002)	84.1 (0.049)	74.5 (0.002)	0.010 (0.000)	0.099 (0.208)	0.009 (0.000)
20	12.9 (0.000)	85.8 (0.070)	77.3 (0.002)	0.025 (0.003)	0.170 (0.261)	0.010 (0.001)
40	13.9 (0.015)	91.0 (0.015)	79.3 (0.033)	0.098 (0.190)	0.370 (0.341)	0.038 (0.107)

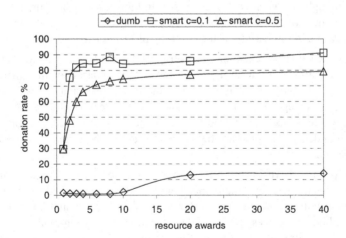

Fig. 2. A chart showing the donation rate data given in table 2 (above) for the 3 different population types in the 5-skill scenario. This can be compared to figure 1 – notice that with more skills less donation occurs – particularly for the dumb population type.

But how is this happening? Intuitively, it would appear that, in the b-type runs the population should be invaded by "cheating" agents with a low tolerance that would restrict donation to agents with tag values much closer to their own while benefiting from donations from more tolerant agents.

But a moment's reflection indicates that agents may not benefit by reducing tolerance in the small decrements produced by the gaussian mutation method (described above) when the cost of donation is low and the initial tolerance is high. This is because a small decrement in the tolerance would mean that agents with higher tolerances could still be recipients of donations. Only if an agent was produced (via mutation) that had a very uncommon tag and a very low tolerance could a substantial increase in fitness be produced. It should be noted that when the cost is increased to $c=0.5$ the b-type runs disappear. This could be explained by the additional evolutionary advantage that the extra cost gives to "cheaters". But do these reflections explain the results? In tables 1 and 2, the b-type runs only occur in resource rich (i.e. when awards (P) are high) environments. We currently do not have an explanation for this. Consequently the b-type runs are under closer investigation.

The forms of interaction and specialisation possible in this model are limited. The assumption that donation only takes place between two individuals (i.e. donation results from dyadic pairing of a donor and recipient) precludes the possibility of an agent donating to several agents at once. The environmental scenario, in which agents are rewarded individually for diverse skills, does not allow agents to become *full-time* specialists in other roles – such as internal group organisation roles (e.g. redistribution agents, that collect and redistribute resources to the in-group or policing agents that punish potential free-riders within the group). Intuitively, it would seem, agents would need to have *smarter redistribution* (or donation) strategies than those presented in the present model and richer interaction abilities. Future work will explore the evolution of smarter redistribution strategies.

5 Conclusions

We have demonstrated with an evolutionary algorithm that altruism, group formation and specialisation are intimately linked in the formation of integrated higher-level social entities which are better adapted to their environment than atomised individuals. Specifically we are trying to show that the underlying processes that bring about such organisations can be driven by essentially self-interested (boundedly rational) learning behaviour at the individual level – e.g. by copying the behaviour of those who achieve higher utility. From the results presented here we question the intuition that evolution (based on individual self-interested learning) can be understood by reducing explanation to the low level selfish replicators[9]. We argue that even in our simple scenario, this intuition would lead to confusion and a failure to understand the

---

[9] This is not a new idea of course, inclusive fitness (kin selection) and reciprocal altruism are both mechanisms that identify social level organisation effecting the evolution of individuals – we advance the processes shown here as a further such mechanism.

behaviour of individual agents observed over time – but simply, the intuition would say that tags would make no difference to the evolutionary trajectory of the population.

Table 3. The first 15 individual runs for the smart strategy (c=0.1 and P=40, 5-skills). Each run represents a single execution of the model to 30,000 generations starting with a different pseudo-random number seed. The Donation Rate shows the proportion of awards that resulted in a successful donation. The Tolerance Average shows the average tolerance over all agents and generations. The Tag Clone Donations shows the proportion of successful donations made to an agent with an identical tag value.

Run No.	Donation Proportion	Tolerance Ave.	Tag Clone Donations
1	0.811	0.020	0.768
2	1.000	0.779	0.013
3	1.000	0.673	0.015
4	0.881	0.188	0.429
5	0.998	0.600	0.018
6	1.000	0.669	0.015
7	0.861	0.109	0.499
8	0.811	0.021	0.750
9	1.000	0.659	0.015
10	0.829	0.045	0.699
11	1.000	0.768	0.013
12	1.000	0.901	0.012
13	0.917	0.418	0.297
14	0.834	0.046	0.641
15	0.813	0.022	0.760

This final observation seems particularly poignant when applied to the concept of "cultural evolution". In modern human societies we appear to observe large numbers of institutions and social groups composed of many individuals with highly specialised roles and seemingly altruistic behaviours within and even between groups. We argue that such complexity and seemingly "unselfish" behaviour does not necessarily undermine the project of attempting to explain such phenomena from an evolutionary perspective[10].

Acknowledgements. Work presented here has greatly benefited from discussions with, and ideas from, Bruce Edmunds, Centre for Policy Modelling, Manchester Metropolitan University, UK. Also thanks go to the reviewers who made very perceptive and constructive comments on previous drafts of this work.

---

[10] Since this model is not based on observations of real social interactions however, we only claim the status of analogy and hypothesis when considering real (human) societies.

References

1. Hales, D.: Cooperation without Space or Memory: Tags, Groups and the Prisoner's Dilemma. In Moss, S., Davidsson, P. (Eds.) *Multi-Agent-Based Simulation.* Lecture Notes in Artificial Intelligence 1979. Berlin: Springer-Verlag (2000)
2. Hales, D.:*Tag Based Cooperation in Artificial Societies.* Unpublished Ph.D. Thesis, Department of Computer Science, University of Essex (2001)
3. Hales, D.: Cooperation and Specialisation without Kin Selection using Tags. *CPM Working Paper 02-88.* The Centre for Policy Modelling, Manchester Metropolitan University, Manchester, UK (2002a).
4. Hales, D.: Smart Agents Don't Need Kin – Evolving Specialisation and Cooperation with Tags. *CPM Working Paper 02-89.* The Centre for Policy Modelling, Manchester Metropolitan University, Manchester, UK (available at: http://www.cpm.mmu.ac.uk/cpmreps.html), (2002b).
5. Hales, D.: Wise-Up! - Smart Tag Pairing Evolves and Persists. *CPM Working Paper 02-90.* The Centre for Policy Modelling, Manchester Metropolitan University, Manchester, UK (available at: http://www.cpm.mmu.ac.uk/cpmreps.html), (2002c).
6. Holland, J.: The Effect of Labels (Tags) on Social Interactions. *SFI Working Paper 93-10-064.* Santa Fe Institute, Santa Fe, NM, (1993)
7. Riolo, R.:The Effects of Tag-Mediated Selection of Partners in Evolving Populations Playing the Interated Prisoner's Dilemma. *SFI Working Paper 97-02-16.* Santa Fe Institute, Santa Fe, NM. (1997).
8. Riolo, R., Cohen, M. & Axelrod, R.: Cooperation without Reciprocity. *Nature* 414, 441–443. (2001).
9. Pedone, R. & Parisi, D.:In What Kinds of Social Groups can Altruistic Behaviour Evolve? In Conte, R., Hegselmann, R. and Terna, P., Eds., *Simulating Social Phenomena – LNEMS 456, Springer-Verlag, Berlin.*(1997).
10. Sigmund & Nowak: Tides of tolerance. *Nature* 414, 403–405. (2001).
11. Watts, J. D.: *Small Worlds – The Dynamics of Networks between Order and Randomness.* Princeton, New Jersey, USA. (1999).

The Need for and Development of Behaviourally Realistic Agents

Wander Jager[1] and Marco Janssen[2]

[1] Faculty of Management and Organisation, Dept, of Marketing, University of Groningen. PO Box 800, 9700 AV, Groningen, The Netherlands. w.jager@bdk.rug.nl

[2] Center for the Study of Institutions, Population, and Environmental Change, Indiana University. 408 North Indiana Avenue Bloomington, IN 47408-3799 USA. maajanss@indiana.edu

Abstract. In this paper we argue that simulating complex systems involving human behaviour requires agent rules based on a theoretically rooted structure that captures basic behavioural processes. Essential components of such a structure involve needs, decision-making processes and learning. Such a structure should be based on state-of-the-art behavioural theories and validated on the micro-level using experimental or field data of individual behaviour. We provide some experiences we had working with such a structure, which involve the possibility to relate the results of simulations on different topics, the ease of building in extra factors for specific research questions and the possibility to use empirical data in calibrating the model. A disadvantage we experienced is the lack of suiting empirical data, which necessitates in our view the combined use of empirical and simulation research.

1 Introduction

Reynolds [1] developed an approach to simulate flocks as a distributed behavioural model. His work on the flocking boids has become a key example how simple local rules lead to complex macro behaviour. Reynolds used three rules for each agent: avoid collisions with nearby flockmates, attempt to match velocity with nearby flockmates and attempt to stay close to nearby flockmates. Due to measurement errors by the flockmates, an impressive flocking like behaviour comes out of this model. Reynolds mentions that "success and validity of these simulations is difficult to measure objectively. They do seem to agree well with certain criteria and some statistical properties of natural flocks and schools which have been reported by the zoological and behavioural sciences. Perhaps more significantly, many people who view these animated flocks immediately recognize them as a representation of a natural flock, and find them similarly delightful to watch" [1, p.26].

One might derive the impression that we have a better understanding of flocking behaviour. However, research on schooling of fish illustrate that we lack a good understanding of the micro-behaviour of fish in relation to schooling. Indeed, information about the behaviour of nearby neighbours is found to be a crucial factor

J.S. Sichman, F. Bousquet, P. Davidsson (Eds.): MABS 2002, LNAI 2581, pp. 36–49, 2003.

in empirical studies, but which behavioural rules are in use is a puzzle and so far computational models fail to reproduce observed behaviour in detail [2].

Reynolds showed that simple local rules could be used to simulate interesting macro-behaviour. As a computer scientist, he was not studying how flocking behaviour was happening in the real world. If that was the case a more rigorous analysis of the micro-behavioural rules tested in controlled experiments would have been necessary. In fact, this is what is happening in biology. In [2] an excellent overview is given on the study of self-organization in biological systems. It shows that the puzzles in their field are recently successfully being approached by combining field work, controlled laboratory experiments and models. They stress that the models "should be developed solely based on observations and experimental data concerning subunits of the system and their interactions" [2, p.70].

If we look at the use of multi-agent models for the study of social phenomena, we have to conclude that the fruitful combination of fieldwork, laboratory data and modelling is lacking. Key publications in social simulation like segregation by Schelling [3] and the evolution of cooperation by Axelrod [4] could explain macro-phenomena, by assuming simple logical rules for the behaviour of the agents. However, like the flocking boids the behavioural rules are not validated by empirical research or based on decision-making theories. We do not want to reduce the importance of the contributions of Schelling and Axelrod, they are evidently milestones. No, we want to argue that the use of simulation models should more often be based on empirically tested theoretical models of human decision-making combined with rigorous empirical research in the field and in the laboratory. This is happening in some areas, although they are often not included in the work of multi-agent simulation. A nice example of such a combination of empirical and simulation research is done by Erev & Roth [5]. They studied learning in experiments in games with a unique mixed strategy. Using a large data set of experimental data, they calibrated different versions of reinforcement learning and tested its predicted value. They showed that reinforcement learning model robustly outperforms the equilibrium predictions. Duffy [6] performed experiments on speculative behaviour with simulated agents, which were modelled on the basis of prior evidence from human subject experiments. Hommes [7] uses experimental data on financial markets in his simulation models of market behaviour. Gigerenzer et al. [8] study which theoretically-sound heuristics explain the observations in laboratory experiments.

Rational choice theory is one of the dominant theories in social science. Although it might often be nicknamed as Homo economicus, the rational agent is also used in other social sciences than economics as the theoretical construct of human decision-making. There is an increasing amount of anomalies of the rational choice theory found in experimental work. For example, subjects cooperate, when theory predicts defection, and framing of the problem leads to different results of the decision [9]. Nobel Laureate in Economics Reinhard Selten states "Modern mainstream economic theory is largely based on an unrealistic picture of human decision-making. Economic agents are portrayed as fully rational Bayesian maximisers of subjective utility. This view of economics is not based on empirical evidence, but rather on the simultaneous axiomisation of utility and subjective probability." [10, page 13].

Many researchers thus felt uncomfortable with the rational-actor assumption, and started to experiment with 'bounded rational' formalisations of human choice behaviour. These researchers were not satisfied with using a model that yielded the same outcomes but on the basis of different processes (heterologous or analogous metaphor, see e.g. [11]). Rather they were interested in trying to capture the same laws that apply to real human behaviour into agent rules (unificational metaphor). However, searching for generic laws of human behaviour quickly causes one to get lost in the abundance of psychological theories on motivation, emotions, norms, social comparison, imitation, habit formation, attitudes, and many more. So instead of making a Don Quixoteian endeavour in capturing all those theories in a single agent, they adhered to the adagio of 'keep it simple, stupid' in order to keep the model simple and the simulation results transparent for interpretation. Hence many simple formalisations of bounded rational agents were and are being developed and tested in different virtual environments. Most of these models demonstrated clearly that different assumptions of agent rules on the micro level had serious consequences for the outcomes at the macro level. A very neat series of experiments was performed already in 1994 by Bousquet *et al* [12], who gradually increased behavioural realism in the decision-making process of a society of fishermen. Currently François Bousquet and his colleagues use role games to extract rules-in-use by the community of interest [13].

Yet, looking at most formalisations of 'bounded rationality' in agent rules they leave the impression of being developed rather 'ad hoc' from the perspective of programming rules rather than reflecting a formalisation on the basis of theoretical considerations. Bounded rationality is not an excuse for using sloppy decision rules. For example, it is very interesting to study the effects of introducing an 'imitation' strategy in agents within a system. However, not considering the issues of under what conditions the agents are likely to imitate, and which other agents they are most likely to start imitating, may yield results that do not originate from the 'psychological laws' on imitative behaviour.

A number of psychologists have started to formalise existing theories in agent rules as to explore the derived behavioural assumptions in a more dynamical context. A very nice example is the formalisation of the Elaboration Likelihood Model by Mosler, Schwarz, Ammann and Gutscher [14]. Here the simulation contributed to the dynamic shifting of attitudes as depending on processing intensity. Also in the fields of social cognition, emotion, social behaviour and normative behaviour more and more simulation models are being used as a complementary tool to study how these empirical validated 'psychological laws' perform in a dynamical context. Returning to human behaviour in complex systems, we may conclude that many behavioural theories may be of importance at different moments in time. People perform habits, they will change their attitudes, develop habits and the like, and all these processes have been described in psychological theories. In fact, we should not only look at theories from psychology, but also integrate theories from other disciplines. Wilk [15] discusses how different approaches to study consumer behaviour, like individual choice theories, social theories and cultural theories, lead to different insights and different policy recommendations. Hence, many theories should be formalised in agent rules as to capture the spectrum of human behaviour in agent rules. However, the many theories, - formalised in simulation models or not (yet) - would yield a far too complex agent as to keep the model programmable and the results transparent for interpretations. Moreover, it would be a very tricky task linking the various theoretical formalisations together in a theoretically and conceptually sound manner. This is especially difficult because so many psychological theories show overlap or describe partly the same processes at a different aggregation level. To do so, we state that a simplified meta-theory is required that organises the various theories in a conceptual framework. Vallacher & Nowak [16] have already identified the need for such a meta-theory. Such a meta-theory would be helpful in developing agent rules that are aimed to capture a broad spectrum of human behaviour in a very simplistic manner as to represent the full spectrum of human behaviour in simulating complex systems. Three main issues that deserve critical attention in the development of such a meta-theory are agent rules are needs, the decision-making process and learning. We will discuss these issues separately in the next sections.

2 Agent Needs

In our daily lives we often have to compromise between conflicting interests. For example, many people find it difficult to find a good balance between working and spending time with family and friends. Every action we perform costs time, which decreases the opportunity to perform other actions. In our view this compromising reflects the multidimensionality of human needs: different actions may satisfy different needs, and in the end we try (we do not always succeed) to make decision over different activities such as to satisfy our various needs. This matches with theoretical conceptions of needs in psychology and economy (e.g., [17], [18]). For example, Maslow [17] discerns physiological and safety needs, needs to belong and be loved, and esteem, cognitive, aesthetic and self-actualisation needs. Yet many artificial agents are (implicitly) equipped with a single need, because they 'live' in a simple one-dimensional world, where only one 'good' can be consumed. This good is formalised in terms of abstract points, and an agent is implicitly assumed to have an everlasting motivation to consume more of these points, irrespectively of the number it has consumed before. Consequently, the agents are equipped with a single unsatisfiable need for points. The first point consumed is considered to be equally satisfying as the consumption of point number 100. Thus, a next unit of goods will contribute the same to the agents need satisfaction, independent of the number of goods consumed previously. This formalisation does not allow for the modelling of conflicting interests between different needs.

Forty years ago, Sauermann and Selten [19] presented a framework to tackle the problem of making decisions when you have different needs, in their approach different aspirations, without transforming the needs into one utility function. In [20] a more formal approach was presented, but so far this approach never been operationalised. Hence, an interesting task for the MAS community.

The modelling of different needs is in our view very important as to avoid this 'single need maximisation' of agents. This does not require that agents will be equipped with e.g., the seven needs as distinguished by Maslow [17]. Formalising two needs already allows for conducting experiments where agents have to compromise. For example, formalising a need for belongingness would stimulate agents to conform to the actions of the group, whereas a need for identity would stimulate deviant actions. Hence the two needs may require different actions for their satisfaction, implicating that the agent has to compromise.

3 Agent Decision-Making

Human structures, as well as human psychological mechanisms, at some fundamental level of description, can be analysed in terms of the problems they solve [21, p 321]. For example, social adaptive problems were so crucial for human survival and reproduction, that many of the most important features of our evolved psychological mechanism will necessarily be social in nature [21, p 323]. As a consequence, we developed socially and individually oriented psychological mechanisms that help us in making decisions, such as imitation, forming habits and following norms.

The various psychological mechanisms we have developed to solve problems are called 'heuristics'. These heuristics simplify complex decision problems, and save on cognitive effort involved in a decision. The work of Simon [22] on bounded rationality offers a perspective on why habits and complying with a norm may be a rational thing to do. The essential argument is that humans optimise the full process of decision-making (*procedural rationality*), not only the outcomes (*substantive rationality*, [22]). This holds that people may decide that a certain choice problem is not worth investing a lot of cognitive effort, whereas another choice problem requires more cognitive attention. Hence it is possible to describe the conditions that favour the use of certain types of heuristics. This would be helpful in formulating bounded rationality in artificial agents as a set of conditions that determine the use of certain strategies. For example, in formalising an imitation rule in an agent, one would also be able to formalise under what conditions this strategy will be employed.

In the last years, we have made considerable effort in trying to develop a framework to organise various heuristics [23], [24]. Here, we make a distinction regarding the cognitive effort that is being invested in the decision-making process, and the degree to which social information is being used. Generally, the less important a decision problem is (low contribution to multiple need satisfaction), the less cognitive energy (time) one is willing to invest in the decision, and hence, the simpler the heuristic that will be employed. Next to that, the degree of social information being used in heuristics differs significantly. Often people rely on their own previous experiences in a heuristic. For example, they may simply repeat previous behaviour. On the other hand, people may effectively use their cognitive capacity in considering the behaviour of others as to quickly find out attractive opportunities. Hence it appears that the heuristics that people employ can be organised on two dimensions: (1) the amount of cognitive effort that is involved, and (2), the individual versus social focus of information gathering [23].

In organising the various heuristics that people employ, we find it instructive to use the two dimensions of cognitive effort and proportion of social processing as depicted in Figure 1 (see e.g., [24]). Here, C stands for the cognitive effort invested in a decision heuristics, and β for the contribution of social information. In the figure we positioned several heuristics.

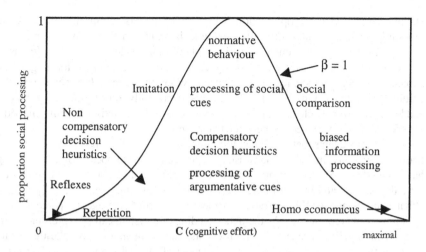

Fig. 1. Different heuristics organised along the dimensions of cognitive effort and use of social information

Figure 1 shows that heuristics that hardly require any cognitive effort (reflexes), or require very much cognitive effort (the prototypical homo economicus resembling the rational actor) do not use social information. Strategies that require an intermediate cognitive effort may use both social and non-social information. Here, uncertainty is a key factor that determines the degree to which social information is being used in the decision-making process.

The selection of a heuristic may not necessarily be conscious [25], but be an automaticity that has been learned (education, experience and looking at other people) and inherited (personality). Hence in the formalisation of agent rules it is possible to formalise under what condition which heuristic will be used.

Note that decision-making heuristics determine *how* agents make a choice, not what they choose. One of the main puzzles in social science is non-selfish behaviour observed in laboratory experiments and field work. This can be explained by need satisfaction where social value orientation, such as cooperative and competitive attitudes can be an important factor.

4 Agent Learning

People interacting within a system will learn about the system and the behaviour of other people, and may use this learned information in their decision-making. For example, after experiencing a number of droughts, people may have learned that occasional droughts belong to the behaviour of the natural system. Or a fisherman may learn from observation that cheating on the harvest quota may yield a substantial extra income. On the basis of this learning from system behaviour and other people's behaviour, people may decide on their own actions. For example, they may store food for droughts, exceed their harvest quota, or, on the contrary, decide to address the other cheater on his immoral behaviour. The latter example shows that learning may be a precondition for the emergence of norms.

Having learned what a proper action is in a given situation diminishes the necessity of investing as much cognitive effort the next time the same situation is encountered.

Learning may occur in situations where more or less cognitive effort is being invested. For example, by experiencing certain outcomes after performing particular behaviour a behaviouristic learning may occur, where the strength between the two events gradually increases. On the contrary, a person carefully scrutinising a problem may suddenly discover a relationship, and by means of this cognitive learning immediately experience a strong connection between two events.

Many agents that have been formalised up till now have no or only a very limited learning capability, including the consumat approach we developed. However, also agents have been developed that primarily focus on developing a cognitive structure that allows for a theoretical valid way of modelling processes of learning (e.g., [26], [27], [28], [29]). What is necessary for this learning is a memory in which the agent's perception of the system is being represented. As the understanding of a system can be represented in terms of the combined occurrence of certain events, such a memory may take the form of a neural network, which is in fact a stylised model of the real human brain. The principle that guides the learning process can be described using Hebb's learning rule [30]. This learning rule describes connection growth and - strengthening as a consequence of simultaneous activity of two neurons. Replacing the concept of neurons by events implies that the closer the occurrence of two events, e.g. behaviour and consequences, the stronger these two events will be connected. On the other hand, when two events cease to occur together, the connection between these two events also decreases. Hence, formalising the memory of agents in such a way allows for continuous learning in a changing system. Moreover, modelling the memory using a neural network approach allows for combining a continuous learning process with relative straightforward heuristics as derived from theory on decision-making.

5 The Need for Integration

In the previous sections we discussed needs, decision-making and learning as critical components of a meta-model of behaviour. These components are very strongly connected. For example, a person may be hungry during a famine (low need satisfaction), and therefore invest a lot of cognitive effort in finding new ways of storing food (decision process), and discovering a new way of conserving vegetables over a long period of time (learning). Learning this new way of storing food also diminishes the urgency of the problem and of investing a lot of cognitive effort in satisfying the need for food. Other persons may observe this new food storage technique, and decide to adopt it. These people learn to satisfy their need for food by using social heuristics. Hence it is clear that needs, heuristics and learning processes should be considered in combination in understanding how people adopt themselves to the system they take part of.

Also when formalising artificial agents that take part of a larger system, it is necessary to address the questions of needs, heuristics and learning, and especially to explicate how these issues are related in the model. Here the model builder is faced with the challenge to pick those theories from the abundance of information that are hypothesised to play a crucial role in the system behaviour under survey, and translate them into simple agent rules that still have a clear relation with the original theory. Hence, models that are focussing on different systems may employ agent rules that differ with regard to the formalisation of needs, heuristics and learning processes, and yet are based on the same basic structure. In Figure 2 we propose such a basic structure that can be used to formalise agent rules.

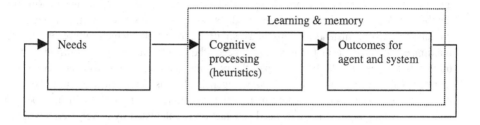

Fig. 2. A basic structure of artificial agents in complex systems

Essential in this basic structure is the feedback loop. This loop involves that the outcomes of behaviour, both on an individual level as on a system level, feedback to the individual needs. For example, the decision to over-harvest may cause a surplus of food now (individual) and a depletion of the food resource (system), which may satisfy the need for food now, but not in the long run.

6 An Example: The Consumat Approach

In recent years we developed the consumat approach as a tool aimed at the integration of various behavioural theories in a relative simple agent architecture [23], [31]. In [23] a review of relevant theories is provided, as well as a formalisation of various theories. The consumat approach emphasised especially the role of different needs and cognitive processes (heuristics), whereas learning processes have hardly been the subject of elaborate conceptualisation. The consumat approach has now been applied to common-pool problems [32], [33] and market dynamics [34], [35]. Like the boid flocking, we mainly showed in our previous publications that differences in needs and cognitive processes matters. But unlike the boid flocking our starting point was to define rules on agents based on theories from psychology. Although a number of theoretical problems are still waiting to be challenged, we now shifted our focus combining our theoretical agents with laboratory experiments and field work. In [36] we report on using the consumat approach to explain a set of laboratory experiments on common-pool resources.

All these simulation experiments are based on the same agent architecture. That is, first we formalise a number of needs. Here, we use the empirically grounded taxonomy of human needs as developed by [18]. This taxonomy comprises nine needs: subsistence, protection, affection, understanding, participation, leisure, creation, identity and freedom. Because formalising nine needs in an agent yield a very complex agent, we condense two or three needs out of this set to implement in the agent. Often we use a personal need, a social need and a need for identity. The personal need relates to how well a specific behaviour (product) satisfies the personal needs for the agent, and hence relates to nutritional value of food or the match of product characteristics with personal preferences. Next, the social need expresses the agent's preference to be in the neighbourhood of other agents (physical distribution) and/or to consume the same products/opportunities as other (similar) agents. Finally, the status need expresses the agent's need to possess more food, goods or capital than other agents (in the neighbourhood). Formalising different needs is essential to model conflicting interests in human behaviour. Instead of (implicit) single need agents, which ultimately try to maximise the satisfaction for this single need, the consumats may be confronted with trade-offs between needs. For example, the personal need may be a motivator to go to a location with a lot of food and a few other agents, whereas the social need may motivate the agent to go to a location where many other agents are, and where food may be less abundant. An aggregated level of need satisfaction is calculated by a weighted summing of the various needs. To express heterogeneity in agent's need valuation it is possible to attach different weights to the different needs in the weighted sum.

Another critical variable in the consumat is uncertainty of the agent. Uncertainty is a key factor that promotes the use of social processing in human beings (e.g., 37). In the consumat approach we formalise uncertainty often as a function that comprises both the expected outcomes and the actual outcomes. The larger the difference (over time) between these values, the larger the uncertainty gets. It is also possible to formalise uncertainty directly as a function of the perceived resources. In this way oscillations in e.g. food availability may cause uncertainty.

The level of need satisfaction and uncertainty determine the type of decision strategy an agent engages in. Critical factors here are the aspiration level and the uncertainty tolerance of the agent. Aspiration level indicates with what level of need satisfaction the agent is satisfied. Agents with a low aspiration level will be easy to satisfy, and hence do not engage quickly in intensive processing. On the contrary, agents with a high aspiration level are hard to satisfy and invest a lot of cognitive effort in their decision-making process. Aspiration level can conceptually be linked to personality traits that have been described in the Abridged Big Five Dimensions Circumplex of personality traits [38]. Uncertainty tolerance also fits very well on this taxonomy of personality traits. People having a low uncertainty tolerance are more likely to look at other people's behaviour, whereas people having a high uncertainty tolerance are more self-confident, and less sensitive to other people's behaviour.

Depending on the multiple need satisfaction of the agent (state), the agent's aspiration level (trait), the uncertainty of the agent (state) and the uncertainty tolerance of the agent (trait) it may engage in six decision rules that resemble cognitive processes (heuristics). Consumats having a very low level of need satisfaction are assumed to *deliberate*, that is: to determine the consequences of all possible decisions given a fixed time-horizon in order to maximise their level of need satisfaction. Consumats having a medium low level of need satisfaction and a low degree of uncertainty are assumed to engage in *satisficing*. This implies a strategy where the agent determines the consequences of decisions one by one, and selects the first decision that satisfies its needs. Consumats having a medium low level of need satisfaction and a high degree of uncertainty are assumed to engage in *social comparison*. This implies comparison of its own previous behaviour with the previous behaviour of consumats having roughly similar abilities, and selecting that behaviour which yields a maximal level of need satisfaction. Consumats having a medium high level of need satisfaction and a low degree of uncertainty are assumed to engage in *improving*. This implies determining the consequences of decisions one by one, and selecting the first decision that improves its need satisfaction. When consumats have a medium high level of need satisfaction, but also a high level of uncertainty, they will *imitate* the behaviour of other similar consumats. Finally, consumats having a very high level of need satisfaction simply *repeat* their previous behaviour. In the following Figure 3 it can be seen that these six rules resemble the organisation of heuristics as depicted in Figure 1.

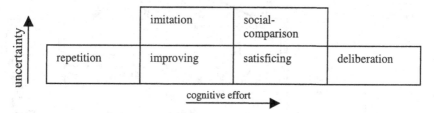

Fig. 3. The six decision rules as used in the consumat approach

When consumats invest more cognitive effort in their decision-making (deliberation, satisficing and social comparison) they will update the information in their mental map, which serves as a memory to store information on abilities, opportunities, and characteristics of other agents. This can also be understood as a more cognitive learning style. When consumats invest less cognitive effort in their decision-making (repetition, improving and imitating) they do not update their memory before making a decision. However, in as much the resulting outcomes will change the strength between events in the memory a more behaviouristic learning process will take place.

Modelling the six rules as requiring different quantities of time allows for the formalisation of cognitive effort. Here repetition costs hardly any time (close to 0% of the maximum), improving and imitation somewhat more (say 33%), social comparison and satisficing even more (say 66%) and deliberation the most (100%). The important consequence of such a formalisation is that the use of simpler rules may yield better outcomes due to the saving of time. For example, imitating the foraging behaviour of others may cause one to obtain a satisfactory quantity of food. Whereas a deliberating agent may find richer opportunities, the associated extra search costs (time) in finding these 'greener pastures' may cause that the quantity of food gathered is lower than the imitating agents gather.

After the consumption of opportunities, a new level of need satisfaction will be derived, and changes will occur regarding consumats' abilities, opportunities and uncertainty. Moreover, the environment the consumats behave in, e.g. a collective resource, will change as a consequence of their behaviour, thereby affecting the behaviour in subsequent time steps. The full consumat model is being depicted in the following Figure 4.

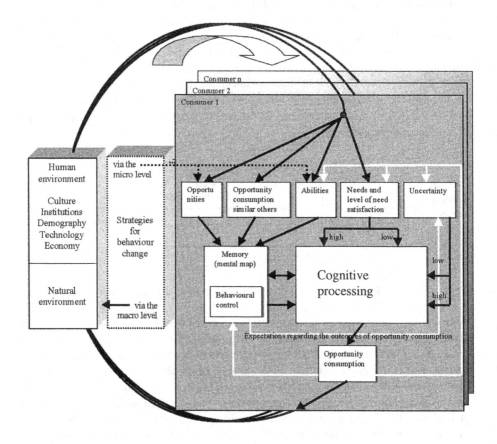

Fig. 4. The full consumat model

Working with the consumat approach on different topics has led us to some conclusions that may hold for the use of a basic agent structure in general. First of all, the results of experiments on different topics are often easy to relate. For example, when identified an 'imitation effect' in a series of relative simple simulation runs, it appeared that this effect also could explain part of the results we found in simulation runs where we formalise a more complex world. Hence the common basic structure facilitates the interchange of experimental results. Especially when the formalisation of the system varies with regard to complexity, it may be so that experiments with a simple system may reveal dynamics that contribute to interpreting the results obtained with a more elaborate formalisation of a system.

A second advantage we experienced working with our consumat approach is that it appeared to be easy to formalise adaptations to study the effects of certain variables. As such we have done experiments in which we formalised Social Value

Orientation (e.g. individualistic, cooperative) in agents by adapting the formalisation of needs [36]. In experiments on preferences we explored the effects of assuming that socialisation and repetitive consumption would alter the preferences agent have for certain opportunities [34]. In [32] we experimented with learning, by assuming that consumats may discover more effective fishing techniques when they deliberate, which subsequently may spread through the population by social processes. Currently we are experimenting with consumats that generate offspring when successful, which allows for experimenting the evolution of consumat characteristics.

A third advantage is that data from laboratory experiments may be used in calibrating the rules of the agents. Whereas it appeared that it is hard to compare micro-level data of artificial agents with data from real subjects [36], it appeared that this comparison stimulated our thinking about which needs and processes should be incorporated in the model. More importantly, a perspective emerged of combining empirical and simulation studies as to explore the dynamics of e.g. simple resource systems, and provide a validation of the agent rules which can not be obtained when modelling more complex systems.

All these experiences convinced us of the value of using an integrated agent model when modelling behaviour in more complex systems.

We also found a number of disadvantages. Our models like many MAS models are artificial worlds, and are limited to explain real world phenomena. But starting to use micro-level data, we are confronted with the problem that a number of our hypotheses cannot be empirically tested because the appropriate data are not available. To strive towards such a validation at the micro level would require rigorously studying the use of heuristics in laboratory and field settings.

7 Prospects of Integrated Agent Models of Behaviour

The simulation of behaviour in systems is increasingly being recognised as a valuable tool to explore the dynamics of various systems. It is very important to capture the relevant micro-level dynamics in these models. For example, if a MAS-model is being used for policy development and support, it may be dangerous to base suggestions for policy measurements on false assumptions of the micro-level behavioural dynamics. To increase the validity of the behavioural dynamics as generated by artificial agents it is recommended to use a basic structure of the agent structure that is based on empirical findings in social sciences such as economics, psychology, sociology, political science and anthropology. Using such a basic structure also facilitates the discussion on how to formalise agent rules in a certain context, and contributes to the comparability of simulation results. Up till now the discussion is often unclear because of the fundamental differences in the behavioural architecture of agents, and hence the incomparability of results. Using a joint basic structure, how different the eventual formalisations may be, will contribute to the exchange of information between research groups, and hence benefit both the growth of knowledge on human dynamics in complex systems, and the application of this knowledge.

Including behavioural dynamics in a more empirically grounded way in simulation models of more complex systems would also allow for experimenting with real people managing artificial systems. Hence it would be possible to experimentally study the management of e.g. large organisations or ecosystems including policy measures aimed at changing the behaviour of the simulated agents.

Acknowledgment. The second author gratefully acknowledges support from the Center for the Study of Institutions, Population, and Environmental Change at Indiana University through National Science Foundation grants SBR9521918 and SES0083511.

References

1. Reynolds, C.W. (1987) Flocks, Herds, and Schools: A Distributed Behavioral Model, *Computer Graphics, 21(4):* 25–34.
2. Camazine, S. J.-L. Deneubourg, N.R. Franks, J. Sneyd, G. Theraulaz and E. Bonabeau (2001). *Self-Organization in Biological Systems,* Princeton University Press.
3. Schelling, T.C. (1971), 'Dynamic Models of Segregation', *Journal of Mathematical Sociology, 1:* 143–186.
4. Axelrod, R. (1984), *The evolution of cooperation,* Basic Books, New York.
5. Erev, I., A. Roth (1998) Prediking How People Play Games: Reinforcement Learning In Experimental Geamas with Unique, Mixed Strategy Equilibria, *American Economic Review 88:* 848–881.
6. Duffy, J. (2001). Learning to speculate: Experiments with artificial and real agents. *Journal of Economic Dynamics & Control, 25:* 295–319.
7. Hommes, C.H., (2001). Financial Markets as Nonlinear Adaptive Evolutionary Systems, Quantitative Finance, 1: 149–167.
8. Gigerenzer, G., P.M. Todd, and the ABC Research (1999), *Simple Heuristics That Make Us Smart.* New York: Oxford University Press.
9. Gintis, H. (2000), 'Beyond Homo economicus: evidence from experimental economics', *Ecological Economics,* **35**: 311–322.
10. Selten, R. (2001) What Is Bounded Rationality?, in Gigerenzer, G, and R. Selten (eds). *Bounded Rationality: The Adaptive Toolbox,* Cambridge, MA: MIT Press, pp.13–36.
11. Khalil, E.L. (1996). Social theory and naturalism. An introduction. In: E.L.Khalil and K.E. Boulding (Eds.). *Evolution, order and complexity.* London: Routledge. pp. 1–39
12. Bousquet, F., Cambier, C., Mullon, C., Morand P. and Quensiere, J., (1994). Simulating fishermen's society. In: N. Gilbert and J. Doran (Eds.) (1994). *Simulating societies: The computer simulation of social phenomena.* London: UCL Press.
13. Bousquet, F., O. Barreteau, P. d'Aquino M. Etienne, S. Boissau, S. Aubert, C. Le Page, D. Babin and J.C. Castella (2002) Multi-agent systems and role games : collective learning processes for ecosystem management, , in Janssen, M.A. (ed.) *Complexity and Ecosystem Management: The Theory and Practice of Multi-agent Systems,* Edward Elgar Publishers, Cheltenham UK/ Northampton, MA, USA.
14. Mosler, H.J., Schwarz, K., Ammann, F., Gutscher, H. (2001) Computer simulation as a method of further developing a theory: Simulating the Elaboration Likelihood Model. *Personality and Social Psychology Review, 5 (3):* 201–215.
15. Wilk, R. (2002) Consumption, human needs, and global environmental change, Global Environmental Change, 12: 5–13.
16. Vallacher, R.R. and Nowak, A., (1994). The chaos in social psychology. In: R.R. Vallacher and A. Nowak, (Eds.). *Dynamical systems in social psychology.* San Diego: Academic Press, Inc.
17. Maslow, A.H. (1954). *Motivation and Personality.* New York, USA: Harper and Row.

18. Max-Neef, M., (1992). Development and human needs. In: P. Ekins and M. Max-Neef (Eds.): *Real-life economics: Understanding wealth creation*. London, New York: Routledge.
19. Sauermann, H., & R. Selten (1962). Anspruchsanpassungstheorie der Unternehmung. *Zeitschrift für die gesamte Staatswissenschaft*. 118: 577–597.
20. Selten, R. (1998). Aspiration Adaptation Theory. *Journal of Mathematical Psychology*. 42: 191–214.
21. Buss, D.M. (1997) Evolutionary Foundations of Personality. In: R. Hogan, J. Johnson, and S. Briggs (Eds.), *Handbook of personality psychology* (pp. 317–344). London: Academic Press.
22. Simon, H.A. (1976). *Administrative behavior: a study of decision-making processes in administrative organizations*. New York: Harper.
23. Jager, W., (2000). Modelling consumer behaviour. Doctoral thesis. Groningen: University of Groningen, Centre for Environmental and Traffic psychology. http://docserver.ub.rug.nl/eldoc/dis/ppsw/w.jager/
24. Jager, W., & Janssen, M.A. (2002). *How to decide how to decide: An integrated and dynamical perspective on human decision-making*. Working paper: University of Groningen, Faculty of Management and Organisation, Dept. of Marketing.
25. Payne, J.W., Bettman, J.R., & Johnson, E.J. (1993). *The adaptive decision maker*. New York: Cambridge University Press.
26. Weiss, G., & Sen, S. (Eds.)(1996). *Adaptation and learning in multi-agent systems*. Lecture Notes in Artificial Intelligence, Volume 1042. Heidelberg: Springer-Verlag
27. Weiss, G. (Ed.) (1997). *Distributed artificial intelligence meets machine learning: Learning in multi-agent environments*. Lecture Notes in Artificial Intelligence, Volume 1221. Heidelberg: Springer-Verlag
28. Conte, R., (1999). Social Intelligence Among Autonomous Agents. *Computational and Mathematical Organization Theory 5(3)*, 203–228.
29. Conte, R. & Paolucci, M. (2001). Intelligent Social Learning. *Journal of Artificial Societies and Social Simulation vol. 4, no. 1*, http://www.soc.surrey.ac.uk/JASSS/4/1/3.html
30. Hebb, D.O. (1949). *The Organization of Behavior*: New York: John Wiley and Sons, Inc.
31. Jager, W., Janssen, M.A. and C.A.J. Vlek (1999). Consumats in a commons dilemma: Testing the behavioural rules of simulated consumers. COV report no. 99–01. 56 pages. Groningen: Centre for Environment and Traffic   Psychology, University of Groningen
32. Jager, W., Janssen, M.A, De Vries, H.J.M., De Greef, J. and Vlek, C.A.J. (2000). Behaviour in commons dilemmas: Homo Economicus and Homo Psychologicus in an ecological-economic model. *Ecological Economics, Vol. 35*:357–380.
33. Jager, W., Janssen, M., & Vlek, C., (in press, 2002). How uncertainty stimulates over-harvesting in a commons dilemma: the imitation effect. *Journal of Environmental Psychology*.
34. Janssen, M.A. and Jager, W., (2001). Adoption of new products in a market of heterogeneous and changing preferences and social networks Journal of Economic Psychology, 22: 745–772.
35. Janssen, M.A. & Jager, W. (in press 2002) Stimulating diffusion of green products. Co-evolution between firms and consumers. *Journal of Evolutionary Economics*
36. Jager, W., Janssen, M.A. (in press 2002). Using artificial agents to understand laboratory experiments of common-pool resources with real agents, in Janssen, M.A. (ed.) *Complexity and Ecosystem Management: The Theory and Practice of Multi-agent Systems*, Edward Elgar Publishers, Cheltenham UK/ Northampton, MA, USA
37. Festinger, L. (1954). A theory of social comparison processes. *Human Relations, 7,* 117–140.
38. Hofstee, W. K. B., De Raad, B., & Goldberg, L. R. (1992). Integration of the Big Five and Circumplex approaches to trait structure. Journal of Social and Personality Psychology, 63, 146–163.

Relating Structure and Dynamics in
Organisation Models

Catholijn M. Jonker[1] and Jan Treur[1,2]

[1]Vrije Universiteit Amsterdam, Department of Artificial Intelligence
De Boelelaan 1081a, NL-1081 HV Amsterdam, The Netherlands
{jonker, treur}@cs.vu.nl
http://www.cs.vu.nl/~{jonker, treur}
[2]Utrecht University, Department of Philosophy
Heidelberglaan 8, 3584 CS Utrecht

Abstract. To understand how an organisational structure relates to dynamics is an interesting fundamental challenge in the area of social modelling. Specifications of organisational structure usually have a diagrammatic form that abstracts from more detailed dynamics. Dynamic properties of agent systems, on the other hand, are often specified in the form of a set of logical formulae in some temporal language. This paper addresses the question how these two perspectives can be combined in one framework. It is shown how for different aggregation levels within an organisation structure, sets of dynamic properties can be specified. Organisational structure provides a structure of interlevel relationships between these multiple sets of dynamic properties. Thus organisational structure relates to specification of the dynamics of organisational behaviour. As an illustration, for Ferber and Gutknecht's AGR organisation modelling approach it is shown how a foundation can be obtained for integrated specification of both structure and dynamic properties of an organisation.

1 Introduction

Societies are characterised by complex dynamics involving interaction between large numbers of actors and groups of actors. If such complex dynamics takes place in an completely unstructured, incoherent manner, any actor involved has not much to rely on to do prediction, and is not able to function in a knowledgeable manner. This has serious disadvantages, which is a reason why in history within human societies organisational structure has been developed as a means to manage complex dynamics. Organisational structure provides co-ordination of the processes in such a manner that a process or agent involved can function in a more adequate manner. The dynamics shown by a given organisational structure are much more dependable than in an entirely unstructured situation. It is assumed that the organisational structure itself is relatively stable, i.e., the structure may change, but the frequency and scale of change are assumed low compared to the more standard dynamics through the structure.

J.S. Sichman, F. Bousquet, P. Davidsson (Eds.): MABS 2002, LNAI 2581, pp. 50-69, 2003.

Within the field of Organisation Theory such organisational structures regulating societal dynamics are studied; e.g., [18], [21]. In summary, organisational *structure* is used to obtain *dynamics* (or organisational *behaviour*) of a desired type. For further analysis a crucial issue here is how exactly structure is able to *affect* dynamics.

This implies in particular that to devise an appropriate approach to organisation modelling, both the *structural* aspects and the *dynamic* aspects and their *relation* have to be covered in an appropriate manner. Multi-agent or organisation modelling approaches have been developed in three manners.

Firstly, informal or semi-formal graphical representations of the organisational structure have been developed; i.e., pictures with boxes and arrows; e.g., [21]. Such organisation models, although they provide a detailed account of the organisation structure, remain on a rather abstract level. In particular they do not give indications how the more detailed dynamics takes place; it does not specify how these structures relate to dynamics.

Secondly, within the area of Computational Organisation Theory and Artificial Intelligence, a number of organisation modelling approaches have been developed to simulate and analyse dynamics within organisations in society; e.g., [23], [19], [22], [6], [11], [12], [13]. Some of these approaches explicitly focus on modelling organisational structure, abstracting from the detailed dynamics. Other approaches put less emphasis on organisational structure but focus on the dynamics in the sense of implementing and experimenting with simulation models. Often these simulation models are based on some implementation environment and not specified in an implementation-independent manner using a formally defined conceptual language. The Strictly Declarative Modelling Language SDML [22] (see also [4]) , and the use of the agent-oriented modelling approach DESIRE in social simulation as presented in [3] are some of the few exceptions. Both modelling approaches focus on specification and simulation; however, they do not offer dedicated support for a specific type of organisational structure. Moreover, simulation of dynamics is the main purpose; not much formally defined support is offered for analysis of dynamics, such as checking whether a given simulation or empirical trace satisfies a given dynamic property.

Thirdly, temporal modelling is one of the dominant approaches for specification and analysis of dynamic properties in agent systems in general; e.g., [1], [9], [9], [22], [16], [11]. One of the strong points in this area of research is the declarative modelling of simulation models, for example based on the paradigm of Executable Temporal Logic [1]. However, the temporal languages or logics usually adopted do not provide explicitly specified organisational structure.

The Agent/Group/Role (AGR) approach (previously called Aalaadin) introduced in [6] is an example of an approach initially focussing on organisational structure, abstracting from the details of the dynamics. However, [7] and [8] are some first steps to relate specifications of dynamic properties to the organisational structure provided by AGR. In [1] the MOCA system presented combines the AGR model with Madkit into a platform, based on a theoretical foundation. This paper shows how dynamics of the organisational structure itself can be modelled: agents that can dynamically create, join, or quit groups.

This paper presents a foundation that can be used to develop an organisation modelling approach that takes into account organisation structure, organisation behaviour (i.e., the internal dynamics) and their relation. First it is explored in more detail (Section 2) how *organisational structure* can be specified based on a formally defined foundation. Section 3 addresses how, given a formalisation of organisational structure, *dynamic properties* can be associated to each element within this structure. These dynamic properties can be used for simulation (especially when expressed in executable format) and analysis of empirical or simulated traces.

As different parts or aggregation levels are structurally related within an organisational structure, a next question in the context of the relation between organisation structure and dynamics is how the associated sets of dynamic properties can be related accordingly. To this end, in Section 4, as part of an analysis of how organisational structure relates to organisational dynamics, *logical interlevel relationships between sets of dynamic properties* of different parts or aggregation levels within an organisational structure are described. Finally, for realisation of an organisation, requirements can be specified on *agents allocated to roles* within an organisation model (Section 5). The paper provides a generic foundation for integrated specification languages covering both structure and dynamics. However, what such a language specifically would look like (for example, using semi-formal and graphical elements) is left open. The foundational approach is illustrated for AGR organisation models, but has a wider applicability.

2 Specification of Organisation Structure

This section presents an approach to a foundation for the specification of organisation *structure*. Organisation structure is often depicted in diagrammatic form (for example, as kind of labelled graph; e.g., see Figures 1 and 2) consisting of different types of elements within the organisation (such as roles, groups, interactions), and relationships between these elements. A suitable formalisation approach for such structure descriptions is the notion of semantic structures (or models, in terms of logic) for many-sorted predicate logic; e.g., [20]. These structures will be denoted by tuples

$$< S_1, \ldots S_n; R_1, \ldots R_p; F_1, \ldots, F_q >$$

where S_i are sorts, R_j relations over sorts, and F_k functions on sorts. This formalisation approach is adopted as a foundation for specification of organisational structure, and illustrated for AGR organisation structures.

Within the Agent/Group/Role or AGR organisation modelling approach [6], an organisation structure consists of a set of *groups*, *roles* in each group and *agents* fulfilling roles; moreover, *connections* between roles are possible; see Figure 1. Here the smaller ovals indicate roles and bigger ovals groups. Connections are indicated by the two types of arrows (dashed indicates an intergroup interaction, not dashed indicates a transfer). To indicate which role belongs to which group is depicted by drawing the smaller role oval within the bigger group oval.

A factory is considered that is organised at the highest aggregation level according to two divisions: *division A* that produces certain components and *division B* that assembles these components to (composite) products. At one aggregation level lower the division A is organised according to two departments: *department A1* (the work planning department for division A) and *department A2* (component production department). Similarly, division B is organised according to two department roles: *department B1* (for assembly work planning) and *department B2* (product production department).

The two divisions are modeled as *groups* (depicted by the larger ovals), with the departments as their *roles* (depicted by smaller ovals within larger ones). A third group, the Connection Group C, models the communication between the two divisions. This group consists of the two *roles* 'division A representative' and 'division B representative'. *Intergroup role interactions* (depicted by pairs of dotted lines) are modeled between the role 'department A1' in the division A group and the role 'division A representative' within the connection group, and between the role 'department B1' in the division B group and the role 'division B representative' within the connection group. *Intragroup role transfers* model communication between the two roles within each of the groups (depicted by the arrows).

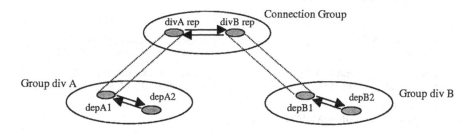

Fig. 1. An example AGR organisation structure

Connections have destination roles (indicated by the arrow points) and source roles (no pointing). Based on the semantic structures of many-sorted predicate logic a more precise formal definition is the following.

Definition 1   (AGR Organisation Structure)
Let IDENT be the set of all identifiers, and let Groups, Roles, Transfers, and Intergroup_interactions be subsets of IDENT which subsequently contain the names of groups, roles, transfers, and intergroup interactions in the organisation. An AGR *organisation structure* is defined by a tuple of sets and relations in the following manner:

AGROrg =   <   Groups, Roles, Intergroup_interactions, Transfers,
                          role_in, source_of_interaction, destination_of_interaction,
                          source_of_transfer, destination_of_transfer >

Each group involves a set of roles. The relationship

role_in: Roles × Groups

defines which role is in which group. The source and destination roles that an intergroup interaction connects are specified by

source_of_interaction, destination_of_interaction: Roles × Intergroup_interactions

Furthermore, transfers relate source roles to destination roles. The relationships

source_of_transfer, destination_of_transfer: Roles × Transfers

specify the roles a transfer connects. It is demanded that source and destination of a transfer belong to the same group:

∀sr, dr ∈ Roles, ∀ t ∈ Transfers:

(source_of_transfer(sr, t) ∧ destination_of_transfer(dr, t)) ⇒
              ∃g ∈ Groups: (role_in(sr, g) ∧ role_in(dr, g))

The example organisation of Figure 1 has

Groups	= {divA, divB, C},
Roles	= {depA1, depA2, depB1, depB2, divArep, divBrep},
Intergroup_interactions	= {iAC, iCA, iBC, iCB}
Transfers	= {tA12, tA21, tB12, tB21},

Some of the relationships are:

within divA

role_in(depA1, divA),
role_in(depA2, divA),

source_of_transfer(depA1, tA12),
destination_of_transfer(depA2, tA12),

source_of_transfer(depA2, tA21),
destination_of_transfer(depA1, tA21),

organisation level

source_of_interaction(divA, iAC),
destination_of_interaction(C, iAC),

source_of_interaction(C, iCA),
destination_of_interaction(divA, iCA),

Note that, for simplicity, no difference is made between a role and role instances that inherit properties of the role. When desired, within a specific language developed on the basis of the formalisation presented here such a difference can be made. Furthermore, intergroup interactions are defined between two roles; this can easily be generalised for intergroup interactions involving more than two roles.

For all i ∈ Intergroup_interactions (resp. t ∈ Transfers or g ∈ Groups), let involved_roles(i) (resp. involved_roles(t), and involved_roles(g)) denote the set of all roles that are involved in interaction i (resp. transfer t or group g):

involved_roles(i) = { r ∈ Roles | destination_of_interaction(r, i) ∨ source_of_interaction(r, i) }
involved_roles(t) = { r ∈ Roles | destination_of_transfer(r, t) ∨ source_of_transfer(r, t) }
involved_roles(g) = { r ∈ Roles | role_in(r, g) }

3 Dynamic Properties in an Organisation

After a foundation of an organisation structure has been defined, foundations for specification of dynamic properties in an organisation are addressed. The aim is not only to cover simple types of dynamics, such as simple reactive behaviour, but also more complex dynamics. For specification of more complex dynamic properties, often temporal logical languages are used; such language have no internal structuring (other than the manner in which formulae can be formed by logical connectives). The challenge here is to incorporate somehow the organisational structure within the logical description of the organisation's internal dynamics. To this aim, the following approach is introduced:

- for each *element* within the organisational structure characterise its dynamics by a *specific set of dynamic properties*; this is addressed in Section 3

- based on *structural relations between elements* in an organisational structure, identify *relationships between the sets of dynamic properties* corresponding with these elements; this is addressed in Section 4

In general, the dynamics of an element within an organisation structure can be characterised by specification of dynamic properties expressing relationships of states of that element over time. For a role the concept 'state' needs to be defined both for the input and the output of the role. Since transfers and intergroup interactions are assumed to operate only on input and output states of roles, without having their own internal state, no further state is assumed for transfers and intergroup interactions. To define states the notion of state property is useful, which is expressed in terms of a state ontology. Moreover, the notion of trace as a sequence of states over a time frame is used to formalise dynamics.

Definition 2   (Ontology, State, Trace)
(a) A *state ontology* is a specification (in order-sorted logic) of a vocabulary, i.e., a signature. A state for ontology Ont is an assignment of truth-values {true, false} to the set At(Ont) of ground atoms expressed in terms of Ont. The *set of all possible states* for state ontology Ont is denoted by STATES(Ont).
(b) A fixed *time frame* T is assumed which is linearly ordered. A *trace* T over a state ontology Ont and time frame T is a mapping $T : T \rightarrow$ STATES(Ont), i.e., a sequence of states $T_t (t \in T)$ in STATES(Ont). The set of all traces over state ontology Ont is denoted by TRACES(Ont).

Depending on the application, it may be dense (e.g., the real numbers), or discrete (e.g., the set of integers or natural numbers or a finite initial segment of the natural numbers), or any other form, as long as it has a linear ordering.

Definition 3   (State Properties and Dynamic Properties)
Let Σ be a given set of state ontologies.
(a) The set of *state properties* STATPROP(Σ) is the set of all propositions over ground atoms expressed in the ontologies from Σ.
(b) Let L be a language for dynamic properties. The set of *dynamic properties* DYNPROP$_L$(Σ) is the set of formulae that can be formulated in language L with respect to traces based on the set of state ontologies Σ.

The subscript L is dropped, when no confusion is expected and when the usage of the set is irrespective of a choice of language. For the paper such a language L is assumed with semantic consequence relation $\models$. The approach is independent of the choice of this language. Two examples of such languages are

- temporal logic with operators that are specific for elements of the organisational structure or multi-agent system; e.g., [9], [4].
- the Temporal Trace Language TTL; e.g., [16], [11].

In order to characterise the dynamics within an organisation, dynamic properties for each of the elements of an organisation structure have to be specified: for the AGR modelling approach for each role, each transfer, each group, each intergroup interaction, and for the organisation as a whole. A specification of the dynamics requires a specification of the state ontologies used (for expressing state properties) for input states and output states of roles. The specifications of the dynamic properties are based on the given state ontologies.

Definition 4   (AGR Organisation Dynamics)
Let ONT be a set of (state) ontologies and O an AGR organisation structure over ONT:

$$O \; = \; < \; \text{Groups, Roles, Intergroup\_interactions, Transfers,}$$
$$\text{role\_in, source\_of\_interaction, destination\_of\_interaction,}$$
$$\text{source\_of\_transfer, destination\_of\_transfer} >.$$

(a) The dynamics of the AGR organisation O is formalised by a tuple as follows:

AGRDyn = < O,   role_input_ontologies, role_output_ontologies,
         role_dynproperties, transfer_dynproperties,
         group_dynproperties, intergroup_interaction_dynproperties,
         organisation_dynproperties >

where

role_input_ontologies, role_output_ontologies:	Roles $\to \wp(\text{ONT})$
role_dynproperties:	Roles $\to \wp(\text{DYNPROP(ONT)})$
transfer_dynproperties:	Transfers $\to \wp(\text{DYNPROP(ONT)})$
group_dynproperties:	Groups $\to \wp(\text{DYNPROP(ONT)})$
intergroup_interaction_dynproperties:	Intergroup_interactions $\to \wp(\text{DYNPROP(ONT)})$
organisation_dynproperties:	$\{O\} \to \wp(\text{DYNPROP(ONT)})$

For these mappings the constraints C1 … C5 listed below are assumed to be fulfilled.
(b) For any part P of organisation O (here a part P is a set of groups, roles, intergroup interactions and/or transfers), ONT(P) denotes the ontology defined as the union of the ontologies used in the elements of P. For example, ONT(O) denotes the ontology defined as the union of all of the ontologies used somewhere in the organisation structure O. For shortness, ONT denotes ONT(O)
(c) For the given organisation structure O, the set DYNPROP$_L$(R, Σ) is the set of dynamic properties that can be formulated in language L with respect to a set R of identifiers of parts (i.e., roles, and/or groups) of the organisation structure and with respect to a set Σ of ontologies. The subscript L is dropped, when no confusion is expected and when the usage of the set is irrespective of a choice of language. The set DYNPROP(O, ONT(O)) is the set of all dynamic properties of O. If no confusion is ex-

pected, DYNPROP refers to DYNPROP(O, ONT(O)). For readability, DYNPROP({ r }, Σ) is abbreviated to DYNPROP(r, Σ).

C1 Role dynamic properties

Role dynamic properties relate input to output of that role:

$$\forall r \in \text{Roles: role\_dynproperties(r)} \subseteq \text{DYNPROP(r, ONT(r))}$$

For example, the gossip role behaviour: 'whenever somebody tells you something, you will tell it to everybody else' is expressed in terms of input of the role leading to output of the role in a reactive manner. An example relating to Figure 1:

DP(depA1)   **Progress Information Generates Planning in depA1**
If within division A department A1 receives progress information on component production, then an updated planning will be generated by department A1 taking this most recent information into account.

C2 Transfer dynamic properties

Transfer properties relate output of the source roles to input of the destination roles:

$\forall t \in$ Transfers: transfer_dynproperties(t) $\subseteq$

DYNPROP(involved_roles(t) , $\bigcup$\{ role_output_ontologies(r) | source_of_transfer(r, t) \}

$\cup \bigcup$\{ role_input_ontologies(r) | destination_of_transfer(r, t) \})

Typically, such sets contain properties like, information is indeed transferred from source to destination, transfer is brought about within x time, arrival comes later than departure, and information departs before other information also arrives before that other information.

C3 Group dynamic properties

Group dynamic properties relate input and/or output of roles within a group.

$$\text{group\_dynproperties(G)} \subseteq \text{DYNPROP(G, ONT(G))}$$

An example of a group property is: "if the manager asks anyone within the group to provide the secretary with information, then the secretary will receive this information". A special case of a group property is an *intragroup interaction* relating the outputs of two roles within a group. A typical (informal) example of such an intragroup interaction property is: "if the manager says 'good afternoon', then the secretary will reply with 'good afternoon' as well". Other examples may involve statistical information, such as "3 out of the 4 employees within the organisation never miss a committed deadline". Example relating to Figure 1 for division A:

DP(A)   A Progress Information Generation
This property is the conjunction of the following properties.
DP1(A) Initial A Progress Information Generation
Department A1 receives initial progress information on component production processes, involving already available components.
DP2(A) Subsequent A Progress Information Generation
Within the division A group, for any component production planning generated by department A1, incorporating a specific required set of components, progress information on the production of these components will be received by department A1.

C4 Intergroup interaction dynamic properties

Intergroup interaction properties relate the input of the source role to the output of the destination role:

∀ i ∈ Intergroup_interactions:

intergroup_interaction_dynproperties(i) ⊆ DYNPROP(involved_roles(i) ,

∪{ role_input_ontologies(r) | source_of_interaction(r, i)   }

∪ ∪{ role_output_ontologies(r) | destination_of_interaction(r, i) })

For example, a project leader is asked by one of the project team members (input of role 'project leader' within the project group) to put forward a proposal in the meeting of project leaders (output of role 'member' within the project leaders group). An example relating to Figure 1:

Intergroup Role Interaction between A and C: IrRI(A, C)

For the connectivity between the groups A and C, the following intergroup role interaction properties are considered, one from A to C, and one from C to A.

IrRI(depA1, divArep)   Progress Information Provision A to B

If within division A progress information on component production is received by department A1, then within the connection group this will be communicated by the division A representative to the division B representative.

IrRI(divArep, depA1)   B Progress Information Incorporation by A

If within the connection group the division A representative receives information from the division B representative on which components are needed, then within division A a component production planning will be generated by department A1 taking these into account.

C5 Organisation dynamic properties

Organisation dynamic properties relate to input and/or output of roles within the organisation.

organisation_dynproperties(G) ⊆ DYNPROP(O, ONT(O))

A typical (informal) example of such a property is: "if within the organisation, role A promises to deliver a product, then role B will deliver this product". An example relating to Figure 1:

DP(F)   Overall Progress Notification

If a request for a product is made (by a client),
then progress information will be provided (for the client).

The different types of dynamic properties all relate to different combinations of input and output. Table 1 provides an overview of these combinations. Note that with respect to simulation, the above dynamics definition can contain elements that are redundant: a smaller subset of dynamical properties can form an executable specification of the dynamics of an AGR type organisation. For example, on the basis of the role and transfer dynamic properties and intergroup interactions the organisation can be simulated. The group dynamic properties, including the intragroup role interaction properties, and the organisation properties should emerge in the execution, and testing for them can validate the model.

Table 1. Types of Dynamic Properties for an AGR Organisation Model

Property type	Relating	
Role r	Role r Input	Role r Output
Transfer from r1 to r2	Role r1 Output	Role r2 Input
Group G	Input or Output of roles in G	
Intragroup interaction	Role r1 Output	Role r2 Output
Intergroup interaction	Role r1 Input	Role r2 Output
Organisation	Input or Output of roles in O	

In order to make an executable organisation model the dynamical properties need to be chosen from the set of executable dynamical properties EXEDYNPROP $\subseteq$ DYNPROP, for example Executable Temporal Logic [1], or the 'leads to' format presented in [17].

4 Interlevel Relations between Dynamic Properties

An organisational structure defines relations between different elements in an organisation. In Section 3 the dynamics of these different elements were characterised by sets of dynamic properties. An organisational structure has the aim to keep the overall dynamics of the organisation manageable; therefore the structural relations between the different elements within the organisational structure have to impose somehow relationships or dependencies between their dynamics. In the introduction to their book Lomi and Larsen [19] emphasize the importance of such relationships. Organisations can be seen as adaptive complex information processing systems of (boundedly) rational agents, and as tools for control; central challenges are [19]:

- from the first view: 'given a set of assumptions about (different forms of) individual behaviour, how can the aggregate properties of a system be determined (or predicted) that are generated by the repeated interaction among those individual units?'
- from the second view: 'given observable regularities in the behaviour of a composite system, which rules and procedures - if adopted by the individual units - induce and sustain these regularities?'.

Both views and problems require means to express relationships between dynamics of different elements and different levels of aggregation within an organisation. In [19] two levels are mentioned: the level of the organisation as a whole versus the level of the units. Also in the development of MOISE (cf. [11], [12], [13]) an emphasis is put on relating dynamics to structure. Within MOISE dynamics is described at the level of units by the goals, actions, plans and resources allocated to roles to obtain the organisation's task as a whole. Specification of the task as a whole may involve achieving a final (goal) state, or an ongoing process (maintenance goals) and an associated plan specification.

As in our formalisation introduced in Section 3, dynamics are characterised by sets of dynamic properties for the respective elements of the organisation, the next step to be made is to identify how organisational structure determines (mathematically defined) relationships between these sets of dynamic properties for the different elements and aggregation levels within an organisation. Preferably such relations between sets of dynamic properties would be of a logical nature; this would allow the use of logical methods to analyse, verify and validate organisation dynamics in relation to organisation structure. Indeed, in our approach presented below, logical relationships between sets of dynamic properties of elements in an organisation turn out an adequate manner to (mathematically) express such dynamic cross-element or cross-level relationships. This will be illustrated for the AGR approach. Within AGR organisation models three aggregation levels are involved:

-   the organisation as a whole; the highest aggregation level.
-   the level of a group
-   the level of a role within a group

A general pattern for the dynamics in the organisation as a whole in relation to the dynamics in groups is as follows:

>   dynamic properties for the groups &
>   dynamic properties for intergroup role interaction
>   ⟹ dynamic properties for the organisation

Moreover, dynamic properties of groups can be related to dynamic properties of roles as follows:

>   dynamic properties for roles &
>   dynamic properties for transfer between roles
>   ⟹ dynamic properties for a group

The idea is that these are properties dynamically relating a number of roles within one group. To get the idea, consider the special case of an intragroup role interaction from role r1 to role r2, characterised by dynamic properties, that relate output of one role r1 to output of another role r2. Assuming that transfer from output of r1 to input of r2 is adequate and simply copies the information, this property mainly depends on the dynamics of the role r2.

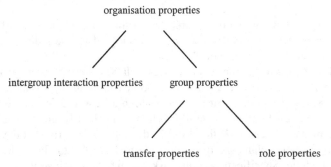

Fig. 2. Overview of interlevel relations between dynamic properties

Therefore in this case the relationship has the form:

>   dynamic properties for role r2 &
>   dynamic properties for transfer from role r1 to role r2
>   ⟹ dynamic properties of intragroup interaction from r1 to r2

An overview of the logical relationships between dynamic properties at different aggregation levels is depicted as an AND-tree in Figure 2. The logical relationships put forward above can be formalised in the following manner. In Definition 5 below the following notations are used, where G is a group:

con(F)   is the conjunction of all dynamic properties in a finite set F

role_dynproperties(G)   = $\cup$ { role_dynproperties(t) | role_in(r, G) }
transfer_dynproperties(G)   =

$\cup$ { transfer_dynproperties(t) | t: Transfer, involved_roles(t) $\subseteq$ involved_roles(G) }

transfer_dynproperties(O)   = $\cup$ { transfer_dynproperties(t) | t: Transfer }
intergroup_interaction_dynproperties(O) =

$\cup$ { intergroup_interaction_dynproperties(i) | i: Intergroup_interaction }

Definition 5 (Role-Group and Group-Organisation Interlevel Relations)

Let AGRDyn be a model for the dynamics of an AGR organisation structure O.

(a) A *logical role-group interlevel relation* for G is a logical statement of the form

$$DP_1 \;\&\; ... \;\&\; DP_n \;\&\; TR \qquad\qquad \Rightarrow \qquad DP$$

where

DP   a group dynamics property for G, from
       group_dynproperties(G)
DP$_i$ a role dynamics property or conjunction thereof from
       role_dynproperties(r$_i$),
TR   a transfer dynamics property or conjunction thereof from transfer_dynproperties(G),

The set of all role-group interlevel relations for G is denoted by RGIR(G); the union of all of them over all groups is denoted by RGIR.

(b) A *logical group-organisation interlevel relation* for O is a logical statement in of the form

$$DP_1 \;\&\; ... \;\&\; DP_n \;\&\; TR \;\&\; IID \qquad \Rightarrow \qquad DP$$

where

DP   an organisation dynamics property from
       org_dynproperties(O)
DP$_i$ a group dynamics property or conjunction thereof from
       group_dynproperties(G$_i$)
TR   a transfer dynamics property or conjunction thereof from
       transfer_dynproperties(O),
IID   an intergroup interaction property or conjunction thereof
       from intergroup_interaction_dynproperties(O)

The set of all group-organisation interlevel relations is denoted by GOIR.

(c) A *logical interlevel relation assignment* for an AGR organisation model AGRDyn is a mapping

interlevel_relations: {O} $\cup$ Groups $\rightarrow$ $\wp$(RGIR $\cup$ GOIR)

such that the set interlevel_relations(O) consists of logical group-organisation interlevel relations for O (i.e., from GOIR), and for each group G the set interlevel_relations(G) consists of logical role-group interlevel relations for G (i.e., from RGIR(G)).

(d) The *standard logical interlevel relation assignment*

standard_interlevel_relations: {O} $\cup$ Groups $\rightarrow$ $\wp$(RGIR $\cup$ GOIR)

for an AGR organisation model AGRDyn is the mapping defined by:

standard_interlevel_relations(G) is the set of logical relations
{ con(role_dynproperties(G) ∪ transfer_dynproperties(G)) ⇒ DP | DP∈group_dynproperties(G) }
standard_interlevel_relations(O) is the set of logical relations
{ con(role_dynproperties(O) ∪ transfer_dynproperties(O) ∪
    intergroup_interaction_dynproperties(O)) ⇒ DP | DP ∈ organisation_dynproperties(O) }.

Notice that this definition provides a formalisation for the type of relations that Lomi and Larsen [19] put forward as one of the challenges in organisation modelling (see above). Following the general implication pattern given above, the following specific relationships between dynamic properties at different aggregation levels can be established:

From group properties and intergroup role interaction properties to organisation properties

$$DP(A) \,\&\, DP(B) \,\&\, DP(C) \,\&\, IrRI(F) \qquad \Rightarrow \qquad DP(F)$$

From intragroup role interaction properties to group properties

$$IaRI(A) \,\&\, TRD(A) \qquad \Rightarrow \qquad DP(A)$$
$$IaRI(B) \,\&\, TRD(B) \qquad \Rightarrow \qquad DP(B)$$
$$TRD(C) \qquad \Rightarrow \qquad DP(C)$$

From dynamic role properties to intragroup interaction properties

$$DP(depA1) \,\&\, DP(depA2) \,\&\, TRD(A) \qquad \Rightarrow \qquad IaRI(A)$$
$$DP(depB1) \,\&\, DP(depB2) \,\&\, TRD(B) \qquad \Rightarrow \qquad IaRI(B)$$

Such relationships between dynamic properties can be visualised in the form of an AND-tree; see Figure 3 (the names have been kept short to keep the picture concise).

Given these definitions notions such as 'valid' and 'complete' can be defined and a proposition can be formulated.

Definition 6 (Valid and Complete)
Let AGRDyn be a model for the dynamics of an AGR organisation structure O
(a) A logical interlevel relations assignment interlevel_relations is called *valid* if all involved logical interlevel relations are valid statements in the logic used, i.e., for any trace, if the antecedent holds, also the consequent holds.
(b) The model AGRDyn is called *grounded* if its standard logical interlevel relation assignment is valid.
(c) A logical interlevel relations assignment interlevel_relations is called *connected* if for any group G each group property occurring (in an antecedent) in interlevel_relations(O) also occurs (as a consequent) in interlevel_relations(G).
(d) A logical interlevel relations assignment interlevel_relations is called *complete* if for any group G each group property from group_dynproperties(G) occurs (as a consequent) in interlevel_relations(G) and each organisation property from organisation_dynproperties(O) occurs (as a consequent) in interlevel_relations(O).

Notice that the standard logical interlevel relation assignment is connected and complete. However, the antecedents used are not minimal in the sense that many irrelevant conjuncts may occur in them.

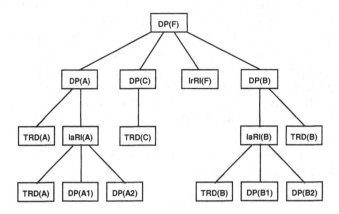

Fig. 3. Example interlevel relations between dynamic properties in the form of an AND-tree

Proposition

Let AGRDyn be a model for the dynamics of an AGR organisation structure O, and interlevel_relations an interlevel relation assignment. Moreover, let $\mathcal{T}$ be a trace that satisfies all dynamic properties in role_dynproperties(r) for all roles r, all transfer properties in transfer_dynproperties(t) for all transfers t, and all intergroup interaction properties in intergroup_interaction_dynproperties(i) for all intergroup interactions i.

(a) If the interlevel relation assignment interlevel_relations is valid, then trace $\mathcal{T}$ satisfies all dynamic group properties occurring in interlevel_relations(G) for any group G.

(b) If the interlevel relation assignment interlevel_relations is valid and complete, then the trace $\mathcal{T}$ satisfies all dynamic group and organisation properties in organisation_dynproperties(O) and group_dynproperties(G) for any group G.

(c) If a valid and complete logical interlevel relations assignment for AGRDyn exists, then AGRDyn is grounded.

This Proposition implies the following for an organisation model with a valid and complete interlevel relation assignment. If the properties for roles, transfers and intergroup interactions are in executable format, and used for simulation (e.g., based on the paradigm of Executable Temporal Logic), then a generated trace will satisfy these properties, and, hence by the Proposition satisfy all group and organisation properties as well. Among others, this gives means to validate (in the sense of falsification) an organisation model.

5 Organisation Realisation

In this section criteria are discussed when allocation of a set of agents to roles is appropriate to realize the organisation dynamics, illustrated for the AGR approach. One of the advantages of an organisation model is that it abstracts from the specific agents fulfilling the roles. This means that all dynamic properties of the organisation remain the same, independent of the particular allocated agents. However, the behaviours of these agents have to fulfil the dynamic properties of the roles and their interactions. The organisation model can be (re)used for any allocation of agents to roles for which:

- for each role, the allocated agent's behavior satisfies the dynamic role properties,
- for each intergroup role interaction, one agent is allocated to both roles and its behavior satisfies the intergroup role interaction properties, and
- the communication between agents satisfies the respective transfer properties.

Expressed differently, for a given allocation of agents to roles the following logical relationships between dynamic properties hold:

agent – role
from dynamic agent properties to dynamic role properties:

> agent A is allocated to role r &
> dynamic properties of agent A $\Rightarrow$
>   dynamic properties of role r

agent – intergroup role interaction
from dynamic agent properties to dynamic intergroup role interaction properties:

> agent A is allocated to roles r1 and r2 in different groups &
> dynamic properties of agent A $\Rightarrow$
>   dynamic properties of intergroup role interaction between r1 and r2

agent communication – role transfer
from dynamic agent communication properties to dynamic transfer properties:

> agent A is allocated to role r1 and agent B to role r2 in one group &
> dynamic properties of communication from A to B$\Rightarrow$
>   dynamic properties of transfer from r1 to r2

Notice that in these relationships, if an agent is allocated to a role, it might be assumed that the input and output ontologies of the agent are subsets of the role's input and output ontologies, but this assumption is not necessary. However, to satisfy the logical relationships specified above, at least a relevant overlap between the agent's ontologies and the role ontologies will be needed; for more discussion on this issue, see [24]. Moreover, note that if in the last relationship, A = B (an agent fulfilling two roles in one group), then dynamic properties of communication from A to A are required, i.e., that A will receive (at its input state) what it communicates (at its output state): 'A hears itself talking'. The logical relationships can be depicted as in the extension of Figure 2 shown as Figure 4. The following formalised criteria are required for an organisation realisation.

Definition 7   (AGR Organisation Realisation)
To realise an organisation, agents fulfil roles in the groups in the AGR organisation modelling approach. A realisation of an AGROrg organisation structure is then:

> AGRReal = <AGROrg, Agents, fulfils>

A set of agent names is given, so Agents $\subseteq$ IDENT. The relationship

> fulfils: Agents × Roles

specifies which roles an agent fulfils. The realisation dynamics specifies dynamic properties and ontologies for the agent input and output.

AGRRealDyn = < AGRReal , AGRDyn, agent_input_ontologies, agent_output_ontologies,
                agent_dynproperties>

where

   agent_input_ontologies, agent_output_ontologies: Agents → $\wp$(ONT)

   agent_dynproperties: Agents → $\wp$(DYNPROP)

The agent must have the required ontologies on input and output, as well as the required properties must be implemented for the roles it fulfils:

   $\forall$a ∈ Agents, $\forall$r ∈ Roles: fulfils(a, r) $\Rightarrow$

   role_input_ontologies(r) ⊆ agent_input_ontologies(a) ∧
   role_output_ontologies(r) ⊆ agent_output_ontologies(a) ∧   agent_dynproperties(a) $\models$
   role_dynproperties(r)

For all i ∈ Intergroup_interactions and for all a ∈ Agents, let involved_in(a, i) denote:

   ∃ r ∈ Roles: fullfils(a, r) ∧ (destination_of_interaction(r, i) ∨ source_of_interaction(r, i))

The dynamical properties of intergroup interactions are assumed to be realised by having the same agent fulfil all roles in the intergroup interaction and having this agent process from its input to its output according to the intergroup interaction dynamical property; under this assumption, the intergroup interaction formally has to satisfy:

$\forall$a ∈ Agents, i ∈ Intergroup_interactions:

   ($\forall$r ∈ involved_roles(i): fulfils(a, r)) $\Rightarrow$ agent_dynproperties(a) $\models$ inter-
   group_interaction_dynproperties(i)

The transfers also need to be realised by successfulness of sending messages by the involved agents:

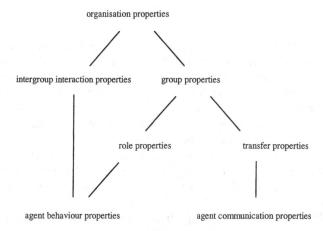

Fig. 4. Interlevel relations between dynamic properties for a realised organisation model

$\forall$t ∈ Transfers, r1, r2 ∈ Roles:
       source_of_transfer(r1, t) ∧ fullfils(a,r1) ∧
       destination_of_transfer(r2, t) ∧ fullfils(b,r2) $\Rightarrow$
       agent_commproperties(a, b) $\models$ transfer_dynproperties(t)

For the example, the following allocation of agents agentA1, agentA2, agentB1, agentB2 to roles is possible:

| agentA1 - depA1 | agentB1 - depB1 | agentA1 - divArep |
| agentA2 - depA2 | agentB2 - depB2 | agentB1 - divBrep |

To realise the organisation model, for example agentA1 has to satisfy the following dynamic properties:

DP(agentA1)

| If | agent A1 receives progress information on component production, |
| then | an updated planning will be generated by agent A1 taking this most recent information into account. |

IrRI(agentA1)

If	progress information on component production is received by agent A1,
then	this will be communicated by agent A1 to agent B1
If	agent A1 receives information on which components are needed,
then	a component production planning will be generated by agent A1 taking these components into account.

Alternatively, if the roles in an intergroup interaction would not be fulfilled by one agent, but by several, this would create a mystery, since input to one agent creates output for another agent, even though the agents are not connected by any transfer since the roles they fulfil are from separate groups. This would suggest that the organisation structure is not complete. Therefore, in an AGR organisation model it is assumed that the roles in an intergroup interaction are fulfilled by one agent.

6 Discussion

Both in human society and for software agents, organisational structure is a means to make complex multi-agent dynamics manageable. To understand and formalize how exactly organisational structure constrains complex dynamics is a fundamental challenge in the area of organisational modelling. The framework combining structure and dynamics introduced in this paper provides support in addressing this challenge. Specification of organisation structure usually takes the form of pictorial descriptions, in a graph-like framework. These descriptions usually abstract from dynamics within an organisation. Specification of the dynamic properties of agent systems, on the other hand, usually takes place in a completely different conceptual framework; these dynamic properties are often specified in the form of a set of logical formulae in some temporal language.

This paper shows how these two perspectives can be combined in one framework. It is shown how for different types of elements within an organisation structure different sets of dynamic properties can be specified. Illustrated for [6]'s AGR organisation modelling approach, it has been shown how a foundation can be obtained for integrated specification of both structure and dynamic properties of an organisation. The organisational structure provides structural relations between different elements of the organisation; these relations induce logical relationships between the sets of dynamic properties for the different elements of the organisation. Such logical relationships make explicit dependencies between dynamic properties of parts of an organisation. The logical relationships express the kind of relations between dynamics of parts of an organisation, their interaction and dynamic properties of the organisation as a whole, which were indicated as crucial by (Lomi and Larsen, 2001) in their introduction. Besides for AGR organisational models approach, the foundational approach presented in this paper also has been successfully applied to compositional organisation models.

The framework presented here contributes directly to the foundations of some of the criteria proposed by [4] (e.g., the criteria regarding the identification of constraints and flexible analysis) for an ideal social simulation language (ISSL), and it illustrates for some of the other criteria how such an ISSL can come about (e.g., the criteria regarding modeller's intentions, compositionality, and emergence) in the context of the structure and dynamics of organizations. Furthermore, a shared basis of the work of [4] and the work presented here lies in the view that the different simulation processes need to be specified separately from the significant outcomes of the simulation, and that the processes that emerge from the simulation are typically more interesting than the resulting states of the simulation.

Also in MOISE and MOISE+ (cf. [11], [12], [13]), as for AGR, organisational structures are based on roles and groups and on links between roles. A difference with AGR is that tasks are taken into account explicitly and specified by goals, plans, resources and actions. These specifications can be considered one of the specific instantiations possible for the notion of dynamic property that is central in our foundational perspective as developed. In this case interlevel relations take the form of relations between tasks for roles and tasks at a higher aggregation level, for example for groups or (parts of) the organisation.

Having one framework that integrates the two perspectives, as well as the logical relationships between the two perspectives enables formal economic diagnostic analysis. Any simulation or empirical trace can be checked against a given dynamic property. Assuming the logical relationships, diagnosis of dysfunctioning within an organisation can be performed see, for example, [15].

For further work, this framework provides a basis for development of more specific organisation specification languages, covering both structure and dynamics. Such languages could make use of semiformal and graphical elements, and specification would be supported by software tools. The specification tools can mediate between a user and further software environments for simulation and analysis.

Acknowledgements. The authors are grateful to Wouter Wijngaards who has contributed to some elements of this paper, in particular in Section 2.

References

1. Amiguet, M., Müller, J.-P., Baez-Barranco, J.-A., and Nagy, A., (2003), The MOCA Platform Simulated the Dynamics of Social Networks. This volume.
2. Barringer, H., Fisher, M., Gabbay, D., Owens, R., and Reynolds, M., (1996). The Imperative Future: Principles of Executable Temporal Logic, Research Studies Press Ltd. and John Wiley & Sons.

3. Brazier, F.M.T., Eck, P.A.T. van, and Treur, J., (2001). Modelling a Society of Simple Agents: From Conceptual Specification to Experimentation. Journal of Applied Intelligence, vol. 14, pp. 161–178.
4. Edmonds, B., (2003), Towards an Ideal Social Simulation Language. This volume.
5. Engelfriet, J., Jonker, C.M., and Treur, J. (2002). Compositional Verification of Multi-Agent Systems in Temporal Multi-Epistemic Logic. Journal of Logic, Language and Information, **11**: 195–22.
6. Ferber, J. and Gutknecht, O. (1998). A meta-model for the analysis and design of organisations in multi-agent systems. In: Proceedings of the Third International Conference on Multi-Agent Systems (ICMAS'98), IEEE Computer Society Press, pp. 128–135.
7. Ferber, J., and Gutknecht, O. (1999). Operational Semantics of a role-based agent architecture. Proceedings of the 6th Int. Workshop on Agent Theories, Architectures and Languages (ATAL'1999). In: Jennings, N.R. & Lesperance, Y. (eds.) Intelligent Agents VI, Lecture Notes in AI, vol. 1757, Springer Verlag, 2000, pp. 205–217.
8. Ferber, J., Gutknecht, O., Jonker, C.M., Müller, J.P., and Treur, J., (2001). Organization Models and Behavioural Requirements Specification for Multi-Agent Systems. In: Y. Demazeau, F. Garijo (eds.), Multi-Agent System Organisations. Proceedings of the 10th European Workshop on Modelling Autonomous Agents in a Multi-Agent World, MAAMAW'01, 2001. Lecture Notes in AI, Springer Verlag. To appear, 2002.
9. Fisher, M. (1994). A survey of Concurrent MetateM — the language and its applications. In: D.M. Gabbay & H.J. Ohlbach (eds.), Temporal Logic - Proceedings of the First International Conference, Lecture Notes in AI, vol. 827, pp. 480–505.
10. Fisher, M., and M. Wooldridge (1997). On the formal specification and verification of multi-agent systems. International Journal of Co-operative Information Systems, vol. 6, pp. 37–65.
11. Hannoun, M., Sichman, J.S., Boissier, O., and Sayettat, C., Dependence Relations between Roles in a Multi-Agent System: Towards the Detection of Inconsistencies in Organization. In: J.S. Sichman, R. Conte, and N. Gilbert (eds.), Multi-Agent Systems and Agent-Based Simulation (Proc. of the 1st. International Workshop on Multi-Agent Based Simulation, MABS'98), Lecture Notes in Artificial Intelligence, vol. 1534, Springer - Verlag Berlin-Alemanha, 1998, pp. 169–182.
12. Hannoun, M., Boissier, O., Sichman, J.S., and Sayettat, C., MOISE: An organizational model for multi-agent systems. In: M. C. Monard and J. S. Sichman (eds.), Advances in Artificial Intelligence, (Proc. International Joint Conference 7th. Ibero-American Conference on Artificial Intelligence (IBERAMIA'00) and 15th. Brazilian Symposium on Artificial Intelligence (SBIA'00), Atibaia, Brasil). Lecture Notes in Artificial Intelligence, vol. 1952, Springer-Verlag, Berlin, 2000, pp. 152–161.
13. Herlea, D.E., Jonker, C.M., Treur, J., and Wijngaards, N.J.E., (1999). Specification of Behavioral Requirements within Compositional Multi-Agent System Design. In: F.J. Garijo, M. Boman (eds.), Multi-Agent System Engineering, Proceedings of the 9th European Workshop on Modelling Autonomous Agents in a Multi-Agent World, MAAMAW'99. Lecture Notes in AI, vol. 1647, Springer Verlag, Berlin, 1999, pp. 8–27.
14. Hubner, J.F., Sichman, J.S., and Boissier, O., A Model for the Structural, Functional and Deontic Specification of Organizations in Multiagent Systems. In: Proc. 16th Brazilian Symposium on Artificial Intelligence (SBIA'02), Porto de Galinhas, Brasil, 2002. Extended abstract: MOISE+: Towards a Structural, Functional and Deontic model for MAS Organizations. In: C. Castelfranchi and W.L. Johnson (eds.), Proceedings of the First International Joint Conference on Autonomous Agents and Multi-Agent Systems, AAMAS'02. ACM Press, 2002, pp. 501–502.

15. Jonker, C.M., Letia, I.A., and Treur, J., (2002). Diagnosis of the Dynamics within an Organisation by Trace Checking of Behavioural Requirements. In: Wooldridge, M., Weiss, G., and Ciancarini, P. (eds.), Proceedings of the 2nd International Workshop on Agent-Oriented Software Engineering, AOSE'01. Lecture Notes in Computer Science, vol. 2222. Springer Verlag, 2002, pp. 17–32.
16. Jonker, C.M. and Treur, J. (1998). Compositional Verification of Multi-Agent Systems: a Formal Analysis of Pro-activeness and Reactiveness. In: W.P. de Roever, H. Langmaack, A. Pnueli (eds.), Proceedings of the International Workshop on Compositionality, COMPOS'97. Lecture Notes in Computer Science, vol. 1536, Springer Verlag, 1998, pp. 350–380.
17. Jonker, C.M., Treur, J., and Wijngaards, W.C.A., (2001). Temporal Languages for Simulation and Analysis of the Dynamics Within an Organisation. In: B. Dunin-Keplicz and E. Nawarecki (eds.), From Theory to Practice in Multi-Agent Systems, Proceedings of the Second International Workshop of Central and Eastern Europe on Multi-Agent Systems, CEEMAS'01, 2001. Lecture Notes in AI, vol. 2296, Springer Verlag, 2002, pp. 151–160.
18. Kreitner, R., and Kunicki, A. (2001). Organisational Behavior, McGraw – Hill.
19. Lomi, A., and Larsen, E.R. (2001). Dynamics of Organizations: Computational Modeling and Organization Theories, AAAI Press, Menlo Park.
20. Meinke, K., and Tucker J.V. (eds.) (1993). Many-sorted Logic and its Applications, John Wiley & Sons, Inc. Publishers - Chichester; New York.
21. Mintzberg, H. (1979). The Structuring of Organisations, Prentice Hall, Englewood Cliffs, N.J.
22. Moss, S., Gaylard, H., Wallis, S., and Edmonds, B. (1998). SDML: A Multi-Agent Language for Organizational Modelling, Computational and Mathematical Organization Theory 4, (1), 43–70.
23. Prietula, M., Gasser, L., Carley, K. (1997). Simulating Organizations. MIT Press.
24. Sichman, J.S. and Conte, R., On Personal and Role Mental Attitudes: A Preliminary Dependence-Based Analysis. In: F. Oliveira (ed.), Advances in AI (Proc. 14th Brazilian Symposium on Artificial Intelligence, SBIA'98), Lecture Notes in Artificial Intelligence, vol. 1515, Springer Verlag, Berlin-Alemanha, 1998, pp 1–10.

The MOCA Platform
Simulating the Dynamics of Social Networks

Matthieu Amiguet[1], Jean-Pierre Müller[2], José-A. Baez-Barranco[1], and
Adina Nagy[1]

[1] Institut d'Informatique et d'Intelligence Artificielle, Université de Neuchâtel, Suisse
{matthieu.amiguet, jose.baez, adina.nagy}@unine.ch
[2] CIRAD, Montpellier, France
jean-pierre.muller@cirad.fr

Abstract. This paper presents a theoretical model and a platform that
allow to describe individual and collective recurrent patterns of behaviour, called respectively roles and organizations, and let agents dynamically choose to create, join or quit groups instanciating these patterns at execution time.

1 Introduction

One of the aims of simulating organizations is to understand the relationship between the recurrent patterns of group behaviour, called organizations, and recurrent patterns of individual behaviour, called roles. These recurrent behavioural
patterns can be formally described either by fixed protocols for interaction between roles at the organizational level and with the external environment at the
individual level, or by constraints on the possible behaviours by means of collective and individual norms. Individual norms are represented in various ways:
as mental attitudes [1,2], as obligations, authorizations and conventions [3] or as
commitments [4], etc. Several different ways to individually reason about norms
have been suggested in [5,6,7,8]. One can think of collective norms as specifying
a set of possible structures of interaction in a group. This last option is generally
linked to a Belief-Desire-Intention (BDI) agent architecture unless collective attitudes are used (as in [9]). As we don't want to impose such a strong structure on
agents, we consider in this paper only the descriptions of structures of interaction
as a set of protocols between roles. Therefore, the roles played by the individuals are completely determined by these structures in a kind of methodological
holism (see [10,11]). It is in contrast with the use of norms explicitly taken into
account by the individuals as in methodological individualism (or mentalism).
This last option has not been taken into account because we are not interested
in this paper to investigate the emergence of norms and institutions but the
dynamics of social networks once these institutions are socially established[1].

---

[1] For an in-depth discussion about the necessity of including the methodological collectivism approaches (defended by R. Conte, S. Moss and B. Edmonds) and thus the
modeling of social-scale phenomena in MABS see [11].

J.S. Sichman, F. Bousquet, P. Davidsson (Eds.): MABS 2002, LNAI 2581, pp. 70–88, 2003.

We further have to distinguish whether the recurrent patterns of behaviour refer to the actual or expected behaviours. The expected behaviours would be a specification of the kind of interactions we would like to emerge from the dynamics of the multi-agent system but which does not necessarily happen. The actual behaviour would be the description of the detailed interactions which has necessarily to occur when the agents interact with each other. In this paper, we mainly focus on the description of the actual behaviour, letting specification as constraints and/or expectations on actual behaviour for further work.

We use a formalism of the structures of interaction as a set of protocols between roles to describe the dynamics of the groups instantiating these structures with individuals creating, entering and leaving groups. Our aim is to provide both a formalism and a tool to investigate the dynamics of social networks in a simple way. More precisely, the aim of this paper is

- first to propose to use a formalism of the structures of interaction as a set of protocols between roles and
- second to describe the dynamics of the groups instantiating these structures with individuals creating, entering and leaving groups

in order to investigate the dynamics of social networks in a simple way. Thus, we partially address the challenge of allowing for open systems in social simulation, which have since a while been recognized as a difficult class of system to design [12,13]. We recall that, in software engineering, open systems are defined [14] as encapsulated, reactive and spatially and temporally extensible systems, whose components are entities that a designer has no knowledge of at the design time and which may dynamically join and leave the system at run-time.

There are mainly two types of approaches of organizational multi-agent systems in literature: some systems, like Aaladin [15], allow for dynamic social organization but social structures do not impose anything on the agents' behaviour; other models do consider social structures as recurrent patterns of interaction, but then the social structures are usually static (see [16,17,12]). Our contribution is to combine these two approaches by allowing the designer to describe the organizations with their roles, relationships and dynamics (protocols), but simultaneously allowing any agent to dynamically create a group instantiating an organization, to enter and to leave such a group.

The belonging of an agent to an organization is constraining: once it is part of this organization, it has to follow the corresponding protocols. The agent autonomy is mainly in his free choice to enter or exit such social networks; once again, the emphasis of our platform is put on social networks dynamics. Additionally, the agents have to define their competences and manage the possible conflicts when playing several roles at once.

Concretely, our approach is illustrated by the realization of an organizational layer above MadKit [18] called MOCA (for Model of Organizations Centered on Agents).

The rest of this paper is organized as follows. Next section discusses the sociological background of organzational models. Section 3 discusses the notion of role in the literature. Section 4 presents the Aalaadin methodology and the MadKit platform, upon which our work is based. Section 5 introduces the main concepts of our architecture and how they are related. Section 6 exposes an example using the MOCA platform and finally section 7 discusses the strength and weaknesses of our approach, together with research perspectives.

2   The Sociological Background of MABS Organizational Models

The way duality agent - society is modeled in the MAS domain reflects several of the approaches to the sociological understanding of the relationships between local properties (individuals, agents) and global properties (society, institutions, organizations). Several sociological theories that constitute a background for the multi-agent based modeling are described by [10] and [11], in the context of social simulation. We found useful to resume this discussion in order to situate MOCA in the context of the MABS literature.

According to these authors, the main sociological frameworks which could represent the background of MABS systems are the methodological individualism, the methodological holism, the social realism, the methodological collectivism and the structuration theory. According to [11], most of the MABS models are based on a methodological individualist approach.

The individualism asserts that macro phenomena must be accounted for by the situations, dispositions and beliefs of individuals, that is the micro-level properties and behavior of individuals. Thus, methodological individualism is a bottom-up emergent-flavored approach. It means that even if in many approaches the focus is on the emergent macro patterns which influence the behavior of individuals, these patterns are derived from models of individual cognition and of interactions between individuals. This is certainly a backdraw as many agent-based emergence models may be less efficient for explanation and prediction that an explicit model of social wholes.

According to holist sociologists, social institutions, as well as social phenomena, are external to and impose to the individuals. For Durkheim, the mentality of the group is not the mentality of the individuals - it has its own laws. If follows that at least a part of the social representations have to be examined independently of the individuals who compose the society. Briefly, the central assertion of methodological holism is that social behavior of individuals should be explained in terms of positions these individuals occupy within the society and in terms of the laws which govern it, which, at their turn, are modeled in terms of social wholes and not in terms of individuals. Methodological holism supports social-entity based models rather that agent-based models.

The notions of role and organization are central to methodological holistic multi-agent based simulation models. Unfortunately, only a few works, as [16, 17] and the MOCA approach belong to this framework. However, these notions may appear in other sociological frameworks, particularly in methodological collectivism.

Methodological collectivism doesn't assert the reality of the social phenomena, arguing that collective entities in a social model are not necessarily real. However, due to the complexity, high-dimensionality and non-linearity of certain phenomena one wishes to model, it can be a useful design strategy to treat them as real. In the organizational research on multi-agent systems design, the MadKit approach for organizations can be classified as framed by methodological collectivism: organizations are abstractions without any reification at the design level. In the specific discipline of multi-agent based simulation (MABS), methodological collectivism is supported by a few designers (B. Edmonds, D. Byrne, A. Dean, M. Bartley) - see [11].

Structuration theory attempts to describe the circular relationship between the macro and the micro level and thus to conciliate the individual-centered and the collective-centered approaches. According to Giddens (1984), social structure or society is produced or reproduced by the means of structuring properties, that is of institutional practices, rules and resources. Individual action has these structures and properties embedded and - through action - individuals (agents) reproduce the society. Thus a structure is both the outcome of knowledgeable action and the medium that influences (as the norms which constrain and enable) the way action is conducted. There is a duality between society and the (human) agents: B. Edmonds (in [11]) states that the micro and the macro level have coevolved and "there are coevolved complex dependencies and causal loops between individuals and society". We agree with B. Edmonds when he emphasizes the necessity to build "models that have both levels, so we can start to entangle the main interdependencies and interactions between the two". In further research on MOCA, we plan to use hiss organizational formalism as one of the building blocks of a structuration-oriented model.

Social networks are a formalism, based on graph theory , for representing relations as nodes and links. Depending on the level or focus of analysis, nodes may represent entities such as people, technology, groups, or entire firms themselves - whatever units of analysis form the organization being studied [19]. Thus a social network can be defined as a set of interacting social entities (individuals, groups, organizations, etc.) related by the flow of information they exchange and their contacts (expressed in general through relations between these entities). The notion of social network in multi-agent organizational systems allows the user to simulate the two sociological approaches specific to such a network. [20]. The first is the personal network in which an actor is considered as the referential for building up - 'de proche en proche' - a network of relations. The second is the global network, where the behaviour of groups of actors is studied, usually in a limited universe of observation (a city, a company, etc.). According to [21], quoted in [20], it is difficult to build up a global social network if the starting point is the set of personal nets.

MOCA represents a tool allowing to simulate both the levels of social nets. On the one hand, the multi-agent system built through the MOCA organizational model is agent-centered (then fitted for the study of dynamics of personal social nets). On the other hand, we look at the global network as being built up not as a snow-ball result of personal networks' analysis, but through interactions between pre-modeled competences and protocols related to the patterns of behaviour (roles) agents follow. The organizational model we propose is a tool allowing to model and simulate different types of social networks, inspired by different sociological theories.

3   The Notion of Role in the Literature

Roles represent a central notion to social structures simulation, as they allow for approaching the social simulation from the methodological holism perspective. Protocols and/or norms are then designed with regard to the chosen role model. In literature roles are viewed either from a behavioral (it is the case of "pure" organizational models with roles as recurrent behaviors [16,17,22]) or from a mentalist perspective - which includes norms, see [23, where a role is explicitly played as such] and [24,25] — depending upon the observer's point of view (see [22] for further details). Most mentalist approaches are extensions of the BDI architecture (Belief-Desire-Intention, see [23]) unless they are used to describe the organization itself as in MOISE+ [9], or notions as joint intention [26], social norms or collective goals.

A valuable attempt to give a mixed behaviorist-mentalist model is the Gaia methodology. In [12, and related papers] authors give an organizational methodology for agent oriented analysis and design, which bears some similarities with MOCA, as it is based onto two abstract models - a "mixed" role model and an interaction model. These two abstract levels are declined at the multi-agent level in an agents model, a service model and an acquaintance model. The roles are defined by four attributes: responsibilities, permission, activities and protocols. The interaction model consists in a set of protocol definitions, focused on the nature and purpose of the interaction, rather than on the precise ordering of message exchange. According to the authors, the representation of inter-agent protocols with Gaia is somewhat impoverished and the need to specify, in a further work, a much richer protocol specification framework is emphasized. Within all these models, the dynamic aspect of socials networks is a perspective for further research.

In [22] the authors use the analogy to object oriented methodology when they propose AUML, an extension to UML meant to represent social structures. The authors mix the works coming from [15], dependency theory [27,28,29, and related papers], interaction protocols and the holonic manufacturing paradigm [30], into a theoretical model of groups, which extends [15] in different directions. Particularly, roles are seen as labellings of recurring patterns of dependency, action templates and (speech and other) interactions. We join the authors when they estimate that such a behaviorist perspective on role "is more useful [than the mentalist ones] to the system analyst, confronted with heterogeneous systems, whose elements are often opaque". As far as the problem of an agent assuming several roles at once (at run-time) is concerned, this approach allows to deal with the composition of roles and the creation of new roles at design time only.

In MOCA, we assume that the composition of roles within an agent is a problem to be treated at the run-time and we give the tools for dealing with the run-time composition.

Closer to MOCA's philosophy, in [31,32], the authors propose another type of behaviorist model of roles, which allows for the regulation of social laws and thus for a dynamics of norms and relations. In [32] social aspects — represented through a participation model — are included in the design of groupware. A participation model is a mean to describe a system from the perspective of group's members implication in a joint activity — an activity which requires the collaboration of several agents in order to reach a common goal described both from the cooperation and from the conflicts' perspective.

Next, the authors propose (see [31]) to build the design of organizational multi-agent systems around the modeling of joint activities of its actors. They suggest to transpose regulation — a groupware concept meant for dynamics and reorganization — to multi-agent systems. Regulation allows participants to organize and reorganize all along the performance of an activity, to negotiate and define the conditions of its realization. They fix together the working rules — laws, rights and responsibilities — of the group.

Regulation is at the opposite of coordination: coordination is meant as the set of mechanisms allowing a group to comply to the established rules and norms, while regulation concerns the establishment and evolution of these rules. In our opinion, this approach has the merit of opening a way toward relations dynamics, thus constituting a complementary approach to MOCA.

In the participation model [31,32], roles are defined as the competences an actor can have in different interactions and are declined as being both thematic and activity-based. Concepts as status (the social position of an individual in a group, independent of its interactions), place (with respect to the social hierarchy — chief, subordinate, etc.) and position (representing individuals factors as the interest, the availability, the acquaintances, etc.) give a hierarchical dimension to roles.

We see the possibility to model such a type of behaviorist roles, as well as the holonic aspects made possible by AUML [22], as natural extensions to the MOCA platform but, for the time being, we decided to limit ourselves to a simplified but clear structure of the basic concepts in order to explore their usefulness and operationality.

4 Aalaadin, Madkit, and MOCA

Our work is based on the Aalaadin methodology [15], which includes two conceptual levels: the *concrete* level, which includes the notions of *agent*, *group*, and *role* (only as names for agents in a group), implementing the actual multi-agent structure; the *abstract* level describes valid interactions and structures of groups (which we call organizations). However, the abstract level is methodological: although the concrete level is fully formalized [33], the abstract level is never formalized nor implemented. In [9], both levels are formalized and implemented but in mentalistic terms.

MadKit [18] is a multi-agent platform based on the Agent-Group-Role model [15], on which the Aaladin methodology is targeted [15]. The services provided by this platform are of two kinds:

1. The agent services
    - Message management (addressing, sending, receiving and queuing)
    - Agent life cycle management (birth, execution and death)
    - Acquaintance management
2. The group services
    - Group creation
    - Group entering and leaving
    - Getting informations about existing groups and roles, and about which agents hold a given role

Notice that a group is explicitly not a recursive notion in MadKit in the sense that a group cannot be an agent. The platform also provides simulation facilities in the form of a synchronous engine but these facilities are not used by our implementation.

Even if methodologically the groups are thought as instantiations of organizations and roles are seen as instances of behaviour patterns, this is not implemented in the platform. In fact, roles and groups are just names for structuring the MAS architecture. In order to overcome this limitation, we want to introduce explicitly *organization* and *role descriptions* as first order objects of which groups and roles are instantiations. Therefore, our contribution with MOCA is to propose formalizations for representing the concepts of Aalaadin and to enrich MadKit with a reification of the *abstract* level concepts, thus providing a complete, operational formalism to build multi-agent systems in an organizational-centered approach [34]. MOCA is implemented in such a way that any multi-agent platform providing communicating agents and group structures could be used in place of MadKit.

Additionally, to ensure maximal independence and reusability of organizations and role descriptions, we limit the possible interactions to those that take place inside a given group. The only opportunity for two different groups to exchange and cooperate is when some agents participate in both of them at the same time. This last option is mentioned in the Aaladin methodology but not currently enforced by MadKit.

5   The Concepts of MOCA

To describe the organizational structure on the one hand and the multi-agent system on the other, our model is composed of two different levels: the descriptive or organizational level and the executive or multi-agent level. Additionaly, we distinguish the external or behaviorist point on view on the system from the internal point of view of the agent. In the external point of view we observe interacting (through influence) agents achieving acquaintance structures or groups whose recurrence can be abstracted away as relationnal structures forming organizations. In the internal point of view, we describe the agent architectures classified into agent types (Reactive, deliberative, BDI, etc.) and providing competences. Role descriptions and their instantiations articulate both by providing at the same time the recurrent pattern of interactions from an external point of view and the way it is achieved from an internal point of view, using and relying on agent competences. Most probably, separating these two aspects would allow further flexibility but have not been taken into account in MOCA. The figure 1 represents the important concepts for each level and from each point of view and the correspondence between them.

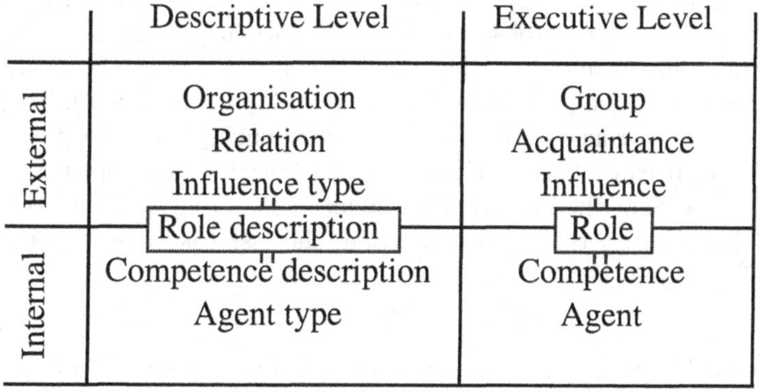

	Descriptive Level	Executive Level
External	Organisation Relation Influence type	Group Acquaintance Influence
Internal	Role description Competence description Agent type	Role Competence Agent

Fig. 1. The concepts of MOCA

Most of the notions of the MAS level exist in MadKit, except for the notions of *influence* and *competence* which will be described further in this section. Our major contribution is hence the explicit representation of the Organization level. We will now describe in detail the notions of the figure 1.

5.1   The Organization Level

Organizations. An organization is defined as a recurrent pattern of interactions from a given point of view (financial exchanges, goods exchanges, ants collective behavior, etc.) and very often attributed with a rationale (ensure equilibrium, feed the ant colony, etc.). In our case, it is formalized as a set of role descriptions and relationships between them. Cardinalities can be specified on both role descriptions and relationships, to describe how many times they can be instantiated as roles and acquaintances, respectively. Figure 2 pictures an example of an organization for the FIPA Contract Net protocol [35]. There are two role descriptions in this organization: the initiator and the participant; in a given instantiation of the organization, there can be only one initiator, but of course several participants, each of them being possibly in acquaintance with the initiator.

Fig. 2. A simple organization for the Contract Net Protocol

Relationships. The relationships between the role descriptions abstract away the recurrent interactions between two roles within an organization. It is described by the related roles and specifies how many agents can play each of these roles (for example, in the contract net of figure 2, the relation between the initiator and the participant is a relationship one to many). There is a clear duality between roles on one hand and relationships between the roles on the other hand, because it is possible either to describe the interaction protocol between two roles or the individual behavior of each role such that the interaction protocol occurs. In this implementation, the last case was chosen but see [36] and [37] for the other choice.

Influence Types. The influence type specifies the kind of interaction a role can receive and generate. In order to be general, we use the term influence to cover in the same abstraction forces for physically situated roles, events and up to speech acts (ACL, KQML, etc.) for socially situated roles. [38] introduces this notion and shows its usefulness to describe concurrent execution. By separating the causes (i.e. the influences) and the effects (i.e. changes in the environment or the agents), this notion allows to combine simultaneous causes to compute the actual effects of concurrent actions.

Role Descriptions. There is a clear duality between roles on one hand and relationships between the roles on the other hand, because it is possible either to describe the interaction protocol between two roles or the individual behavior of each role such that the interaction protocol occurs. In this implementation, the last case was chosen but see [36] and [37] for the other choice.

A role is defined as a recurrent behavioral pattern within an organization. The role description represents the way this behavioural pattern is generated, being the internal account of the external pattern. To formalize it, we chose to use a formalism strongly based on [17], which is a combination of Statecharts [39,40] and Object-Z [41,42]. The formalism is quite intuitive, so we expose it quickly on an example, without further formal description (for details refer to [17]).

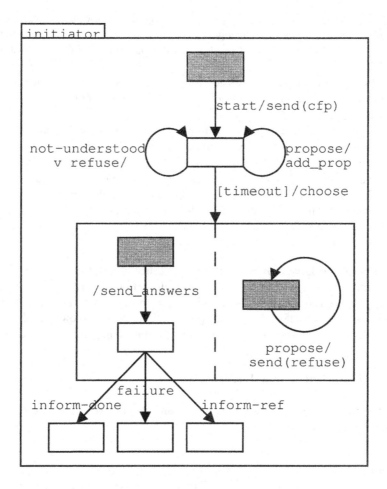

Fig. 3. The *initiator* role description

Figure 3 pictures a typical role description corresponding to the initiator role of figure 2.

This description is based on Hilaire's framework [17], which can be seen in the inheritance statement of the first line. The heart of the description is of course the statechart specifying the behavior. Statecharts are an extension of finite state automata used in UML, with and-or hierarchy of states; hence the dotted line in figure 3 means that the two halves of the super-state have to run in parallel. Note that we use a slightly non-standard notation for default states, which are pictured as gray boxes.

Transitions are labeled with three-parts expressions of the form *influence[condition]/action*. This means that the arrival of *influence* triggers the firing of the transition, which can take place only if *condition* holds. If the transition is fired, then *action* is executed. Each part of the expression can be omitted.

All actions in this figure are calls to agent competences (e.g. *send*); the required competences of the agent must be listed (variable *req_competences*) in order to check if the agent is able to take the role. Usually, at least *send* will be listed there, as it corresponds to the capacity of sending influences to other agents. Our model also allows for internal methods and variables, specified in object-Z notation, but we will not expose this feature here as it is not the focus of this paper.

In addition to what is described above roles must provide a few services: they must be able to give the list of influence types they are able to recognize, the list of those they are actually ready to receive, etc. . For example, the list of the influences a role can actually receive is computed from the set of fireable transitions minus the transitions which are blocked because of role conflicts (described in another paper [43]). They can also possibly provide competences to the agent who takes them (see section 5.3).

Competence Descriptions. The competence descriptions are specifications of the services an agent has to provide in order to be able to play the role; typical examples are the ability to send and to receive messages, to compute an offer or evaluate between offers for a contract net. This notion allows the description of the role at a very abstract level, essentially the management of interactions.

5.2   The Multi-agent Level

At the multi-agent level we find the instantiation of the various concepts at the organizational level.

Groups. A group is an instance of an organization made of agents playing the various roles of the organization. The only difference from the same notion in MadKit is the explicitation of this instantiation.

Roles. The role in MadKit is just a name in a group; it is not expected that roles with the same name in different groups are linked to the same behavior. In our higher abstraction level, two roles with the same name in two different organizations can produce different behaviors, but two roles with the same name in two different groups instantiating the same organization will have the same behavior. Each role in an agent is the instantiation of the role's state (automaton state and internal variables) and a reference to the role description.

Acquaintances. The acquaintances of an agent are, as usual, the agents it can communicate with. The link between acquaintances and relationships is that an agent can be in acquaintance with another agent if and only if there is at least one relationship between the roles played by the respective agents.

Agents, Influences, and Competences. An agent is an autonomous entity able to create new groups by instantiating organizations, to take and to leave roles in existing groups. An agent can play none to many roles at any given time. In the following, we assume that an agent can only play different roles in different organizations or in the same organization but not several times the same role. In order to preserve its autonomy, the agent not only provides its competences to execute the roles but has complete execution control on the roles it acquires. In particular, the agent dispatches the received influences to and from the roles and can take care of possible role incompatibilities. Thus the typical execution of an agent includes:

1. Get the influences coming from other agents.
2. Dispatch them on the different roles.
3. Provide its competences when required by the roles.
4. Send the influences emitted by its roles to other agents.
5. Control the roles execution in order to avoid negative interferences.
6. Manage its social networks (create, enter and leave groups).

There are many ways of handling these different tasks. It is a part of the autonomy of an agent — along with its competences — to do it one way or another. We quickly comment on these tasks.

The first task is the less problematic, as it is already part of the MadKit Platform. The dispatch of the second point is made by asking each role which types of influence it is ready to accept, and passing them to everybody interested[2]. The other ones are kept in a queue; this is necessary because the asynchronous nature of the MAS can not ensure the order of arrival of messages. The design is made for preserving the operational semantics of statecharts [40].

When the roles execute, they can make calls to the agent's competences. As said before, these can be for example to send and to receive messages, to compute an offer or evaluate between offers for a contract net.

One of the most difficult task of the agent is of course the control of role execution in order to avoid destructive interferences. There is no simple general way of handling this task, and for the time being we have to treat it case by case. We have developed a mecanism based on a weak version of mutual exclusion of potentially conflictual use of roles which is automatically computed from the statecharts [43].

The platform does not provide a default mechanism for social network management, because it is the object to investigate, and so it is very likely to change in every experimental case. We can think of the agent creating or entering groups depending on its goal. For example, an agent whose goal is to buy an object could have to enter first a contract net to try and earn some money.

---

[2] If necessary, the influences can be indexed by the current conversation to avoid confusion.

5.3   Social Networks Dynamics

In order to be able to create a group instantiating an organization and to enter and leave it, we need a mechanism to do so. This is clearly a "meta" level with respect to the organizational one, but to preserve conceptual homogeneity of our model, we choose to implement this mechanism as an organization.

So there is a *Managing group* in the system in which all agents take part[3] (see figure 4). The corresponding *Managing organization* has three role descriptions (RD's) which are the YellowPages RD, the *Manager* RD and the *Requester* RD.

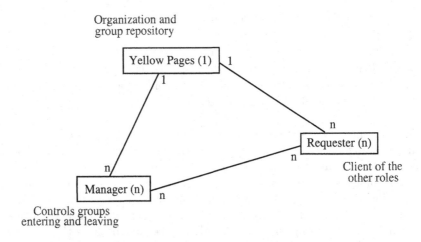

Fig. 4. The management organization

The first task of the YellowPages RD is to provide an organization repository; every agent in the system can consult it and ask for the creation of a new instance of one of them. This agent then becomes the manager of the resulting group, that is it gets a Manager role in the Managing group. The second task of the YellowPages role is to maintain a group repository and inform requesting agents about existing groups.

The Manager RD is attached to a specific existing group in the system and consists in controlling the acquisition of roles in that group by requesting agents (that is, agents playing the Requester role in the Managing group). Responding to a role request, it controls the identity and competences of the agent before attributing the requested role. Thus the minimal requested competence of this RD (in addition to the standard communication competence) is to be able to match the competences of the agent to the competences of the requested role.

The Requester role can ask YellowPages about existing groups and organizations and ask for the instantiation of a new group from a given organization

---

[3] In a large system, it is possible to have several of them to avoid a bottleneck effect.

(then becoming its manager). It can also ask a manager to enter an existing group.

This mechanism allows for group creation and management without any inter-group communication. However, if we want our system to be more than a few groups functioning independently, we have to provide a collaboration mechanism between groups. The way to do this without introducing explicit inter-group communication is to allow agents to have several roles in different groups at the same time.

Hence the local coordination of roles inside the agents achieves groups coordination at the system level. The way roles are coordinated by an agent is of course part of the agent's autonomy, but in order to ease the agent's design we provide a generic and powerful implicit communication mechanism: we allow roles to provide competences to the agent. Hence the role executions rely only on agent competences, but the agent has the possibility to use roles to implement some of them. This way allows elegant implicit role communication inside the agent, together with a powerful mechanism to achieve agents' evolution: by acquiring more capacities, the agent will possibly be able to take new roles, which in turn can provide him with new capacities, and so on.

6 Example of Use

Our architecture has been implemented in Java above MadKit. The organization level has been completely reified with a set of classes for describing the organizations, roles (and their state-charts) and the relationships between the roles. The class MOCA-Agent is just a subclass of Agent (from MadKit) implementing the interface of an organisational agent able to enter and to leave a group and to acquire or to leave a role. The first two services are provided by MadKit. The last two services are implemented by a dynamic component manager which executes the agent algorithm described in section 5.2. The implementation is made in such a way that any platform providing communicating agents and the notion of group can be used instead of MadKit. The instantiation of the organizations into groups and of the roles is managed by a meta-organization as described in section 5.3.

This architecture has been tested on a number of examples among them the famous prey/predator benchmark [44] and a foot-and-mouth epidemic simulation. This last example was first proposed by [16], and was restated in a somewhat simplified formulation by [17]. We have based our experiment on Hilaire's model.

Figure 5 pictures the structure of the system, which consists of three agent types and two organizations. The meaning of the *Stockbreeder* and *Livestock* agent types is straightforward; note that the *Disease* has also been reified as an agent. We now quickly describe the two organizations:

The Production Organization is composed of two roles: the *Herd Management* role is responsible for selling animals, and moving them to grass-land

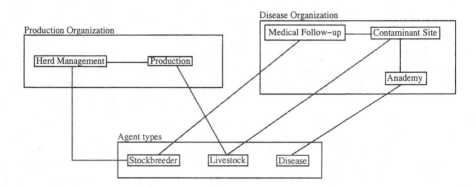

Fig. 5. The foot-and-mouth epidemic example

in spring and back to stalls in fall. The *Production* role is responsible for
simulating the birth of calves.

The Disease Organization is composed of three roles: the *Medical Follow-up*
role is responsible for detecting the presence of the disease and initiating a
treatment; The *Contaminant Site* role deals with the effect of the treatment
and the *Anademy* role simulates contagion and healing.

A more complete description of this simulation, including the full specification
of the roles, can be found in [17].

Figure 6 pictures the result of the simulation: the number of sick animals
increases in winter, because they are located in stalls, were contamination rate
is high; it decreases in summer when the animals are outside. The total number
of cows varies as a result of the births and selling. Our results are very similar
to those of [17] and could be obtained with a low cost in term of development
time.

7 Conclusion and Perspectives

We have presented formalisms which allow to abstract, describe and reuse recurrent patterns of individual (role) and collective (organization) behavior at design
time, such that agents can dynamically adopt one or several of these behavioural
patterns at run-time. The MOCA platform is an original implementation with
organizations and roles as first class citizens. This gives a fully operational meaning to the Aaladin methodology [15]. It also constitutes an advance on [6] or [16]
where the social networks are static and on [22] where run-time coordination of
several roles is not considered.

For the time being, the organizational descriptions have to be written directly
in XML files, but we plan to have a graphical interface in a few months that
will allow to design new organizational patterns with ease and almost without
typing any code, allowing to concentrate on the content of the simulation.

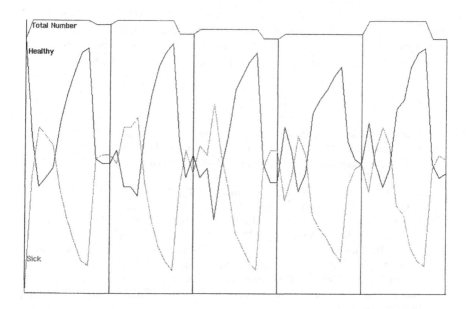

Fig. 6. The results of the simulation

A major issue of our approach is to establish a reasonable mechanism for role conflict management in the agent. We are currently developing an approach based on mutual exclusion of roles on some critical zones. The main difficulty is to find a relevant and efficient way of detecting such critical zones.

The model is being implemented as an organizational layer above MadKit; there are three immediate perspectives to extend this work:

1. For the time being, only simple simulations have been realized using MOCA, to demonstrate its usability. Of course, it is now necessary to implement larger scale examples based on more meaningful situations.
2. The scheduling techniques are introduced in an ad-hoc way (a simple step by step scheduler for the given example) and do not even use the tools provided by MadKit. It is foreseen to specify a specific scheduling technique with each organization to be instantiated as a scheduler for each group. The groups would to be synchronized with each other, allowing for distributed simulation.
3. A major issue, as already mentionned, is the distinction between the external description of roles, i.e. the expected interactions and the way it is generated internally allowing for even more flexible agent architectures. In particular, it would introduce a description of expected behaviour rather than an actual one separating what from how.

Finally, the possibility for a role to provide new competences to an agent just by being acquired when entering a group (no learning here), first thought as an implicit communication mechanism between groups, could allow for the design of incrementally learning agents: taking a new role provides new capabilities to the agent, which could allow him to take other roles, and so on. This constitutes a very promising longer-term perspective for the MOCA platform.

References

1. Conte, R., Castelfranchi, C.: Cognitive and Social Action. UCL Press (1995)
2. Conte, R., Castelfranchi, C.: Norms as mental objects. from normative beliefs to normative goals. In Castelfranchi, C., Müller, J.P., eds.: From reaction to Cognition (MAAMAW'93). (1995) 186–196
3. Dignum, F. Artificial Intelligence and Law **7** (99) 69–79
4. Jennings, N.R. The Knowledge Engineering Review **8** (1993) 223–250
5. Castelfranchi, C., Dignum, F., Jonker, C., Treur, J. In Jennings, N., Lesperance, Y., eds.: Intelligent Agents VI (ATAL99), Springer-Verlag (2000)
6. Conte, R., Castelfranchi, C., Dignum, F.: Autonomous norm-accpetance. In Müller, J., Singh, M., Rao, A., eds.: Intelligent Agents V (ATAL98). (1999) 319–333
7. Dignum, F., Morley, D., Sonenberg, E., Cavendon, L. In: Proceedings of the Fourth International Conference on MultiAgent Systems (ICMAS2000), IEEE Computer Society (2000) 111–118
8. López y López, F., Luck, M., d'Inverno, M.: A Framework for Agent Architecture, Dependence, Norms and Obligations. In: MAAMAW'2001. (2001)
9. Hübner, J.F., ao Sichman, J.S., Boissier, O.: Spécification structurelle, fonctionnelle et déontique d'organisations dans les sma. In Mathieu, P., Müller, J.P., eds.: Systèmes multi-agents et systèmes complexes, JFIASMA'02, Hermès (2002)
10. Gilbert, N.: Emergence in social simulations. In Gilbert, N., Conte, R., eds.: Artificial Societies. UCL Press Limited (1995) 144–156
11. Conte, R., Edmonds, B., Moss, S., Sawyer, K.: Sociology and social theory in agent based social simulation : A symposium. Computational and Mathematical Organization **7** (2001) 183–205
12. Wooldridge, M., Jennings, N.R., Kinny, D.: The Gaia methodology for agent-oriented analysis and design. Autonomous Agents and Multi-Agent Systems **3** (2000) 285–312
13. Gasser, L.: Social conceptions of knowledge and action: Dai foundations and open systems semantics. Artificial Intelligence **47** (1995) 107–138
14. Lea, D., Marlowe, J.: Psl: Protocols and pragmatics for open systems. Technical report, State University of New York (1995) available on ftp://g.oswego.edu/pub/papers/psl.ps.
15. Ferber, J., Gutknecht, O.: A meta-model for the analysis and design of organizations in multi-agent systems. In: ICMAS'98, IEEE Computer Society (1998) 128–135
16. Durand, B.: Simulation multi-agents et épidémiologie opérationnelle. PhD thesis, Université de Caen (1996)
17. Hilaire, V.: Vers une approche de spécification, de prototypage et de vérification de systèmes multi-agents. PhD thesis, Université de Franche-Comté (2000)
18. : The MadKit project (a multi-agent development kit). (http://www.madkit.org)
19. Zack, M.H.: Researching organizational systems using social network analysis. In IEEE, ed.: Proceedings of the 33rd Hawai'i International Conference on System Sciences, Maui, Hawai'i. (2000)

20. Amblard, F.: MODELES MULTI-AGENTS POUR LA DECISION COLLEC-
    TIVE. Technical report, Université de Montpellier II (1999)
21. T.A.B, S.: Estimation on the basis of snowball samples: How to Weight. Bulletin
    de Méthodologie Sociologique 1 (1992) 59–70
22. Parunak, H., Odell, J.: Representing social structures in UML. In: Workshop
    Agent-Oriented Software Engineering, AOSE2001. (2001)
23. Panzarasa, P., Norman, T.J., Jennings, N.R.: Modeling sociality in the BDI frame-
    work. In: Proceedings of First Asia-Pacific Conference on Intelligent Agent Tech-
    nology (IAT'99). (1999) 202–206
24. Kendall, E.: Role modelling for agents analysis, design and implementation. In:
    1st ASA - 3rd MA, Palm Springs, USA (1999)
25. Barbuceanu, M., Gray, T., Mankovski, S.: Coordinating with obligations. In:
    Agents'98, Minneapolis (1998) 62–69
26. Cohen, P.R., Levesque, H.J.: Confirmation and joint actions. In: Proceedings of the
    twelfth International Joint Conference on Artificial Intelligence, IJCAI'91, AAAI
    (1991)
27. Hannoun, M., Boissier, O., Sichman, J.S., Sayettat, C.: MOISE: Un modèle organi-
    sationnel pour la conception de systèmes multi-agents. In: JFIADSMA'99, Hermes
    (1999)
28. Castelfranchi, C.: Founding agent's 'autonomy' on dependence theory. In: ECAI
    2000, IOS Press (2000) 353–357
29. ao Sichman, J.S.: DEPINT: dependence-based coalition formation in an open
    multi-agent scenario. Journal of Artificial Societies and Social Simulation 1 (1998)
30. Fischer, K.: Agent-based design of holonic manufacturing systems. Robotics and
    Autonomous Systems 27 (1999) 3–13
31. Ferraris, C., Martel, C.: Antigone, modélisation pour les activités conjointes: un
    méta-modéle pour les sma? In: JFIADSMA'99, Hermes (1999) 135–148
32. Ferraris, C., Martel, C.: Regulation in groupware, the example of a collaborative
    drawing tool for young children. In: 6th International Workshop on Groupware
    (CRIWG 2000), Madeira, Portugal (2000) 119–127
33. Ferber, J., Gutknecht, O.: Operational semantics of a role-based agent architecture.
    In: ATAL'99. (1999)
34. Lemaître, C., Excelente, C.B.: Multi-agent organization approach. In: Proceedings
    of the second Iberoamerican Workshop on Distributed Artificial Intelligence and
    Multi-Agent systems, Toledo, Spain. (1998)
35. : The foundation for intelligent physical agents (FIPA). (http://www.fipa.org)
36. Yoo, M.J.: Une approche componentielle pour la modélisation des agents
    coopérants et sa validation. PhD thesis, Université de Paris 6 (1999)
37. Dury, A.: Modélisation des interactions dans les systèmes multi-agents. PhD thesis,
    Université Henri Poincaré (2000)
38. Ferber, J., Müller, J.P.: Influence and reaction: a model of situated multi-agent
    system. In: ICMAS'96, Kyoto, AAAI Press (1996)
39. Harel, D.: Statecharts: A visual formalism for complex systems. Science of Com-
    puter Programming 8 (1987) 231–274
40. Harel, D., Naamad, A.: The Statemate Semantics of Statecharts. ACM Trans.
    Soft. Eng. Method. 4 (1996)
41. Duke, R., King, P., Rose, G., Smith, G.: The Object-Z specification Language.
    Technical report, Software Verification Research Center, Departement of Computer
    Science, University of Queensland, Australia (1991)

42. Duke, R., Rose, G., Smith, G.: Object-Z: a specification language advocated for the description of standards. Technical Report 94–95, Software Verification Research Centre, Department of Computer Science, University of Queensland (1994)
43. Amiguet, M., Müller, J.P.: Solving Role Conflicts in Organizational Models. Autonomous Agents and Multi-Agent Systems (2002) submitted
44. Müller, J.P., Amiguet, M., Baez, J., Nagy, A.: La plate-forme MOCA: réification de la notion d'organisation au-dessus de madkit. In El Fallah Segrouchni, A., Magnin, L., eds.: JFIADSMA'01. (2001) 307–310

Towards an Emergence-Driven Software Process
for Agent-Based Simulation

Nuno David[1,2,*], Jaime Simão Sichman[2,**], and Helder Coelho[3]

[1] Department of Information Science and Technology, ISCTE/DCTI, Lisbon, Portugal
Nuno.David@iscte.pt   http://www.iscte.pt/~nmcd
[2] Intelligent Techniques Laboratory, University of São Paulo, Brazil
Jaime.Sichman@poli.usp.br   http://www.pcs.usp.br/~jaime
[3] Department of Informatics, University of Lisbon, Portugal
hcoelho@di.fc.ul.pt   http://www.di.fc.ul.pt/~hcoelho

Abstract. In this paper we propose an emergence-driven software process for agent-based simulation that clarifies the traceability of micro and macro observations to micro and macro specifications in agent-based models. We use the concept of hyperstructures [1] to illustrate how micro and macro specifications interact in agent-based models, and show that the reductionism/ non-reductionism debate is important to understand the reliability of agent-based simulations. In particular, we show that the effort expended in the verification of agent-based simulations increases exponentially with the number of micro and macro specifications, and that the reliability assessment of non-anticipated results in simulation is in practice not possible. According to these results we claim to be impossible in practice to verify that an agent-based conceptual model has been implemented properly as a computational model, since we do not usually know what we want the output to be a priori. We thus advocate that the classic process of verification, validation and exploration of non-anticipated results is not reliable in agent-based simulation, and call into question the applicability of traditional software engineering methods to agent-based simulation.

1   Introduction

The software process is the set of activities and results that produce a software product. In Software Engineering the attributes of a software product refer to the *non-functional* characteristics displayed by the product once it is installed and put to use. These attributes characterize the product's dynamic behaviour and the use made of the product, where reliability and usability are among the most fundamental ones (see [19]).

Meanwhile, the Agent-Based Simulation product differs in various senses from the classical one. Similarly, the process of product development in Agent-Based Simulation (ABS) proceeds from different motivations from the ones originating the

---

* Partially supported by FCT/PRAXIS XXI, Portugal, grant number BD/21595/99.
** Partially supported by CNPq, Brazil, grant number 301041/95-4, and by project MAPPEL (PROTEM-CC, CNPq/NSF), grant number 680033/99-8.

J.S. Sichman, F. Bousquet, P. Davidsson (Eds.): MABS 2002, LNAI 2581, pp. 89-104, 2003.

classical process. By *ABS product* we mean the set of programs and documents required to satisfy the designer and users' goals of running successful and informative simulations. We identify four fundamental aspects that characterize the ABS product:

i) the product is instantiated as such after the first development cycles, throughout the implementation phase with the first simulation experiment;

ii) the product does not stipulate an exhaustive and pre-specified enumeration of requirements that must satisfy once it is put to use; instead, a model is developed along succeeding cycles that simultaneously include specification, implementation, verification, validation and use; the motto is thus *exploration of requirements*;

iii) the product is frequently used to *explore outputs* that are difficult to calculate analytically from complex models;

iv) the product is normally used to *explore qualitative concepts* according to outputs that are neither anticipated nor intentionally specified during the model specification phase, which makes the classical notion of *dynamic verification*[1] very difficult to apply.

Characteristics (i) and (ii) have been well identified and systematized problems in classical **S**oftware **E**ngineering (SE) and **A**rtificial **I**ntelligence (AI), particularly in the field of exploratory programming for knowledge based systems. Typical processes to develop these products are strongly based on formal or informal verification of programs according to requirements that must be specified at some point of the development process. Contemporary models of **A**gent **O**riented **S**oftware **E**ngineering (AOSE) (see [4]) do not add novelty in this respect, for its methodologies concern the interaction of distributed intelligence, so as to define behaviours and solve problems that must be specified at some point of the development process.

Characteristic (iii) has been reasonably systematized in classic **C**omputer **S**imulation (CS) for dynamic system analysis, queuing models or general-purpose engineering (see [13]). In this case, the exploration of requirements and results is more quantitative than qualitative in nature. Most model specifications come in the form of equations, and the verification process usually arises in the form of mathematical analysis.

Characteristic (iv) is potentially more defining of ABS products. It results not only from the product role of *exploring requirements* and *program outputs*, but also from *exploring qualitative concepts* according to such outputs. In effect, a relevant use of ABS is to detect which effects may be drawn from patterns of agent interaction, the emergence of macro-level regularities that are not intentionally specified at micro levels of detail. These observations must be verified *a posteriori*, after program execution trials, and some of them may be hard to verify and validate. Hence, in most cases, the development of ABS products covers additional levels of difficulty if compared with classical products, since the borders between *dynamic verification* and *dynamic validation*[2] are harder to distinguish.

---

[1] The role of verification is to show that the computational model is equivalent to the conceptual model. *Dynamic* verification checks program correctness by evaluating given inputs with program execution outputs (see §2, [17,18,19] and [21] in this volume).

[2] The role of validation is to show that the conceptual model specification is equivalent to an intended application or observed target. In practice the computational model must be

Methodological issues in ABS have been a topic of primary importance in the discipline (see e.g.[5,9,20]). Meanwhile, the research has rarely approached the technical details of software processes and its relationship with the problematic of emergence. While the software process may have been somewhat considered by some authors, the underlying methodological analysis has been invariably understood according to assumptions and principles of classic SE, classic CS, AI and AOSE, whose feasibility of purpose in ABS is far from being clear. At this stage, it is important to include the software process in the ABS research agenda for the following reasons:

i) the ABS product is not only used for technological automation of problem solving and expertise support, but also for purposes of scientific investigation of social theories and models of the real world. While in the former case the results of ABS may be reasonably verified with specifications and most times validated by its users' *desires*, in the latter validation requires independence from the users' and developers' bias;

ii) the crucial role of non-anticipated observation of program execution outputs in ABS hinders the applicability of classic software development principles to ABS. One must remember that validating a conceptual model does not guarantee the correctness and acceptability of non-anticipated outputs in the corresponding computational model. Since in ABS the verification and validation of non-anticipated outputs are superimposed, the existence of development premises for ABS that have not been considered in classic SE, AI and AOSE can be hypothesised. This change of premises may have a profound impact on the product non-functional requirements, especially, with respect to reliability requirements;

iii) most classic CS and AOSE products are not concerned with emergent, non-anticipated, structures. Classic CS is not agent-based. Organisations and institutions in AOSE are both considered as computationally individual entities in the system; here, the interaction between different levels of agent granularity is usually pre-defined; the concept of emergent "wholes", multi-level modelling, and emergent interaction between agents at different levels of abstraction is usually undesirable. The specification of models in ABS must thus be significantly different from classical CS and AOSE. Currently, there are no meta-models to describe the ABS process. For this reason, the methodological and epistemological tension between individualistic and holistic approaches has been discussed from an abstract point of view, with no real connection to practical ways of specifying agent-based simulations. The inexistence of meta-models to specify software is an excellent way to attain incorrect implementations and bad verification and validation. Indeed, specifications need to be *traceable* to implementations and program execution outputs.

In this paper we investigate an abstract model that characterizes the ABS software process with regard to the specification stage. We concentrate on the logical analysis of the method *per se*, rather than validate the discipline through simulation results and case studies. Method examination facilitates detection of inconsistencies and errors

---

validated as well. *Dynamic* validation checks if the computational model outputs agree with the intended application or observed target (see §2, [17,18,19] and [21] in this volume).

related to problem conceptualisation and program construction. It is important to establish systematic development and interpretation principles, particularly with respect to the analysis of emergent phenomena.

This paper is structured as follows. In section 2 we will analyse the role of conceptual and computational models in agent based simulation. Later we will show how to incorporate micro- and macro-observations in agent-based conceptual models, and that the reductionism/non-reductionism debate is important to understand the reliability of simulation programs. In particular, we will demonstrate that the effort expended in static verification increases exponentially with the number of micro and macro observations specified in agent-based models, and that an extensive verification of anticipated results in agent-based simulation is in practice not possible. In section 3 we will use this result to assert that the process of dynamic verification, validation and exploration of non-anticipated results is not reliable in agent-based simulation. We will then point out research directions to solve this problem and give our conclusions in section 4.

2   From Conceptual to Computational Models

It is relatively unanimous that the ABS process begins with the identification of some research object, a "puzzle", for which there are questions whose answer is not known (cf. [11]). The research object leads us to the definition of an abstract or real world *target* for modelling. The target is the real or proposed idea, situation or phenomena to be modelled, from which one constructs a *conceptual model* (a mathematical/logical/verbal representation) based on observations, assumptions and formulation of hypothesis. The conceptual model must be transformed into a corresponding *computational model*.

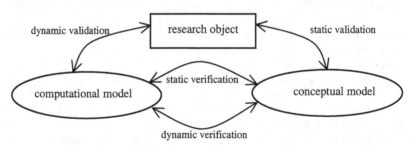

Fig. 1. The modelling process with relation to verification and validation.

Consider the simplified version of the agent-based modelling process in figure 1. The figure relates verification and validation with the modelling process (see [18,21]). *Static validation* is defined as determining that the theories and assumptions underlying the conceptual model are reasonable representations of the research object. *Static verification* is defined as ensuring that the program source code representing the conceptual model is correct. Therefore, static verification is not directly concerned with the evaluation of non-anticipated outputs during the simulation. *Dynamic verification* is defined as determining that the conceptual model entails the computational model outputs. *Dynamic validation* is defined as determining that the computational model outputs are correct according to the research object[3]. In the present section we investigate the stages involving the specification of conceptual models and static verification.

2.1 Multiple Targets in Agent-Based Simulation

The particularity of agent-based modelling is the definition of elements in a model that represent entities in the target, such as human beings, organizations or inanimated objects. Eventually, every passive and active entity in the target may be "agentified". Some approaches differ in respect to the model's level of abstraction in relation to the real world, as well as to the representation granularity of agents in the model:

i) *simulation with artificial societies* - at one extreme of the abstraction axis we find models of artificial societies that do not reference a concrete target or specific theory about the real world (e.g.[10]). This approach is the most akin to requirements exploration in classical SE and AI: the conceptual model is validated according to the designer's *observation perspectives* and *desires* in respect to the computational model outputs. The conceptual and computational models evolve in consecutive refinement cycles according to those judgments. Hence, a major part of the software process is devoted to the *verification* of models: to what extent the macroscopic regularities of interest given by the computational model outputs are caused by the local or micro mechanisms specified in the conceptual model? This tendency often suggests an implicit assumption that does not have to be adopted, when the term *micro* is associated with specifications of conceptual and computational models, and the term *macro* with observations of computational models outputs.

ii) *animation of socio-cognitive theories* - halfway to the other extreme of the axis, we find the simulation of models of socio-cognitive or sociological theories. This approach is usually founded on computational animation of logic formalisms, which represent agents and social structures according to a specific theory, for instance, the Theory of Dependence and Social Power [3]. The animation serves a purpose of theory consistency checking and refinement of social theories (see [6]), as well as to verify the pragmatic feasibility of such theories in MAS engineering [22,8]. In this trend, the structures emerging from the interaction of elements in the model are crucial for theory refinement. By emergent structures we mean new observable categories that do not find a semantic expression in the original vocabulary of the model (e.g. the subjective observation of agent *coalitions* according to patterns of *dependence relations*). Recent methodological discussions propose the explicit specification of given emergent (macro) entities in models, regardless of being reducible or not reducible to levels of description at lower granularity (see, e.g., Sawyer's claim in [5] or [27]). As we will soon show, such practice has always been common in ABS, but it has not been methodologically and appropriately assumed.

---

[3] In the software engineering literature, dynamic verification and validation is also known as "program testing".

iii) *simulations with representations of the real world* - at the end of the axis, we find simulations with models that should desirably represent observations of real social and institutional concrete processes (see, e.g., Moss' claim in [5]). The goal is "the use of MAS to describe observed social systems or aspects thereof and to capture the sometimes conflicting perceptions of the social system by stakeholders and other domain experts". This approach is the most conflicting with the classic process, owing to the practical inevitability of defects in computer programs. Insofar as specification and program coding errors are unavoidable in practice, the *validation* of computational model outputs is susceptible to misjudgements because the *verification* and *validation* processes overlap with respect to the evaluation of such outputs.

We can see that when travelling from approach (i) to (iii) there is an increasing overlap of dynamic verification and validation judgements. Such increasing overlap also parallelizes a change in the scientific role of simulation from *explanation and prediction* to *explanation and representation* of targets. But as we will see, the complexity of the verification process in the former case, and the superposition of verification and validation judgements in the latter, obstructs the feasibility of SE techniques in ABS. If these questions are not appropriately and successfully tackled, this problematic may challenge us to change the scientific role of ABS from the context of *explanation, representation* and *prediction*, to the context of *prescriptive explanation* and *prescriptive representation* of targets.

2.2 Micro or Macro?

One may say that in most ABS approaches there is an association flavour of the term *micro* with the specification of conceptual and computational models, and the term *macro* with the computational model outcomes. But this is not entirely factual. There are at least two cases for which the term macro is underlying the specification process:

i) *implicit in the target* – there are elements in the universe of the model that are indivisible, but represent entities of the target with a higher (macro) [or lower (micro)] granularity than the other indivisible elements with whom the element interacts in the model.

ii) *explicit in the model* – there are elements in the universe of the model that represent aggregates of other indivisible or non-indivisible elements, that is, a set of elements defined in the model as a "whole", having specific, and possibly exclusive, properties.

In the first case the macro concept is subjectively relevant in the target, but irrelevant to the model objective dynamics. In the second case, there are aggregates treated explicitly as "wholes" in the model. Some researchers would agree that the most frequent approach is the first one. However, there are numerous examples of the second, e.g., in Swarm [12] agents may be contained in *swarms* that are in turn contained in other *swarms*. The source of this question and its effects on the product reliability requirements can be found if we further abstractly detail the specification of agent-based models.

2.3 Agentified Conceptual Specifications

We start the specification of a model with its set of indivisible agents. This set will be known as the *Agentified Conceptual Specification* (ACS). An ACS is a set of *Agentified Entities* (AEs) associated with a finite index set I, $ACS=\{A_i\}$, $i \in I$.

An AE is an element in the model specified according to some arbitrary observation process. The role of the observation is to analyse a particular feature of abstract or physical nature in the target. Different AEs can represent entities of different granularity in the target, such as physical objects, humans, organisations, realistic representations of organisational concepts (e.g. a norm). Before we proceed, it should be clear for the sake of generality that it is indeed possible to represent any feature of a target by agentifying it, despite the disadvantage of overstressing the agent metaphor (see [20]).

At this point we have not represented explicit macro concepts in the model. The specification of agentified aggregates can be accomplished with observation processes that explicitly describe macro-observations of the target.

2.3.1 Levels of Observation and Emergence: An Hyperstructural Vision

The ABS product development is an exploratory and iterative process, for which the conceptual model is to a great extent determined by observing properties of entities in the target, and how the entities relate and interact with each other according to those properties. Particularly relevant to ABS is the observation of entities according to different levels of abstraction and perspective. We view an ABS model as a hyperstructural construction [1,26]. The hyperstructural framework is useful to model AEs that can interact with other AEs at different levels of abstraction. Given one or more arbitrary observation processes we define two qualitative distinct levels of observation, called *micro-observation* and *macro-observation*:

Micro-observation – the observation of properties of each individual AE in the target:

$$Obs(A_i), i \in I$$

Macro-observation – the observation of properties of "wholes", according to (i) any subset $K \in P(I)$ of AEs in the ACS; (ii) micro-observation of those AEs; (iii) an interaction process between those AEs using properties observed in (ii):

$$Obs(A_K), \text{ with } A_K = R(A_j, Obs(A_j), Int)), j \in K, K \in P(I)$$

where every whole A_K is indexed by some element $K \in P(I)$.

The conceptualisation of a new structure, a "whole", involves observing an aggregate of AEs in the target, where *Int* is an interaction process between those AEs and R is the result of the construction process. For instance, consider an aggregate of AEs characterized by a macro property, say the gross income. The micro-properties are the AEs' individual incomes, and the construction process is an aggregation of AEs according to an interaction process that calculates the gross income based on the individual incomes. In other cases, the observed macro-properties may be disjoint from the observed micro-properties, for instance, the *cohesion* of an aggregate calculated according to patterns of relations of trust and dependence between its members.

If we want to represent explicit macro-observations in the model, we have to specify a new type of AEs in the ACS. The specification of such wholes is achieved by representing new AEs at higher levels of granularity than its constituent AEs. A structure A_K denotes a *first order macro-AE*, conceptualised in a distinct level of abstraction from the other *micro-AEs*. Thus, in the previous example, the concept *cohesion of an aggregate* would be specified as a new macro-AE in the conceptual model! Nevertheless, note that the construction process defining the macro-AE does not have to be expressed in the specification. Moreover, it can be argued that the observation of macro-properties does not even need to be computationally expressible, i.e., by way of an algorithm. Indeed, like any other micro-AE, the designer can ascribe (by definition) additional macro-properties to a macro-AE. For instance, if one specifies in the model an organisation that contains several agents, one is not necessarily assuming that those agents are sufficient to specify the properties of that organisation. If that is the case, the micro-observations and the interaction process (the construction process R) are thus subjectively represented in the observer's mind. *It is common practice in ABS to define properties of macro-AEs without stating its hypothetic reducibility to properties of its constituent AEs according to a particular theory. Such omission is perfectly acceptable, but it should inhibit the designer from ascribing methodological individualistic principles to his simulation.*

Sawyer [5] is right when he claims that the inspiration principles of ABS are methodological individualistic, but his claim that most agent-based models are methodological individualistic seems to be false; in practice most models represent macro-concepts, regardless of being reducible or non-reducible to other micro-concepts. Nevertheless, as we will soon show, Moss [5] does not seem to be right in suggesting that the reductionism/non-reductionism debate does not influence the verification and validation problematic in ABS.

The set of observed micro-AES and first-order macro-AEs constitute a *first-order ACS*, denoted by ACS^I. The maximum number of elements in a first-order ACS is given by $\#ACS^I = \#P(ACS)-1$. It is evidently possible to consider second order macro observations over first order ACSs, and so on. The process that combines AEs of different order is called a hyperstructure, and is illustrated in figure 2.

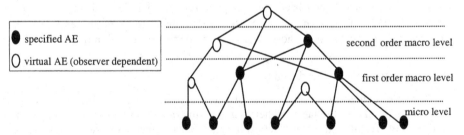

Fig. 2. Specified AEs and virtual emergent AEs. The convergence of lines from lower order to higher order AEs means that lower order AEs interact with each other. This may be ascribed by the specification itself or be only represented in the observer's mind. For instance, the notion of observed 'system" in a simulation, e.g., the construction process given by the interaction between a grid and a set of individual agents, can be understood as a virtual AE; in such example the concept of 'grid' is thus agentified.

We proceed from the principle that the interesting emergent events that involve agent-based simulations reside not only in the simulations themselves but in the ways that they change the way we think and interact with the world. "Rather than emergent devices in their own right, computer simulations are catalysts for emergent processes in our mind" [2]; they help us to create new ways of seeing the research object. In the figure, the black vertexes denote AEs that are explicitly specified in a model. The white vertexes denote possible observable *virtual* AEs, which are not part of the specification. Some of them will constitute the observer's expectations of how the model will behave; consequently, *they must be verified during the software process.* We immediately see that the observer's interest can be the conceptualisation of ACSs of higher order than the one specified, for example, the conceptualisation of the system as whole.

2.3.2 Specifying State Transitions

The ACS modifies its state along the time by modifying the state of its constituent AEs. We denote an arbitrary order ACS in state e by $A_{|e}$, where $A_{|e}=\{A_{i|e}\}$, $i \in I_{|e}$ and $I_{|e}$ is the index set in state e. The notation $A_{i|e}$ denotes an AE with index $i \in I_{|e}$ in state e.

Consider a set of properties given by some arbitrary observation process *Obs* over the AEs in the ACS $A_{|e}$. A state transition $e1 \rightarrow e2$ in the simulation is calculated by submitting the AEs in state $e1$ to an algorithmic process of interaction *AlgInt* that uses the properties registered under the observation process *Obs*. A transition sequence $e1 \rightarrow e2 \rightarrow ... \rightarrow en$ is obtained by successive compositions of the algorithm $A_{|en}=AlgInt_{Obs|e1 \rightarrow en}(A_{|e1})$.

The specification of the interaction algorithm will have a decisive impact in the AEs' evolution. For instance, new AEs may be created and others cease to exist. It is also possible to specify mechanics to observe aggregates composed of AEs at different time states. These observations would allow the agents themselves to establish the *persistence* in time of some regularity. Such observations would have to be *previously* and *algorithmically* specified, which is different from the usual designer-observer's position that *mentally* conceptualizes the emergence of *new* categories *during* or *after* the simulation.

2.4 Static Verification

The need to transform conceptual models into equivalent computational models has always been a major motivation for the substratum of software engineering techniques. Verification techniques involve showing that the detailed design, and implementation of the conceptual and computational models are correct. It involves static and dynamic techniques (see [17,18,19]). Static techniques are concerned with the analysis and checking of system representations such as specification documents and the program source code. *Static techniques are not directly concerned with evaluation of non-anticipated emergent outcomes during the simulation.* For this reason, some static techniques used in classical SE and AOSE can also be used in ABS, although it will probably involve in most cases a higher degree of complexity analysis.

Within an agent-based realm of complexity, static verification involves to a great extent checking the model specification with its detailed design. There is an increasing amount of literature for verifying agent-based systems in AOSE. One approach relevant to ABS is static compositional verification [7]. For macro-properties assumedly reducible to lower order properties, this involves verifying that the properties of macro-AEs derive from its constituent micro-AEs properties, according to some interaction algorithm.

Consider a m-order ACS $A_{|e1}$ with an index set I_{e1}. The state $e1$ is the initial state. Within a hyperstructural framework, verifying the model *expected* behaviour can be described by the following steps:

(i) verify *specified* AEs by composition: given the properties of micro-AEs, verify that the properties of each macro-AE resemble the specification of the macro-observation, i.e., for each j-order macro-AE $A_{i|e1} \in A_{|e1}$ and $j \leq m$, show that there is a subset $I_i \in I_{|e1}$ of AEs with order less or equal to j-1, such that $A_{i|e1} = R(A_{l|e1}, Obs(A_{i|e1}), Int))$, $l \in I_i$. So if A_i is an AE representing the concept *cohesion of an aggregate*, this amounts to show that the algorithm that computes the cohesion according to the set of lower order AEs conforms to its specification R;

(ii) verify the interaction algorithm *AlgInt*: given the properties of micro and macro AEs in state $e1$, verify that for any state en subsequent to $e1$, the properties in $e1$ are preserved in en;

(iii) verify *expected* emergent AEs by composition: given the properties verified in (i), verify that the system will behave according to the designer's expectations. These are emergent properties associated with *virtual* AEs, possibly, with order greater than m. So if we specify that the system should reach some form of equilibrium after some state en, this amounts to show that it will do so according to the properties verified in (i).

The specification of macro-AEs is obviously a complexifying factor in the verification process. But the increase in complexity does not only lie in the compositional verification of step (i). Step (iii) implies the compositional verification of virtual aggregates, i.e., verifying expected emergent properties in the system. The number of observable virtual AEs will possibly increase with the number of micro- and macro-AEs specified in the model. For an ACS or order m, the highest number of observable virtual macro-AEs at order m+1 is:

$$N_{virtual}(m) = 2^{n+n_1+...+n_m} - n - n_1 - ... - n_m - 1$$

where n is the number of micro-AEs and n_k denotes the number of k-order AEs.

Thus, for a program without macro-AEs that manipulates 15 micro-AEs, the highest number of observable virtual AEs is 32753. If we include in the ACS one additional micro-AE and two second-order AEs the number increases to 262125. Of course, the number of virtual AEs that must be statically verified is much lower. This is the case if the goal of ABS is the *exploration* of emergent events rather than the *specification* of emergent events. *What this formula tells us is that even if we limit the number of observation processes to observe a simulation (limit the set of observable properties), the increase in the number of micro and macro-AEs in the model implies an exponential increase of observable virtual macro-AEs in the simulation.* But if they are indeed observable, can we verify them? And if not, can they be validated without being verified?

3   Exploration of Results

We have now reached the conditions to confirm our claims in respect to assumptions in the classical process that cannot be used in the ABS process. For this purpose we make a short circuit in the development process, jumping directly to stages of dynamic verification, dynamic validation and exploration of results. It should be clear that we left behind many development steps that we have not approached here, such as static validation, detailed design and implementation.

For the time being, the unstated tendency in ABS to associate the term micro with the conceptual and computational model specifications, and the term macro with the computational model outcomes should now have been understood. For this reason, it should not be strange the traditional attempt in AOSE to arrive at feasible verification processes, also implicitly adopted in ABS. The rule of thumb in AOSE, "specify few agents so as to get controlled and verifiable systems" is a particular case of "specify few micro and macro concepts so as to get controlled and verifiable systems". Surely, the ABS research community will hardly adopt such rule of thumb, and we would like to stay that way.

3.1 Dynamic Verification and Validation

It is often alleged that one fundamental difference that distinguishes the classical from the ABS process is the need in ABS to validate models with data and/or observations from real world targets. On one hand, the correctness of simulation results that are previously anticipated along the model specification phase is assessed with verification techniques that are similar, to a great extent, to classical SE and AOSE. On the other hand, the emergent tendencies that are not anticipated or intentionally specified are validated with data and observations of the target. The logic underlying this strategy is that if a program is correctly verified then its outputs are entailed by the conceptual model specification. This assertion would in fact be correct if we could rigorously verify the correctness of reasonably complex code.

What is the role of static and dynamic verification? Static verification techniques can partially demonstrate that the conceptual model corresponds to the computational model, but they cannot demonstrate that the computational model is indeed operationally useful and without software faults and failures. A *software failure* occurs when the software is executing, and the software does not behave as expected by the user. A *software failure* is not the same as a *software fault* (see [19]). *Software faults* are programming errors whereby the program does not conform to the specification. Software faults are static and its existence may be inferred through program inspections (i.e. static verification) and from software failures. Software faults cause software failures when the faulty code is executed with a set of inputs that expose the software fault. For these reasons, dynamic testing is the predominant validation and verification technique in SE. Dynamic testing exercises the program using data like the real data processed by the program, and the values obtained are used to test if the computer program behaves as expected. It is both used in classical SE (see [19]) and CS (see [18]). The bad news for ABS is that real data is not easy to obtain. But even if that was not the case, suppose that the ABS program can be verified and validated for a set of known input/output relations. How can the reliability of such simulation be affected after that stage?

3.2   Classic Software Engineering Methods Are Not Reliable in ABS

One result after the forty years of research history in software engineering is that any product that does not have its reliability requirements assessed cannot be validated with any model, whichever it may be. In most cases, classical products are ultimately verified and validated by the users' *desires* and *satisfaction* with the product behaviour. This means that if some dysfunctional result is not predicted before product delivery, then it must be uncovered with *acceptance tests*.

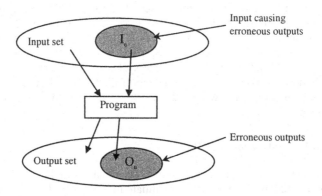

Fig. 3. Software faults cause software failures when the faulty code is executed with a set of inputs which expose the software fault. The software reliability is related to the probability that, in a particular execution of the program, the system input will be a member of the set of inputs which cause an erroneous output. In the classical product, there are usually a number of members of I_e which are more likely to be selected than others (adapted from [19], pp.351).

In fact, empirical data show that more than 50% of all effort expended on a program will be expended after it is delivered to the customer [17,pp.22;14;19]. Such procedures detect software failures, promoting the subsequent distinction between software faults (verification) and invalid specifications (validation). These findings result from empirical analyses that establish the following results (see [19]): (i) not all software faults are equally likely to cause software failures; (ii) transient failures or whose consequences are not serious to the users' needs are of little practical importance in the operational use of the software. In some programs, empirical analysis find that removing 60% of product defects would only led to a 3% reliability improvement [16]. Curiously, these are good results for classical SE. On the one hand, not all software faults imply less system reliability (if the probability of choosing an input which causes an erratic output is low – see figure 3). On the other hand, dysfunctional and annoying software failures can ultimately be detected with dynamic tests, including acceptance testing.

The difference between the classic and the ABS product can be founded precisely here. The first thing that we should be aware is that all simulation results are outcomes of a computational model, which is not necessarily equivalent to the conceptual model. Nevertheless, in the classical product the equivalence of the conceptual with the computational model does not need to be exhaustive. For the classical product, it is software failures not software faults that affect the reliability of a system [19,pp.357]. Hence, the existence of defects in the system is mostly assessed with dynamic and acceptance testing, according to the detection of unexpected outputs. During that stage, the emergence of very undesirable properties is suppressed through program correction or requirements re-specification. *The emergence of undesirable properties that are rare or not very annoying to users are typically not considered and not corrected.* As we have mentioned, removing product defects does not necessarily lead to reliability improvements. The emergence of properties that are irrelevant to users may not even be evaluated (actually, they will be rarely observed). To the users' concerns it does not matter if the system non-dysfunctional characteristics are, or are not, a result of a software fault. *Moreover, to the users' concerns it does not matter if some functional characteristic is, or is not, a result of a software fault.*

Now, dynamic and acceptance tests of this kind are definitely defective, not appropriate, for ABS. This is due to the alteration of the product aims, where the users' satisfaction to accept the classical product is replaced in ABS with symbolic data and stakeholder (subjective) evaluation of social and institutional target realities. For the classic user, it does not matter if the conceptual model is not absolutely equivalent to the computational model, as long as the latter is functional to his desires and needs. Conversely, for the ABS designer and its users the goal is precisely the conceptual model, or/and a set of explanations according to the conceptual model. This may lead us to conclude that the ABS product requires high levels of reliability in much the same way as critical systems in classical SE, for the conceptual specification must be exhaustively equivalent to the computational model[4]. Of course, prescribing high quantitative reliability requirements to ABS programs is at present too much to ask. Furthermore, the nature of critical systems is what we do not need in ABS, since the goal of critical systems is precisely the complete suppression of non-anticipated results.

In reality, the problematic in ABS is far more reaching than reliability and correction *per se*. The problem is situated on the difficult definition of means to distinguish unexpected results from software faults and, therefore, detect incorrectness. In effect, static verification in ABS is hard, as we have seen before; dynamic verification can contribute to enhance the product reliability according to a very limited range of input/outputs; there is no such thing as acceptance testing in ABS. *The distinction between non-anticipated outcomes, entailed by the conceptual model, and software faults in the computational model may, therefore, be virtually impossible to realize.* This indefinition is aggravated when sensitivity analysis and stochastic effects are at stake; for, to what extent is the conceptual model that we analyse sensitive or not to software faults? Or to what extent is some stability and low sensitivity of results not a consequence of a software fault? These indefinitions call into question the applicability of classical SE techniques in the ABS development process. But do we have other techniques? Are we running too fast with the desirable increase in domain diversity, complexity and number of agents in simulations?

---

[4] Critical systems are software systems that require high levels of reliability, like the software installed on a aircraft.

4   Discussion

4.1   Some Prospects on How to Address the Problem

In our vision, reliability is presently the fundamental problem in ABS. The problem of validation has been an important research issue, but are we adopting the right principles? Should we insist with the use of classic approaches and assumptions in regard to verification? We have demonstrated that we should not. Nevertheless, is there an alternative software process for ABS?

At the present maturing stage of ABS there is not yet an answer to these questions. But what this work has demonstrated is that the premises underlying program development and reliability of results have to be substantially revised. At this time such need has not been incorporated in the discipline research trends. A careful reading of the literature of SE teach us how the quantitative analysis of program construction has helped the discipline to find an equilibrium between theoretic and empirical knowledge, allowing large scale production of programs with reasonable reliability patterns in a diversity of domains. Such effort may also be needed in ABS. For instance, are there typical patterns of code complexity in ABS programs? (see e.g. [15]). Is there a relation between the number of corrected software faults and an increase in reliability? As far as we know this type of quantitative analysis does not presently exist in ABS.

Other approaches might involve the so-called *alignment* of models [23], by comparing different models that announce the same type of results and try to see if they actually produce similar results (see e.g. [25] in this volume). There are some scalability limits to these approaches, however; particularly with respect to the level of code complexity (e.g. number of lines). The first is that it is highly biased to validate conceptual models, rather than to verify computational models. The second is that, as we have seen, a same conceptual model can lead to different computational models, which may produce similar or different outputs. The third is that it relies on a social process, the systematic process of re-implementation of programs, transfer of knowledge and assessment of results, which in the specific case of computational models, the implementations themselves, limits in practice the underlying inductive process of verification. In effect, it seems implausible to see programmers willing to collaborate on the massive inspection or re-implementation of programming code, not only because it is a tedious and complex activity; as DeMillo *et al.* [24] would put it, static "(...) verification (of programs) cannot be internalized, transformed, generalized, used, connected to other disciplines, and eventually incorporated into a community consciousness. They cannot acquire gradual credibility, as a mathematical theorem does (...)".

The complementary approach that we have taken in this paper adopted a qualitative methodological course. Such effort allowed us to examine how the micro and macro modelling perspectives interact, affecting static verification and associated reliability requirements. This was possible because we have defined the concept of micro and macro specification in an unambiguous way. These results are also informative to the ongoing methodological and epistemological discussion, with respect to the tension between individualistic and holistic modelling trends in ABS.

4.2   Conclusions

In this paper we have analysed an abstract specification framework as part of an abstract development process for agent-based simulation. We have proposed an emergence-driven software process based on hyperstructures, which clarifies the traceability of micro and macro observations to micro and macro specifications in agent-based models. We have examined how micro and macro specifications interact in a model, and showed that the effort expended in the verification of observable emergent entities in simulation increases exponentially with the number of micro and macro specifications.

According to these results we have showed that it is impossible in practice to verify that an agent-based conceptual model has been implemented properly as a computational model, given that we do not usually know what we want the output to be a priori. Since in agent-based simulation the conceptual and the computational models must be exhaustively equivalent, these results demonstrate that the reliability assessment of non-anticipated results in simulation is in practice not possible. Furthermore, they indicate that the reductionism/non-reductionism debate is important to understand the reliability of simulation programs. According to these results we have called into question the applicability of traditional software engineering methods to agent-based simulation. Hence, we claim that the premises underlying the applicability of classical program development to agent-based simulation have to be substantially revised.

References

1. Baas N.A. and Emmenche C. (1997). On Emergence and Explanation. In: *Intellectica*, 25, pp.67–83.
2. Cariani P. (1991). Emergence and Artificial Life. In: *Artificial Life II*, Addison Wesley, pp.775–797.
3. Castelfranchi C., Miceli M. and Cesta A. (1992). Dependence relations among autonomous agents, *Proceedings of MAAMAW92*, Elsevier Science, pp. 215–227.
4. Ciancarini P. and Wooldridge M. (eds), 2001. *Agent-Oriented Software Engineering*, Springer-Verlag, LNAI1957.
5. Conte R, Edmonds B., Moss S. and Sawyer R.K. (2001). Sociology and Social Theory in Agent Based Social Simulation:A Symposium. In *Computational and Mathematical Organization Theory*, 7(3), pp.183–205.
6. Conte R. and Sichman J.S. (1995). DEPNET: How to benefit from social dependence, In: *Journal of Mathematical Sociology*, 20(2–3), 161–177.
7. Cornelissen F., Jonker C.M. and Treur J. (2001). Compositional Verification of Knowledge-Based Systems: a Case Study for Diagnostic Reasoning. In *Series in Defeasible Reasoning and Uncertainty Management Systems*, vol.6, Kluwer Academic Publishers, pp. 65–82.
8. David N., Sichman J.S. and Coelho H. (2001). Agent-Based Social Simulation with Coalitions in Social Reasoning, In Moss S. and Davidsson P., editors, *Multi-Agent-Based Simulation*, Springer Verlag, LNAI, v.1979, pp.244–265.
9. Davidsson P. (2002). Agent Based Social Simulation: A Computer Science View, In *JASSS*, vol.5, no.1, http://jasss.soc.surrey.ac.uk/5/1/7.html.
10. Epstein J. and Axtell R. (1996). *Growing Artificial Societies: Social Science from the Bottom Up*, MIT press.

11. Gilbert N. and Troitzsch K. (1999). *Simulation for the Social Scientist*, Open University Press.
12. Langton C., Minar N., and Burkhart R., The Swarm Simulation System: A Tool for studying complex systems, http://www.swarm.org.
13. Law A. and Kelton W.D. (1991). *Simulating Modelling and Analysis*, McGraw-Hill.
14. Lienz B. and Swanson E. (1980). *Software Maintenance Management*, Addison-Wesley.
15. McCabe T. and Butler W. (1989). Design Complexity Measurement and Testing, In: *CACM*, vol.32, no.12.
16. Mills D., Dyer M. and Linger R. (1987). Cleanroom software engineering, In: *IEEE Software*, vol.4, no.2.
17. Pressman R. (1994). *Software Engineering: A Practitioner's Approach*, McGraw-Hill.
18. Sargent R.G. (1999). Validation and Verification of Simulation Models. In: *Winter Simulation Conference*, IEEE, Piscataway, NJ, 39–48.
19. Sommerville I. (1998). *Software Engineering*, Addison Wesley.
20. Troitzsch K.G., Brassel K, Mohring M. and Shumacher E. (1997). Can Agents Cover All the World?, In: *Simulating Social Phenomena*, Springer-Verlag, LNEMS 456, pp.55–72.
21. Marietto M.B., David N., Sichman J.S. and Coelho H. (2002). Requirements Analysis of Agent-Based Simulation Platforms: State of the Art and New Prospects. In this volume.
22. Sichman J.S. (1998). DEPINT: Dependence-based coalition formation in an open multi-agent scenario, In *Journal of Artificial Societies and Social Simulation*, 1 (2), http://www.soc.survey.ac.uk/JASSS/1/2/3.html.
23. Axtell R., Axelrod R., J.M. Epstein and M.D.Cohen (1996). Aligning Simulation Models: A Case Study and Results, *Computational and Mathematical Organization Theory* 1(2), pp. 123–141.
24. DeMillo R., Lipton R. and Perlis A. (1979). Social Processes and proofs of theorems and programs, *Communications of the ACM* 22, 5 (May), 271–280.
25. Antunes L., Nobrega L. and Coelho H. (2002). BVG choice in Axerold's tribute model. In this volume.
26. Baas N.A. (1994). Emergence, Hierarchies and Hyperstructures. In Langton C. (eds), *Artificial Life III*, Santa Fe Studies in the Sciences of Complexity, Proceedings, Volume XVII, Addison-Wesley.
27. Sawyer R.K. (2001). Simulating Emergence and Downward Causation in Small Groups. In Moss S. and Davidsson P., editors, *Multi-Agent-Based Simulation*, Springer Verlag, LNAI, v.1979, pp.49–67.

Towards an Ideal Social Simulation Language

Bruce Edmonds

Centre for Policy Modelling,
Manchester Metropolitan University
http://bruce.edmonds.name

Abstract. The problem of social simulation is analysed, identifying what I call 'syntactic' and 'semantic' complexity. These mean that social simulation has particular needs in terms of computational tools. I suggest an approach where one identifies, documents and checks constraints from a variety of sources. Eight criteria for a computational tool to support social simulation are proposed and illustrated using the language SDML. I speculate that a general tool for developing, running and comparing sets of models and results could greatly aid social simulation. This would help manage the clusters of closely related models that social systems seem to necessitate.

1   Introduction

In this paper I discuss the purpose, and design of systems for the computational simulation of social phenomena. I do this by arguing and speculating about what an ideal system of this type might look like. I hope that this will inform and stimulate the further development of social tools.

The ultimate aim of a social simulation is, trivially, to help us understand social phenomena. What is far from trivial is knowing what sort of understanding it can give us and how this may occur. A deeper insight into these issues may help us to design appropriate tools. A good tool will fit well with a good methodology, and an appropriate methodology will depend on the sort of knowledge we are after.

For this reason I will start with an examination of the process of modelling and from this list some of the general characteristics one might expect of an ideal social simulation language (ISSL). A social simulation language called a Strictly Declarative Modelling Language (SDML) [18] is compared against these critieria to illustrate the workings and purpose of the critieria. Finally I will look forward to the possible advances that may take us further towards the ideal. Some of the discussion will be illustrated in terms of the Schelling model [19]. Ths is a simple 2D cellular automata model with black and white counters, which move when they have a low proportion of similar coloured neighbours. The model was designed to illustrate an argument about racial segregation. This model is described in more detail in the appendix.

J.S. Sichman, F. Bousquet, P. Davidsson (Eds.): MABS 2002, LNAI 2581, pp. 105-124, 2003.

2   Modelling Social Systems

Modelling social systems is difficult. It is difficult for (at least) two fundermental reasons: *syntactic* and *semantic* complexity, and two pragmatic reasons: managing clusters of interrelated models and the need to constrain model possibilities.

2.1 Syntactic Complexity

The complex interactions that are involved in social systems mean that the outcomes are difficult to analyse using traditional formal approaches — I will call this the 'syntactical complexity'. One way of thinking about this is that the computational 'distance' from the system's initial set-up to the outcomes is so great that is completely impractical (and probably unhelpful) to attempt to derive general properties of the outcome from the set-up in an analytic fashion.

The presence of syntactic complexity means that there will be at least two different views of a simulation: the interactive processes that are used to specify the simulation; and an appropriate representation of the significant outcomes. The syntactic complexity of the process detail means that it will not be easy to infer the later from the former. It is the presence of this complexity that necessitates the duality in our representations of the simulation: one for the design and one for the outcomes. For example, in the Schelling model: *firstly* there are the detailed rules for the movement of black and white pieces – depending on a critical parameter (specifying the minimum acceptable proportion of like coloured pieces in each piece's locality in order to stay put), and *secondly* there is an 'overview' – the extent to which the colours have 'clumped' together. The former might be expressed as the operation of a cellular automaton and the latter as some sort of statistical measure. The simulation is interesting precisely because it is difficult to see or prove why this clumping occurs from within the computational view for low values of the critical parameter.

If the outcomes are not easily deducible from either views, then I call these outcomes 'emergent'. Many social phenomena fall into this category. In the Schelling model the 'clumping' outcome is *not* emergent for high values of the critical parameter, since it is fairly obvious from within the overview why the clumping occurs. However it *is* emergent for low values where the clumping occurs only because of detailed probabilistic dynamics at the edge of clumps.

Emergence and complexity can not be sensibly defined if one leaves out the frame of reference and the system of representation [8]. Holland's definition of emergence as *"recurring patterns ... regularly associated with events of interest"* ([14] p. 45) simply begs the question of what: 'pattern', 'associated', 'events' and 'interest' mean. Typically the contrasting views of a simulation are talked about in terms of 'micro' or 'macro' levels (e.g. [13], although he generalises this to "complex hierarchies of levels"), which implies that the change in viewpoint is primarily one of *scale*. Scale is often a very important change of representation, however, it is not the only one. For example, it is possible for fine level details to 'emerge' from global properties as in Conway's game of 'life', where the possibility that a particular detailed pattern may act as a sort of travelling 'particle' results from the global rules determining the game. The general shift is one of representation (or modelling), but this makes many uneasy due to the fact that it implies that just studying the phenomena is enough (or even possible).

2.2 Semantic Complexity

The characteristics of social phenomena are frequently best approached using semantically rich representations (purpose, emotions, social pressure etc.) and these are difficult to translate into formal models — I will call this the 'semantic complexity'. I will not discuss here whether there is a fundamental difference between these. I will merely note that there are at least significant practical differences (see [7] for more on the reductionist/holist question, and [8] on complexity).

The existence of semantic complexity means that modellers have three choices:

1. they can concentrate on those parts of social systems that they think *are* effectively modellable by syntactic representation;
2. they can adopt a pseudo-semantic approach, where the simulation manipulates tokens which are undefined inside the simulation (where they are computationally manipulated) but which are meaningful to the humans involved (as found in both the set-up and outcome); or
3. they can avoid computational simulation altogether.

The Schelling model only qualifies as social science because the mechanisms and results can be interpreted into the semantically rich domain of racial relations. Thus for this model (and many other social simulations) there are at least *three* relevant views: the computational view; the 'overview' (usually concerned with the outcomes); and the simulation's intended interpretation in terms of social phenomena. Without this interpretation in terms of social phenomena the simulation is merely a board game of limited relevance and generality.

2.3 Model Clusters and Chains

Of course, frequently there are more than just the three relevant views mentioned above. For example, there might be entirely different views and bases for different parts of a simulation — the cognition of the agents might be viewed in the light of a particular model from cognitive science, the computational mechanisms might be expressed as logic-like rules, the resulting population dynamics might be viewed using the analogy of a market, the communication between agents modelled as a process of mutual convergence and the whole thing interpreted as a representation of a population of web-based information agents. In fact unitary models are the exception in science — it is far more usual to encounter *composite models*, that is clusters of closely related models [10]). This is a theme I will address in the last section.

Another complication comes from the fact that, typically, models will take a lot of their structure from previous models and have outcomes that are validated against yet other models. This 'chaining' of models is inevitable when modelling complex systems. However, it does not discharge the onus to verify its structure or validate its outcomes, this is merely achieved via other models — thus such a model will only become finally acceptable if the whole chain is verified and validated. The chaining of models delays judgement on a model by making its verification and/or validation indirect, but it does not eradicate the need for such checking.

It is frequently the case that in social simulation that what is interesting is not so much the resulting states, but the *processes* that emerge from the simulation in terms of the overview. This is because the highly dynamic nature of many social systems does not allow us even the pretence of *ceteris parabis* prediction of representative states, but rather we often use simulations to inform our semantic understanding of existing social processes. In the case of the Schelling model, social scientists would not presume that they could actually predict the probability of self-organised segregation based on measurements of the critical parameter in real populations, but rather it informs their perception of the likelihood of the emergence of segregation among relatively tolerant populations, which they will then use as a part of their general evaluation of situations. Thus the processes of interpreting the social phenomena into the code of a simulation and interpreting the outcomes back out again are, at least, as important as the internal workings of the simulation. For without good interpretation a simulation is just another computation.

2.4 Constraining Our Models

I shall call the interpretation into a simulation the 'representation' of a social system and the interpretation of the outcomes back out as the 'expression' of the simulation. Using these terms, *verification* is the process of checking that the representation is faithful to the simulator's intentions and *validation* is the process of checking that the epression of the simulation (in terms of outcomes) is faithful to the relevant social phenomena. Both representation and expression provide constraints on acceptable social simulations. The former acts to constrain the *design of the* simulation before it is run, while the later acts as a post-hoc check on its acceptability. They are thus both ways of constraining the simulation so that it relates to the object social phenomena. From a scientific point of view we want our simulations to be as faithfully constrained as possible by the object social phenomena (or process).

Now, of course, things are not quite as simple as the above account of representation and expression might suggest. Not only will our processes of interpretation be biased by the available technology and our world view, but sometimes the social phenomena will be intimately bound up with our perceptions of it — in other words some *real social phenomena are constructed by us*. In this case the constraint comes from society, but not in the guise of an object of our interpretation but as an inescapable result of our perceptual and social processes.

Also it is almost always the case in social simulation, that the object of study (or phenomenon) is not directly modelled, but rather an abstraction of it. The simulation provides understanding of the workings of the abstraction. This abstraction is frequently left implicit and sometimes it appears that some authors have completely conflated their abstraction with the object of study. Even when such an abstraction is carefully introduced, it inevitably introduces a bias into the modelling process; the form of the abstraction will be inevitably biased by abstraction's framework [9]. This is acceptable when: (1) the framework is chosen to suit (i.e. not unnecessarily distort) the original object of study w.r.t. to the modelling goals; and (2) the framework and its biases are acknowledged and documented.

In all cases enough constraints will have to be accumulated if the simulation is to be computationally well defined, i.e. so that a computer can execute it. The important question is *where* these constraints will come from. Some possible sources for these constraints are:

- From the object phenomena under study (either directly or indirectly);
- From previously well-validated models (or chains of models);
- From the processes of interpretation;
- From practical difficulties in implementing the intended specification;
- From theoretical *a priori* restrictions;
- From considerations of simplicity — i.e. general resource considerations;
- Other, essentially arbitrary, sources (e.g. programming error).

These types of constraints are to different degrees desirable and avoidable (depending on the situation). Clearly, progress in the methodology of social simulation should aim to increase desirable constraints, decrease undesirable constraints, clearly separate the different types of constraint and document them all.

A methodology which distinguishes, documents and checks constraints (whatever their origin) deflates the constructivist/realist divide. A model that is categorised as realist is one which happens to be highly constrained by the object under study, it reflects the object of study in those aspects in which it is constrained to the extent that it is constrained (strong constraint *is* the only sensible meaning for a model *reflecting* its target phenomena, [4]). Where the model is weakly constrained by the target phenomena (the usual case in social simulation), then the biasing effect of the language of modelling and the focusing effect of our perceptions will be greatest — such a model is necessarily constructed in some ways, and if it is to have a social use these ways will have to be based on social commonalties.

In the former case the interpretation processes are closely specified by strong constraints which means that the syntactic content of the simulation becomes more important. In the latter there is more latitude for varying interpretations – where the construction of meaningful and useful functions of language are essential – so the focus tends to shift more towards the *token processing* aspect. Although the former case would seem to provide us with more certain knowledge in some sense, it is far from certain that it will be more effective in helping us understand social systems. There are several reasons for this: firstly, our semantic understanding of society is far more powerful and effective than our more formal theorising (at least currently); secondly, it is extremely difficult to obtain useful and reflective models of social phenomena; and finally, the aim of social simulation is frequently not to predict detail but to inform our semantic understanding anyway.

In practice, we will often not be able to tell whether the extent to which our models are constrained by the object social phenomena and how much by the social/linguistic constructive processes (in some cases it not even clear that such a distinction even exists). For example, there may not be any objective viewpoint from which to make such an evaluation. Nevertheless, regardless of this uncertainty, a methodology which attempts to distinguish, document and check the constraints that specify a simulation is helpful. It is helpful because a process whereby we can continue to criticise, specialise, generalise and systematically adapt simulations using explicit knowledge about the source constraints would allow a more rapid and effect simulation evolution. If we are intending to reduce a set of social phenomena to a syntactic simulation (so that the resulting model is relatable to other such models using formal methods) such models can be combined, compared and subsumed using well tried methods. In such a case well-documented constraints can considerably aid this process both in terms of guiding the formal processes and by providing the essential building blocks for the formal representation itself. However, if we are adopting a more pseudo-semantic token-manipulation approachable, being able to distinguish and document the processes and constraints we used to construct the simulation (including our intended interpretation of it) would ease the task of re-evaluating it from within different paradigms. This would increase the chance that parts of the simulation may be separated out and reused. Even if future researchers have a different view to us as to the constraints that are appropriate or even as to the correct attribution of constraints, if they are *documented* the research may still be valuable to them, because they will have the information with which to reinterpret the work.

The sort of constraints we use can also be strongly related to our purposes in building and using simulations. A simulation at the more theoretical end, may only be weakly constrained by observation of social systems because its purpose is to try and map out some of the possible processes that could occur in such systems – it is a sort of 'stand-in' for an effective method of deductive inference from set-up to outcomes. This might be necessary due to the presence of syntactic complexity. Such a model needs to exhibit quite relevant, general and strong patterns of behaviour because its interpretation back into our semantic understanding is necessarily weak – the justification for doing this sort of simulation is that its results will be relevant to *many* other simulations. A simulation at the more applied end will attempt to take the maximum possible constraint from the system under study both in terms of the set-up of the model as well as in terms of the results – the justification for doing this sort of simulation is sufficiently constrained by the object phenomena that insights gained from outcomes of the simulation are also applicable to the phenomena themselves. If these are weak then we can have little confidence that the simulation results *are relevant at all* to the target social phenomena.

3   Consequences for an ISSL

Based on the analysis above I will extract some criteria for an ISSL. These will be far from exhaustive for I am attempting to be as generally relevant as possible.

1.   The system should be as free of any particular social or cognitive theory. Whatever theory exists to structure the system should be clear so that its contribution can be distinguished from the intended content.

This is, of course, true only of an ISSL that is intended to be generally useful. If a system is intended to embody a particular theory, and this theory is clear, then simulators who want to use or who accept that theory can work within this. Even then it is important that the structure that the base system provides is as well understood as possible, so that its influence of the process of implementation may be distinguished.

2.   The system should make the process of translating the modeller's intentions into an actual simulation as straightforward and transparent as possible.

This will never be a simple criterion to apply to a candidate ISSL, due to the presence of semantic complexity. However, steps can be taken to ease the process of implementation and document it. In general there should be structures in the ISSL that correspond as closely as possible to the basic items in the shared ontology of social simulators. This will probably change as the field develops. Presently, such a menu of structures might include: agents, models, scripts, utterances, time, norms, memes, groups etc. The trouble is that these entities are far from being theory-independent! Thus there is an inevitable tension between the ease of implementation and the wish for a computational base whose theoretical base is clearly separable from the focus theory. An approach to this problem is to provide structure for that where there is most agreement and fewest issues of interpretation, which can then be used to construct the others according to some intended (and hopefully documented) theory.

3.   The system should facilitate the introduction, definition and manipulation of tokens and token structures that are readily interpretable in semantic terms.

At a minimum, the system should allow the definition of strings and their syntax so that they can be stored, manipulated and retrieved in a flexible way. Better, it should allow the use of lists, trees and other data structures of tokens in a relational way, so that it can directly represent a whole variety of linguistic and other natural structures. Ideally it should allow the specification and use of general expressions and their associated grammars so that the system can approximate some linguistic abilities.

4.   The system should encourage the identification, clarification, application, manipulation and documentation of different types of constraints.

As far as possible the code that implements the different types of constraint should be able to be differentiated and labelled with the source of the constraint. It should be possible to determine the type of the constraint (e.g. hard, soft, warning, halt etc.) in relation to other constraints. For example, one might be more certain of some constraints than others, so if the simulation gets into a state where it will have to violate one of these constraints in order to continue, it will know which to transgress.

5.   The system should facilitate the controlled exploration of possible trajectories

In most social simulations it is not intended that it predict a unique outcome, but rather pick one of a constrained range of possible trajectories. Quite apart from unintended sources of arbitrariness most simulations are intended not to be completely deterministic – uncertainty and contingency being essential aspects of many social systems. It is the intended constrained *range* of processes that is posited and explored using a simulation. For example, in the Schelling model, it is intended that the choice of which empty location to move to be arbitrary, but it is also intended that this arbitrary choice be constrained to the present location's local neighbourhood. Once one has implemented the intended constraints, one then has to choose how to explore the range of possible trajectories that are left. Possibilities for such exploration include: a statistical sampling; an enumeration of the space; the examination of example trajectories; or some proof of bounds to the space.

6.   The system should support the flexible investigation and analysis of simulation outcomes to enable the development of models of the results.

As noted above, syntactic complexity means that it will be necessary to actively model the outcomes of a simulation in order to understand the results. In other words to find an appropriate viewpoint from which to analyse the outcomes and then the appropriate model of the outcomes from within that viewpoint. This process is frequently exploratory, so one wants to be as flexible as possible. In particular one should have a range of modelling tools and be able to apply them without prior restriction to a subset of the aspects of the simulation. In fact, ideally one should be able to iterate this exploratory process so as to enable the modelling of a model of the simulation outcomes, the modelling of a model of a model of the outcomes etc.

7.   The system should facilitate the construction of composite simulations where different components can be developed separately and then brought together.

This is very similar to the requirement for effective encapsulation in computer science. Social simulators will often wish to incorporate mechanisms from a variety of sources into their models. An approach to this problem is to adopt object-oriented methodology and tools: strong encapsulation of objects which are instances of a hierarchy of types. This still does not quite solve the problem when one wants to deal with inter-object processes or where one needs overlapping clusters of objects. Another recent innovation is to abstract patterns of solutions to frequent problems.

8.   The system should facilitate the understanding of the emergence of process.

Given that many social simulations are not constrained up to uniqueness and that social scientists are primarily interested in emergent process, an ISSL should not impose arbitrary constraints upon implementation. In other words, when implementing an intended specification one would not want to have to include extra constraints merely to make it run. Rather one would want to be able to specify the structure one wishes and explore the processes that are possible within this.

4   SDML as a Step towards an ISSL

The computer language SDML (Strictly Declarative Modelling Language), was not developed with the above criteria explicitly in mind. However, it has been developed specifically to support social simulation, and has closely co-evolved with the CPM's thinking on social simulation methodology — so it is not very surprising that it goes some way to meet the above criteria. Other systems, such as DESIRE [3] have taken a similar route. In the last section of this paper I will make some tentative suggestions as to how we might go about pooling the knowledge gained by different teams to inform the development of the next generation of systems, but first I will look at each of the criteria introduced above and briefly outline how SDML goes towards meeting them. In each case I repeat the criterion for the convenience of the reader and then describe if and how SDML represents a step towards meeting the criterion.

1.   The system should be free of any particular social or cognitive theory. Whatever theory exists to structure the system should be as clear as possible so that its contribution can be cleanly distinguished from the intended content.

The implementation of SDML has a logical basis and is therefore free of any particular social or cognitive theory. It is based on a fragment of Konolige's Strictly Grounded Auto-epistemic Logic [15]. This provides a clear semantics for SDML's computation (i.e. a formal way for understanding and working out what it will do given certain rules). This basis provides an expressive base that allows the implementation of any computational representation of cognitive or social processes – the logic does not specify how an agent in SDML must think but is chosen so as to allow any such process to be implemented. It is unclear the extent to which this particular logical basis is the most natural for implementing social or cognitive theories. This use of logical semantics for grounding real computation is in sharp contrast to the use of logical languages for ungrounded specifications of agent properties at a high level.

2.   The system should make the process of translating the modeller's intentions into an actual simulation as straightforward as possible.

As with other languages, SDML provides some general and flexible structuring mechanisms. A model is composed of a number of interacting agents, which are objects with their own databases and rulebases. An agent's databases record static and dynamic information about the agent (e.g. its perceptions or beliefs), and its rulebases determine its behaviour. Agents are arranged in a container hierarchy, with complex agents composed of simpler ones. Such composite agents can be serial or parallel, depending on whether their sub-agents are simulated in a sequence or (conceptually) in parallel with each other.

SDML also provides a flexible mechanism for the representation of time. Time levels can be defined, and these can also be nested inside each other. For example, a simulation may define the time levels week and day, with seven time periods at time level day for every week. The outermost time level, called eternity, represents information that is always true. Agents have separate databases for different time periods, with databases at more specific time periods inheriting from databases representing information that is true for longer periods of time. For example, something that is true for a whole week is true for every day within that week. Agents can define additional time levels, allowing some agents to be simulated to a greater degree of temporal detail than others.

These two features mean that, to a significant extent, the static structure of the simulation can be taken directly from the perceived structure of the social system being modelled. One can have institutions or groupings of individuals represented as whole entities, but also containing the individuals (or parts) that they derive from or cover. Each part of the simulation can have its own appropriate system of time: so a market might have a trading cycle whilst an individual might work within a finer level of time, withing which the cognition might occur.

The container structure for the SDML implementation of the Schelling model is shown in figure 1. Each counter is represented as a sub-agent of agent schellingModel, which is a serial composite agent because in his model the counters are simulated in a random order that is determined before hand. Agent schellingModel has a single time level denoted iteration.

iteration time level

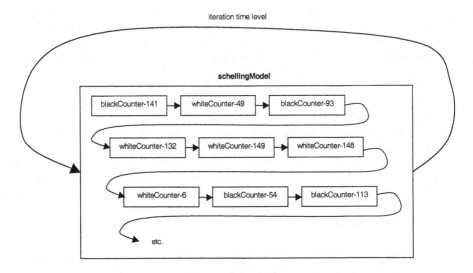

Fig. 1. The container structure of the Schelling Model

3.   The system should facilitate the introduction, definition and manipulation of tokens and token structures that are readily interpretable in semantic terms.

In SDML, an item of information is represented as a clause on a database, consisting of a predicate and a number of arguments. For example, in the Schelling model, the knowledge that whiteCounter-42 is at position (5,7) at iteration 2 is represented by the clause gridCounter 5 7 'whiteCounter-42' on the model's database for iteration 2. The predicate gridCounter must be defined before it can be used. This is done using a clause definition, that includes, among other things, a syntax diagram for clauses with this predicate. In the above example, the clause represents a simple relationship between the tokens (objects) gridCounter and whiteCounter-42, and numbers. Clauses can also be used to build more complex data structures, since clauses can have subclauses. In the Schelling model, clauses are used for lists of agents and lists of points where each point is itself a clause. The fact that the computation is concerning rules acting on such strings of tokens within a given sysntax facilitates the interpretation of the computation in semantic terms.

4.   The system should encourage the identification, clarification, application, manipulation and documentation of different types of constraints.

An SDML rule is composed of an antecedent and a consequent. Every SDML rule is declarative and acts as a kind of truth constraint, specifying that if the antecedent is true, the consequent is also true. Rules can be fired, to infer that the consequent of a rule is true when the antecedent is inferred to be true. The antecedents and consequents of rules are clauses, which may contain subclauses and/or variables. Typically checking if an antecedent is true involves retrieving one or more clauses from a database, and inferring that the consequent is true entails asserting one or more clauses to a database.

In the Schelling model, each counter has a rule called "move or stay still" (inherited from type Counter) which specifies the counter's current position based on its position at the previous iteration and the positions and colours of other counters in its neighbourhood. In effect the various constraints on the possible positions of the counter have been gathered together into a single rule.

SDML has some capabilities for constraint programming, with possibilities marked by assumptions which can then be backtracked to and then re-evaluated. To understand this one needs to know a little how SDML works. In SDML a rule can be written which only fires under some assumption — whether that assumption holds can only be determined by firing further rules. One use of assumptions is in handling negation. The antecedent notInferred <subclause> is defined to be true if and only if the subclause is not inferred to be true (for any bindings of variables used within it). Inferences can be made based on this assumption, by asserting the consequent of the rule to the database tagged with this assumption. If the assumption later proves to be false (because the subclause or a subclause of the subclause is later inferred to be true), this inference is retracted. In order to fire rules efficiently, SDML partitions rulebases based on the dependencies between rules, and assumptions are resolved at the end of each partition. If there are no consistent resolutions for the assumptions in one partition, SDML backtracks to try to find other resolutions for assumptions in previous partitions. SDML also backtracks if false is inferred; i.e. a rule with false as its consequent is fired. Thus a rule with false as its consequent acts as a constraint that the antecedent is not true – if a simulation vialates such a constraint it backtracks to try and find a simulation trajectory where the constraint is resepected. However, this feature provides only limited constraint programming capabilities — such constraints can only be used to eliminate possibilities rather than generate them. Furthermore, this feature only provides one kind of constraint — hard ones that cannot be transgressed in order to continue with the simulation.

5.   *The system should allow for the controlled exploration of a specified space of possible trajectories using a variety of means.*

Often, during a simulation, it is necessary to choose one value from a range of possibilities. SDML has several primitives, which can be used in antecedents of rules, to make such choices. These primitives include randomNumber to yield a random number in the range 0 to 1, randomList to yield a randomly ordered list, and randomChoice to randomly select one value from a set of possible values. There is also an arbitraryChoice primitive, which is similar to randomChoice except that the choice does not have to be random; any choice will do.

When one of the possibilities is chosen, SDML explores that trajectory. The backtracking facility described above can be used with the randomChoice and arbitraryChoice primitives, to make different choices and explore different trajectories if one trajectory leads to a contradiction (such as a constraint failing). There are two alternative primitives, called fixedRandomChoice and fixedArbitraryChoice, to make fixed choices that cannot be altered by backtracking.

In the SDML implementation of the Schelling model, there are three situations where such primitives are required. The initial grid is set up and the order in which the counters are simulated is chosen using the randomList primitive. When a counter decides to move to a neighbouring empty cell, it selects that cell using fixedRandomChoice.

Since the model is itself an agent, it can be embedded in a larger structure. This enables the same model to be iterated many times, and the results can be analysed using statistical techniques for example.

Because of SDML's closeness to logic, it is likely to be more feasible than with other simulation languages to use a theorem prover to prove the bounds of possibilities within a model.

6.   *The system should provide tools for the flexible investigation and analysis of the simulation outcomes to enable the development of an appropriate model of the results.*

One of the features of SDML is an implementation of virtual memory. Instead of discarding databases from previous time periods, SDML writes them to a file and can read them back into real memory when required. This has two uses. Firstly, agents can analyse past data during the simulation, and secondly, users can analyse the data from outside the simulation.

The SDML environment includes a flexible query interface, allowing the databases to be interrogated in the same way as in the antecedent of a rule. SDML has limited built-in visualisation and statistical tools (such as displaying the results of a query in a graph or performing a linear regression). However, it does include a general facility to construct user interfaces (which is used in the Schelling module by the gridDisplayer agent to display the grid in a window on the screen). Also it provides the ability for arbitrary agents to work on past outcomes in order to model them (e.g. using a genetic program to summarise the behaviour of another agent in the simulation).

7.   *The system should facilitate the construction of composite simulations where different components can be developed separately and then brought together.*

In SDML, different components can be developed separately in separate modules. They can be brought together by defining a new module which inherits from the component modules. All types, objects and rules, etc., defined in each of the modules are inherited by the new module. Object-oriented encapsulation is provided using types. The program information is grouped into modules by the programmer which somewht facilitates the separate development of parts of the simulation and their later integration. However, it still remains a challenging task to program in this way, for there are inevitabley many levels and types of interaction between agents in the simulation and they are not, in general, cleanly seperable into encapsulated objects and types.

8.   *The system should facilitate the emergence of process.*

The declarative nature of SDML encourages the specification of facts and relationships, in terms of clauses on databases and rules. The *process* of firing rules in a rulebase is not specified explicitly. To some degree, the process emerges from the declarative structures of SDML. However, as in any declarative programming language, the process is implicit in the structures of the language and the mechanisms used to manipulate those structures.

The extent to which the rules *determine* the resulting simulation process depends upon their nature. In some cases, especially when assumptions and backtracking are used, the process of firing the rules is highly unpredictable and emergent to a high degree. In other cases, such as in the Schelling model, the process of firing the rules in a rulebase is highly predictable and emergent to a low degree (the properties that are particularly emergent are the longer term tendencies for counters to form clusters). It may also be noted that the order in which rulebases are processed is explicitly specified by the modeller (using time levels and composite agents).

There is a trade-off here between avoiding specifying process and obtaining sufficient efficiency. It would be possible to define a simulation entirely in terms of constraints and let the system resolve them. However, this is likely to be extremely expensive in terms of both execution speed and memory usage. SDML allows, but does not require, the process to be partially specified. Thus SDML facilitates the study of emergent process.

5   A Speculation on the Future of Social Simulation Languages

In this we would like to speculate a little bit, on the some of the features an ISSL might have in the near (if we are lucky) or far (if we are not) future. The first two subsections suggest that much greater support might be provided for the processes of mapping to and from social phenomena to the simulation. At the moment the processes are largely a "black art" and undocumented. Whilst we think it highly unlikely that this will be improved by a completely formal specification or analysis methodology, we do think that these mappings might be achievable in a more incremental and testable manner. The third subsection is more ambitious as it envisions a general modelling environment within which *sets* of simulation models can be held, run, manipulated and related.

5.1   The Integration and Management of the Specification and Implementation Processes

In the specification and production of simulation models: the intention of the programmer; a specification of that program; the first prototype of the simulation; and an efficient simulation are all (or should be) strongly related. In particular a prototype of the program should be consistent with the specification of the program; and an efficient implementation of the simulation should exhibit the same outcomes as the prototype simulation. Generally the aim is to move in steps from general intentions to an efficient implementation: each stage being a specific case of the stage before. Thus a typical process might start from some prior knowledge about the social phenomena to be modelled (gained from expert opinion, ethnographic studies, anecdotal accounts etc.); choose or devise an abstraction of the phenomena that was consistent (or, at least, not obviously *inconsistent*) with that knowledge; compose a specification of a simulation to model a part of such an abstraction; write a prototype of the simulation to match the specification; then iteratively improve the efficiency of the simulation without changing its behaviour in the aspects that are relevant to the specification.

The ability to move from a descriptive specification to fixing (or otherwise constraining) some of the structure of the simulation within the same software would allow the provision of tools to capture and keep the motivation and intentions behind the specification. For example at each stage the programmer could choose a new constraint to place upon the model and be prompted to enter a comment about the reasons for the choice. The software framework could support alternative branches in this choice process along with the advantages of each. In the future a simulator (either the same one or another) could be aided in adapting the simulation by backtracking along the choice tree and choosing another branch.

Ideally the simulator would be able to animate the simulation in a rough and inefficient way at an early stage as possible. This might be achieved through a combination of the use of constraint programming techniques which search for a solution that fits loose constraints and the provision of stand-in proxies for unprogrammed parts (e.g. agents that take random actions from a menu provided). Being able to incrementally explore and specify the simulation might enable the simulator to focus down on the desired simulation behaviour in a way that was easier to understand, check and document.

5.2 Aids for the Modelling and Analysis of Simulation Outcomes

To understand the increasingly complex models that we use we have to model our models, either by postulating theories about the processes in those models, by graphing and visualising the results and by producing simpler models that approximate the emergent behaviour of the model. Sometimes we are even forced to model the model of our models. An example of this is when the simulator collects data from simulation runs which are, in turn, modelled in the form of a graph or approximated with an analytic expression.

Understanding our creations can be greatly aided by the provision of flexible query and data visualisation tools so that a researcher can interactively explore what happened (or is happening) during a simulation. Another tool could be one that 'fits' analytic forms to the resultant data by finding the parameterisation that gives the lowest error of the form w.r.t. the data. In general, one would want to be able to 'fix' the first simulation as data and then use another simulation (or runs of a simulation) to model the fixed simulation. Here the first model simply plays the part of the validation data more usually used and the specification of the second meta-model coming from some hypothesis about the processes occurring in the first gained from inspection, visualisation and the like. Of course, there is no end to how far this can be taken in terms of meta-meta-simulations etc. [17] also argue that the provision of analysis tools is important.

5.3 A Software Environment to Aid the Development of Compositional Models and the Chaining of Models

The above are specific instances of a more general case: that of relating different but related models. We often need to compare models which are differently formulated but whose results are related. In fact we routinely use chains of models in our attempts to understand complex phenomena: starting with the data model and ending at quite abstract theories and descriptions. This was foreshadowed by Patrick Suppes in 1960:

"... *a whole hierarchy of models stands between the model of the basic theory and the complete experimental evidence. Moreover for each level of the hierarchy there is a theory in its own right. Theories at one level is given empirical meaning by making formal connections with theory at a lower level.*" [21] p.260.

Thus we may have large chains or even clusters of models (as [10] characterises a theory) which are all interrelated by their content (i.e. their results).

In a typical simulation you might have the following related models:

1. the prior knowledge about the social phenomena with which you intend to make the simulation consistent;
2. the intended abstraction of the phenomena which you will try to simulate;
3. the specification of the simulation;
4. the simulation code;
5. the simulation runs;
6. statistics, graphs or other means of interpreting the results;
7. a data model against which to help validate the results;
8. what the results correspond to in terms of the abstraction;
9. and a picture of what the results might correspond to in terms of the original phenomena.

Here one has nine interrelated models just for one "simulation"! A software framework which could hold and relate multiple runs of these some of these models would be very helpful.

The essence of a simulation is that there is some code that produces some results. There is a mapping between a space of possible programs and a space of possible results. Usually each run of the simulation traces out one 'trajectory' out of a set of possible trajectories that the code could produce. This trajectory is a concrete exemplar of the code. Thus the basic computational framework would need to hold the codes and some representation of the set of possible trajectories that the code could produce. This is illustrated in figure 2a below.

In figure 2a all the trajectories are shown as starting from the same state. This is not necessarily the case – in general a single program corresponds to a subspace of the result space. This subspace might be composed of a set of points, trajectories or even regions. Often we seek to characterise this subspace in terms of the trajectories central tendency and spread using statistics. Another way of characterising it is in terms of the 'envelope' surrounding the set of trajectories [22]. With the increasing complexity of subject matter and the increasing availability of computational power and data storage it will be advantageous to *delay* the simplification of data in terms of such descriptions as one might loose some of the qualitative characteristics that later turn out to be important.

A *data model* [21] is one where there is a particularly direct relationship between the description of the model and what it corresponds to in the result space. This is not necessarily however a completely direct relationship because the data model might include indications about the accuracy of that data (as in "35±2mm"), in which case the description might map into a (maybe fuzzy) region of the result space.

120   B. Edmonds

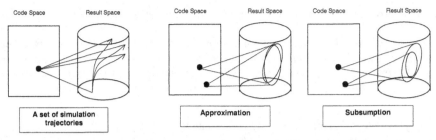

Fig. 2a. Simulation code corresponding to the trajectories from a set of runs;

Fig. 2b. and c. Comparing models via the result space.

It is occasionally possible to relate simple programs (or other formal models) using formal manipulations purely within the code space. This can occur when the operations in the code space have known effects on the result space. For example when a physicists approximate a set of unsolvable equations with a solvable set they use a lot of knowledge as to what changes in the formulae will result in results that are not changed to any significant effect. However with almost all social simulation models this sort of move is completely impractical if not impossible. Usually the only practical way is to check the correspondence of models by their results.

There are two basic ways of comparing models via their sets of trajectories in some space of results. *Firstly*, one can say that the set of results from model-1 *approximates* the set of results from model-2. In other words there is some distance function from the two sets and this is acceptably small. If one such set is the *data model* which can been gained from target phenomena then we use measures such as the root mean squared error. *Secondly*, one can say that the set of results from model-1 *subsumes* those from model-2. In this case the set of the trajectories from model-2 is a subset of those in model-1 (or using less strict criteria) that the *envelope* of the trajectories from model-2 is inside the envelope of the trajectories from model-1. These methods of comparison are illustrated in figure 1b and 1c.

Of course it is possible that models might be related using different result spaces. Thus model-1 could subsume model-2 in result-space-A and model-2 could approximate model-3 in result-space-B. For example, model-2 might be a more efficient version of model-1, so that you could show in result-space-A (which might record the detail of the transactions in the models) that model-1 subsumes model-2. Then you might want to approximate some global outcomes of model-2 using an analytic model-3 in a space of aggregate measures of simulation outcomes (result-space-B). Thus you can get *chains* of models.

A particular case of this is where you have models of different granularities. One might have a detailed model of a farm and a coarser model of many farms in a region which one is checking against aggregate statistics of agricultural output. The model of the farm in the coarser model might be far simpler than in the single farm model but be a good approximation of it in terms of actions with respect to the outside world (purchases, production etc.). Here the comparison is between a projection the multi-farm model by ignoring all but a single farm onto a result space of production. The farms example within such a framework is illustrated in figure 3.

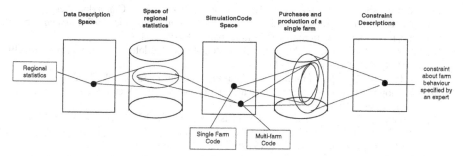

Fig. 3. The farm simulation example within this framework

Thus the envisioned computation framework would have the following abilities:

1. the ability to store multiple descriptions including simulation code, data sets, and possibly other descriptions such as constraints on data;
2. the ability to capture and hold multiple sets of data derived from different simulation runs of the code;
3. the ability to define (maybe many) result spaces into which the simulation runs, data sets and constraints can be mapped;
4. the ability to explore, measure and test the relationships between different subspaces in the result space; and
5. the ability to annotate all these entities and the relationship between entities.

The core of the system would be the result spaces – which can be though of as databases. They would be designed to facilitate the holding of results from a number of different packages and languages, and allow a (possibly different) number of packages and languages to read that data. Thus they allow the relating of different descriptions via mappings into (and from) its space. For example:

1. one might want to make statistical summaries by taking data from one result space of simulation runs and outputting these to another result space using a statistical package;
2. one may wish to generate some example data from a set of constraints using a constraint satisfaction engine;
3. one may wish to compare the results from one simulation model with another within the same result space;
4. one may wish to calculate some measures of the difference of one sets of results from another to inform a change in simulation code.

References

[1] Axelrod, R., Epstein, J. M. and Cohen, M. D. (1996) Aligning Simulation Models: A Case Study and Results. *Computational and Mathematical Organization Theory*, **1**.
[2] Axtell, R. L. and J. M. Epstein (1994). Agent-based Modelling: Understanding our Creations. *The Bulletin of the Santa Fe Institute* **9**: 28–32.

[3]   Brazier, F. M. T., Dunin-Keplicz, B. M., Jennings, N. R. and Treur, J. (1997), DESIRE: Modelling Multi-Agent Systems in a Compositional Formal Framework, *International Journal of Cooperative Information Systems*, **6**:67–94.

[4]   Cartwright, N. (1983). *How the Laws of Physics Lie*. Oxford, Clarendon Press.

[5]   Conte, R., Hegselman, R. and Terna, P. (1997) *Simulating Social Phenomena*, Springer: Lecture Notes in Economics and Mathematical Systems, **456**.

[6]   Cooper, R., J. Fox, et al. (1997). A Systematic Methodology for Cognitive Modelling. *Artificial Intelligence* **85**: 3–44.

[7]   Edmonds, B. (1999). Pragmatic Holism. *Foundations of Science* 4:57–82.

[8]   Edmonds, B. (1999). Syntactic Measures of Complexity. Doctoral Thesis, University of Manchester, Manchester, UK.

[9]   Edmonds, B. (2000). The Use of Models - making MABS actually work. In S. Moss and P. Davidsson (eds.) *Multi Agent Based Simulation*. Berlin: Springer-Verlag. *Lecture Notes in Artificial Intelligence*, **1979**:15–3.

[10]   Giere Ronald, N. (1988). *Explaining science : a cognitive approach*. Chicago ; London, University of Chicago Press.

[11]   Gilbert, N. (1995) Emergence in Social Simulation. In (Gilbert and Conte 1995), . 144–156.

[12]   Gilbert, N. and Doran, J. (1994) *Simulating societies: the computer simulation of social phenomena*. London: UCL Press.

[13]   Gilbert, N. and Conte, R. (1995) *Artificial societies: the computer simulation of social life*. London: UCL Press.

[14]   Holland John, H. (1998). *Emergence : from chaos to order*. Oxford ; New York, Oxford University Press.

[15]   Konolige, K. (1992). Autoepistemic Logic. In D. Gabbay, C. Hogger and J. Robinson. (eds.) *Handbook of Logic in Artificial Intelligence and Logic Programming, Vol. 3*. Oxford, Clarendon. 217–295.

[16]   Lakatos, I. (1983). *The methodology of scientific research programmes*. Cambridge, Cambridge University Press.

[17]   Mariotto, M. B., Nuno, D., Sichman, J. S. and Coelho, H. (2002) Requirements Analysis of Agent-Based Simulation Platforms: State of the Art and New Prospects, this volume.

[18]   Moss, S., H. Gaylard, & al. (1996). SDML: A Multi-Agent Language for Organizational Modelling. *Computational and Mathematical Organization Theory* 4(1): 43–69.

[19]   Schelling, Thomas C. (1971). Dynamic Models of Segregation. *Journal of Mathematical Sociology* 1:143–186.

[20]   Simon, H.A. (1986). The failure of armchair economics [Interview]. Challenge, **29**(5), 18–25.

[21]   Suppes, P. (1962). Models of Data. In Nagel, E. et al. (eds.) *Logic Methodology and the Philosophy of Science: Proceedings of the 1960 International Conference*. Stanford, CA: Stanford University Press, 252–261.

[22]   Terán, O., Edmonds, B. & Wallis, S. (2001) Mapping the Envelope of Social Simulation Trajectories. Multi Agent Based Simulation 2000 (MABS2000), Boston, MA, July, 2000. *Lecture Notes in Artificial Intelligence*, **1979**:229–243.

Appendix — A Description of the Schelling Model of Racial Segregation

This model was originally described in [22]. I describe what I take to be its essence below. Basically one has a board with black and white counters randomly distributed leaving some empty squares; then each 'turn' all counters with below a certain percentage of like-coloured counters next to themselves are randomly moved into an adjacent empty square; the simulation ends when there is no more movement.

Static Structure
There is a large rectangular 2D grid of locations of fixed dimensions. Each location can be occupied by a black counter, a white counter, or be empty. Each location has a 'neighbourhood' of the eight adjacent locations (including diagonally). There are a fixed number of black and white counters, some of the locations are empty.

Temporal Structure
There is a series of discrete time periods, starting at an initial period, over which the dynamics occur. What can change each time period is the position the counters.

Important Parameters
- The number of black counters.
- The number of white counters.
- The width and height of the grid.
- A parameter, C, between 0 and 1 for the proportion of minimum proportion of neighbours that must be the same colour in order to stay put.

Initialisation
The black and white counters are placed randomly on the grid at an initial time period so that there is at most one counter in each location.

Dynamics
For each counter, selected in turn, at each time period do the following:
1. Count up the total number of counters in the neighbourhood, T.
2. Count up the total number of counters of the same colour as the selected one in the neighbourhood, S.
3. If S/T is less than C and there is at least one empty location in the neighbourhood, pick one such empty location at random and move to it, otherwise stay put.

Results Claimed as Significant
There is a critical value for parameter C, such that if it is above this value the grid self-organises into segregated areas of single colour counters. This is lower than 0.5.

Intended Interpretation
Even a desire for a small proportion of racially similar neighbours might lead to self-organised segregation.

Other Details Considered Unimportant But Which Were Necessary for the Implementation
Size, shape and edge topology of the grid: the results can only be depended on when the movement of counters is not additionally constrained by the topology of the grid.

This means that the grid has to be sufficiently large and not have a too extensive edge. Typically simulations have been performed on a 20x20 grid with the edges 'wrapped around' left to right and top to bottom, so that the surface has the topology of a torus and no edges.

The order in which the counters are selected: this does not seem to be significant, but either: counters are randomly selected individually; some order has to be imposed on the selection of counters (e.g. a randomly determined order); or some conflict-resolution method employed if they are processed in parallel and counters select the same location to move to.

The pseudo-random generator: this is used to decide the initial distribution of counters and the location to move to if there is more than one available. In fact, the results would probably still hold even with non-random generators as long as the movements occurred equally in all directions and were not linked to the selected counter's colour or the distribution of other counters on the board.

Source Code
The source code for an implementation of this model in SDML can be found at: http://sdml.cfpm.org/examples/schelling.sdm. This module requires SDML release 3.6 or later. For details of obtaining SDML see: [18] and http://sdml.cfpm.org

Example Output from Running This Code

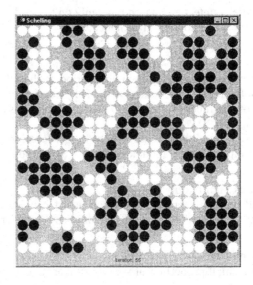

Requirements Analysis of Agent-Based Simulation Platforms: State of the Art and New Prospects

Maria Bruno Marietto[1,*], Nuno David[1,2,**], Jaime Simão Sichman[1,***] and Helder Coelho[3]

[1] Intelligent Techniques Laboratory, University of São Paulo, Brazil
gracas.marietto@poli.usp.br   http://www.lti.pcs.usp.br/~graca
jaime.sichman@poli.usp.br   http://www.pcs.usp.br/~jaime
[2] Department of Information Science and Technology, ISCTE/DCTI, Lisbon, Portugal
Nuno.David@iscte.pt   http://www.iscte.pt/~nmcd
[3] Department of Informatics, University of Lisbon, Portugal
hcoelho@di.fc.ul.pt   http://www.di.fc.ul.pt/~hcoelho

Abstract. In this paper we propose a preliminary reference model for the requirements specification of agent-based simulation platforms. We give the following contributions: (i) aid the identification of general principles to develop platforms; (ii) advance the analysis and prospection of technical-operational and high-level requirements; (iii) promote the identification of shared requirements, addressing them to the development of an integrated work. We present our reference model and make a comparative analysis between three well-known platforms, resulting in an unambiguous and schematic characterisation of computational systems for agent-based simulation.

1 Introduction

Computational platforms and test-beds are becoming increasingly important in Multi-agent Systems (MAS). A first goal of these systems is to release the researchers from low-level technical-operational issues, allowing the researcher to concentrate his/her efforts on the relevant domain application logic. In the area of Multiagent-Based Simulation (MABS) (see [22]), computational platforms are important methodological tools that aid the researcher in the processes of modelling and development of simulation programs. They are especially valuable to conciliate different interdisciplinary perspectives, which in MABS typically involve researchers from various scientific

---

*   Supported by FAPESP, Brazil, grant number 00/14689-0. On leave from Dom Bosco Catholic University.
**   Partially supported by FCT/PRAXIS XXI, Portugal, grant number BD/21595/99.
*** Partially supported by CNPq, Brazil, grant number 301041/95-4, and by project MAPPEL (PROTEM-CC, CNPq/NSF), grant number 680033/99-8.

J.S. Sichman, F. Bousquet, P. Davidsson (Eds.): MABS 2002, LNAI 2581, pp. 125-141, 2003.
© Springer-Verlag Berlin Heidelberg 2003

areas, such as social psychology, artificial intelligence, computer engineering, artificial life, social biology, sociology and economics. The interdisciplinary character of MABS is an important challenge faced by all researchers in this discipline, while demanding a difficult interlacement of different methodologies, terminologies and points of view. To help with this process of integration, simulation platforms that support educational, industrial and scientific research objectives are in increasing demand.

Meanwhile, at the present maturing stage of the discipline, the *requirements analysis* of simulation platforms plays a fundamental role, since there is not yet a consensus with respect to the specification of services and its standards of behaviour. It is important to include this subject in the MABS agenda because:

1. The process of requirements analysis promotes a deeper discussion of many research topics in the area, such as the problem of observation of emergent phenomena, verification and validation of models. If such topics and associated solutions are not well defined than that will become evident during the design of both the general structure and the global behaviour of platforms, helping the researchers to redirect their works. Conversely, if they are already well defined, requirements analysis will bring new dimensions to accepted solutions and further integration with other requirements.

2. The process of requirements analysis identifies shared requirements of many projects, addressing them to the development of an integrated work rather than individual ones.

In effect, when evaluating the importance of requirements analysis in this field it is quite odd to find very few references in the literature about this topic. This observation becomes even more surprising since one can find a considerable number of platforms (though very heterogeneous) available to the research community (see e.g. [3, 12, 16, 19, 20, 25]). The extensive availability of domain specific and general-purpose platforms does not necessarily facilitate the work of researchers in the field. The diversity of functions and diffusion of ends can bring benefits, but also disadvantages in the absence of reference models that help the researcher to systematize his/her choices and needs. Presently, a clear and systematised reference model is in need, in order to stimulate the integration of different works and materialize new prospects for requirements related to common problems in the field, such as the observation and manipulation of emergent phenomena.

Aiming to assist on the construction of a general framework that characterizes an ideal type of platform, the *SimCog* project [23] aims at two independent and cross-fertilizable goals. The first goal is to define a *reference model* for the requirements specification of an ideal type MABS platform. The second goal is the specification, design and implementation of a platform complying with a subset of those requirements, with special focus on the simulation of cognitive agents. With regard to the first goal a set of functional and non-functional requirements guiding the specification of MABS platforms may be found in [17]. Such specification will be further validated and specialized based on two independent approaches: (i) by making a comparative analysis between requirements of different platforms that are presently available to the research community; (ii) by prospecting and exploring requirements with researchers in the field[1]. In this work we report our results with respect to the first approach, the comparative analysis.

This paper is structured as follows. In section 2 we will present a set of requirements that seem to characterize both the general structure and global behaviour of MABS platforms. In section 3 we will evaluate the adequacy of the reference model with a comparative analysis between requirements of three well-known platforms (CORMAS, Swarm and MadKit). The comparative analysis will allow us to trace: (i) the set of common requirements that characterize all platforms; (ii) the set of requirements that do not characterize any platform, bringing new dimensions to the prospection of requirements in the *SimCog* reference model. Finally, in section 4, we draw some conclusions and suggest some general principles that should be considered in the design of MABS platforms.

2 Requirements Analysis of MABS Platforms

Currently, there are a large number of computational systems in MABS. While analysing such systems it is possible to detect several technologies, but among this diversity there are certain groups of requirements that characterize different kinds of technologies. Such groups of requirements will be called *facilities*, borrowing the term from [9]. We identify four facilities that can be found in these computational systems: *technological, domain, development* and *analysis*. In this work, computational systems that present at some degree of development these four facilities, will be called *MABS platforms*.

Meanwhile, there are a number of requirements that are not so well systematized and developed. Most of them focus on the exploration of unexpected outputs or emergent structures that should desirably play causal effects in the evolution of simulation results. These requirements are important to balance the subjective role of observing and validating unexpected results with the objective role of verifying such results. We will cluster these services in a new group called *exploration* facilities.

In [17] we present a requirements specification for MABS platforms. As stated by [21], a requirement is a feature of a system or a description of something the system is capable of doing in order to reach its objectives. Additionally, it aims to detail the structure of a system, establishing its principles of behaviour. The requirements presented in [17] followed a top-down approach, usually adopted in requirements engineering. At first the most general requirements are described and at subsequent levels

---

[1] The survey with researchers in the field can be found at
http://www.lti.pcs.usp.br/SimCog/Doc/M1_Questionnaire.html. This survey has involved more than a hundred and seventy opinions of recognized researchers in MABS. Queries will be available at http://www.lti.pcs.usp.br/SimCog/Doc/Search/M1_Quest.html.

they are made more specific. In that specification there is a description of forty seven (47) requirements, distributed across the five facilities. The requirements were classified in two categories, typical in requirements engineering: functional and non-functional. Functional requirements describe the behaviour and the services that the user expects a system to provide. Non-functional requirements describe restrictions, qualities and/or benefits associated with the system, but usually do not specify a detailed account of services in the system.

In this section we present a small subset of these requirements. We restrict our presentation to functional requirements. The selection was guided with the aim of identifying those that (i) seem to compose a basic structure of MABS platforms; (ii) are common to, or that better differentiate, current existing platforms, and (iii) are not present in any platform that we know, at least in a formal way. In this presentation the following points are considered:

1. A brief description of each requirement and some associated activities in both a precise and unambiguous way. This approach is important in MABS due to its interdisciplinary character; for instance the term "domain" must be interpreted in the same way by a Psychologist, an Anthropologist, an Engineer, and so on;

2. Each functional requirement has a name. In order to connect requirements with UML use cases [2], each name is an active phrase, for instance "Launch Agents".

In the rest of this section we will describe requirements clustered around the foresaid facilities. In section 3 we will use these requirements to guide the comparative analysis.

2.1 Technological Facilities

Technological facilities encompass services that (i) intermediate the platform with both the operational system and the network services; (ii) provide services to support controlled simulation worlds.

A. Manage Scheduling Techniques: The platform should support controlled simulations and allow repeatability. To this end it should provide (i) libraries including at least one commonly used scheduling technique, like discrete-time or event-based simulation; (ii) mechanisms to cluster agents in groups and apply different scheduling techniques to each group.

2.2 Domain Facilities

According to [1], the environment of a problem can be represented by a collection of objects and agents. In our sense, a domain is defined by the environment and causal knowledge of how those objects and agents interact with one another. Domain facilities embrace two sub-types of requirements:

- The first type deals with requirements that have a considerable importance in the modelling and implementation of domains. This importance is assessed by considering how the absence of requirements may hamper, or even inhibit, the modelling and implementation of domains. This is the case of §2.2.A and §2.2.C.

- The second type deals with requirements whose technological and logical functionalities must be modelled in a personalized way according to the relevant domain. They usually demand further implementation work. This is the case of §2.2.B.

A. Launch Agents: The platform should provide agent templates related with different manners to launch agents like threads, applets and objects. For instance, platforms that do not provide multi-threaded agents may hamper the modelling and simulation of distributed network environments.

B. Manage Intentional Failures: From a technical-operational point of view, there are two classes of intentional failures that can be manipulated in a simulation (see [11]). The first class, called *operational failures*, works with disturbances in the technical-operational infrastructure (corrupted messages, server failures, etc.). The second, called *logical failures*, manipulate patterns of behaviour that can be viewed as dysfunctional exceptions in the simulated system. Operational failures can be used to build specific scenarios and serve as the base to build more general logical failures. Logical failures are strongly domain dependent, and the user may have to engage in further implementation work in order to utilize them. The platform should offer: (i) libraries to manipulate basic operational failures; (ii) mechanisms to store and search templates of logical failures created by users.

C. Integrate Controlled and Non-Controlled Environments: Typically the simulation environment must be totally controlled, every event in the simulation world must be performed under the control of the simulator. These situations characterize what we call *controlled environments*. Nevertheless, there are cases where the agents can (or must) perform actions outside the controlled environment, in real environments. This integration can occur in two ways. In a first scenario an agent could use the platform environment to perform some of its actions, while performing others under real conditions. In a second scenario, an agent could be decoupled from the simulator, perform autonomously some action under real conditions, and return to the simulated environment. In both cases this integration demands a time-consuming implementation work from the developer.

To support this functionality a platform should offer agent architectures that separate the agent domain-dependent behaviour from the simulator design patterns. Also, in order to keep the simulation consistent and guarantee a good level of repeatability, when agents are running in non-controlled environments some of their events should be notified to the simulator, which should update its local view (see [25]).

2.3 Development Facilities

Development facilities include mechanisms and tools to construct MAS within an agent-centered approach or organisation-centered approach (see [15]).

A. Develop Agent Architectures: The platform should provide templates of generic agent architectures, from reactive to intentional agents.

B. Manage Messages: Agents should communicate between each other with message passing mechanisms. The platform should also offer: (i) message models with basic attributes and mechanisms to extend or add additional attributes; (ii) APIs and parsers to check the correctness of agent communication languages, eventually according to given standards, like *e.g.* KQML.

C. Use Organisational Abstractions: Organisational abstractions are MAS components that explicitly structure an organisation. Roles and groups are the most common ones. The platform should provide services that define roles in terms of, e.g., functions, activities or responsibilities. It should also be possible to define their interaction protocols (see [26]). The concept of groups is an example of an organisational abstraction that defines different sub-organisations according to modularity and encapsulation principles. The platform should support the creation and management of agent and organisation collections, clustered around common relations.

D. Use Multiple Societies: In the real world we have the ability to create explicit organisational structures, observe them and reason about them, like other agents, institutions or even new societies (for example, artificial agent societies). From the observer's point of view, an artificial society may be seen as an aggregate of agents and organisations, which coexist and interact with each other through social events. This concept of society in agent-based simulation is rarely specified as an explicit structural and relational entity, but usually implicitly defined in formal or informal terms of inclusiveness of agents and other organisational entities [7]. Such tendency complicates the design of artificial agents that are able to observe and reason about other societies, particularly if the environment is composed of multiple interacting social spaces and levels of abstraction. Although some approaches have used models that explicitly define multiple societies, the concept of society in those models is still reducible to the concept of group, where agents are viewed simultaneously both as actors and non-neutral observers in a given society. Therefore the role of opaque artificial observation is not explicitly assigned to agents, being exclusively and implicitly defined in the person of the system designer

The possibility of instantiating multiple societies in an explicit way, as explicit organisational and relational entities themselves, can be very useful in MABS. It is important, for instance, in multi-level modelling approaches (hierarchical organisations of social spaces). Additionally, it can serve as the basic mechanism to integrate controlled and non-controlled environments (see §2.2C). The platform should provide primitives to instantiate topologies of multiple societies, and to instantiate opaque social spaces (see §2.5C, [7]) that may be used as neutral observation windows to other societies and social spaces.

E. Use Ontologies: Ontologies can be used with many objectives like interoperability, reuse, search of information and knowledge sharing and acquisition (see [24, 13]). Ontologies can be powerful tools to assist simulation modelling. The platform should provide: (i) a standard ontology describing its adopted concepts and their causal relationships; (ii) mechanisms to store new ontologies based on the standard ontology; (iii) a search engine to manipulate ontologies; (iv) a browser to query the search engine and visualize results; and (v) mechanisms to relate ontologies with implementation components.

2.4 Analysis Facilities

The researcher's capacity to observe and interpret simulation results can lead someone to ask if those results are verified, validated and relevant to the observed system, questioning if such results are only conclusions associated with a specific observer. This kind of question is found in [4], where the author points out the need to construct structured simulations in order to explain the emergence and "imergence" phenomena.

According to [4], there is not yet a "...real emergence of some causal property (a new complexity level of organisation of the domain); but simply some subjective and unreliable global interpretation". In [8] we show that this problem arises in MABS because the *computational model* may not be complete, or even specified correctly, in relation to the intended *conceptual model* specification – see figure 1. Additionally, the *conceptual model* may not be complete, or even specified correctly, in relation to the observed target system. In fact, even if the observer is able to observe certain patterns in the simulation results that could, according to some possible world, affect the intended conceptual model, the underlying observation (e.g., a law, a theorem) may have not been specified in the computational model, bringing the observed result to the realm of epiphenomenalism with no causal power on the computational model.

Nevertheless, it is possible to specify requirements that can help the researcher to observe objective simulation results. In [8] we view agent-based computational models as a triple composed by (i) a set of *Agentified Entities* (AE); (ii) a set of properties observed over each one of those AEs; and (iii) a set of interaction algorithms. Agentified entities may be (i) atomic entities representing an observed feature, agent or organisation in the target; or (ii) aggregates specified with interaction algorithms that manipulate atomic or other aggregate entities according to properties observed over those entities. The former are called *micro-AEs* and the latter are called *macro-AEs*. Macro AEs may differ in order of level according to different aggregation levels. The AEs interact with each other through primitives that define the set of behavioural events specified in the model (e.g. message-passing, perception mechanics). Requirements related to *analysis* should specify the means to observe behavioural events and the internal state of AEs during the simulation. Furthermore they should specify the means to define windows of observation that can be cross analysed, like the effects produced by some micro-AE's behavioural event in the internal state of some macro-AE (and *vice versa*).

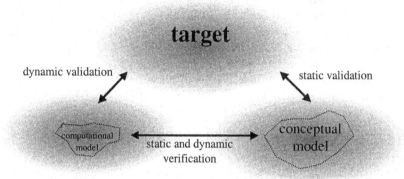

Fig. 1. Conceptual and computational models. Static verification and validation techniques are concerned with the analysis and checking of system representations such as specification documents and the program source code. Dynamic testing exercises the program using (real or experimental) data, and the values obtained are used to test if the computer program behaves as expected by the conceptual model (verification) or as observed in the target (validation) – see [8].

Figure 2 acknowledges the information processing character of computational models, and illustrates lines of information flow which can be observed at different levels of aggregation. The figure emphasizes the effect of macro-AEs on micro-AEs (or lower order macro AEs), and *vice versa*. Continuous lines denote flow of information caused by invocation of behavioural events, where each AE acts as an information transformation function. The symbol "x" denotes observation of behavioural events or internal states of AEs. Dotted lines denote control activity exercised by the simulator.

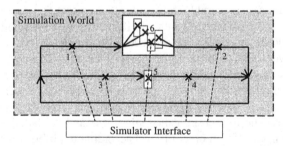

Fig. 2. Points of observation and intervention on behavioural and cognitive events.

A. Observe Behavioural Events: Behavioural events are events that can be observed by an external observer (e.g., message passing, creation/destruction of agents, data base access). The platform should provide mechanisms to select specific windows to observe behavioural events. Observation windows for behavioural events are given in figure 2 by points (1), (2), (3) and (4). Points (1) and (2) observe whole sets of behavioural events issued by AEs associated with a same macro-AE. Points (3) and (4) refer to events associated with a single AE.

B. Observe Cognitive Events: Cognitive events are events in the agents' internal architectures. The observation of such events may be counter-intuitive according to the usual agent paradigm, but indispensable to analyse structured simulations. For example, it may be useful to analyse the effect of some behavioural event in the recipient agent's mental states; or if the effect perceived by the agent who issues the event is in fact objective according to the simulation designer-observer's perspective.

The platform should offer mechanisms to control the agents' internal mechanisms, in order to trigger specific observation methods. In figure 2 point (6) denotes the observation of whole sets of AEs associated with a same macro-AE. Point (5) denotes the observation of single AEs. In order to provide structured observation of cognitive events, the platform should comply with another requirement, called cognitive reflectivity (see §2.5D).

C. Provide Data Analysis: In a simulation the amount of output data is huge and graphical analysis at run time cannot capture all aspects of the simulation logic. This requirement should define technical indicators and decision support (e.g., graphical and statistical packages) to work in more depth with generated data.

2.5 Exploration Facilities

Exploration facilities emphasise the human-computer interactive character of simulations with respect to the exploration of different results and emerging qualitative concepts. This is important because most classic simulation programs and contemporaneous models of agent-oriented software engineering (see [5]) are not concerned with the exploration of emergent, non-anticipated, structures. While most classic software processes concentrate on the analysis and exploration of system requirements and intended behaviours, the MABS software process is also concerned with *exploration of results*. The interactive exploration of different conditions, such as different sequences of method invocation, mental states or assignment of variables, is thus a crucial issue. The exploration can be facilitated if those conditions are allowed to change interactively, during the simulation, in-between simulation steps.

A. Intervene in Behavioural Events: Behavioural events are events that can be observed by an external observer. The platform should offer mechanisms to select specific points to intervene in behavioural events. The intervention should permit the *suppression, modification* or *creation* of behavioural events. For instance, it may be useful to *modify* the content of behavioural events (e.g., the intended recipient agent in a message), or even to *suppress* its arrival to the intended recipient. These experiments give the means to analyse functional effects in the simulation independently from the agents' internal representations that originate other or those same events. In figure 2, points (1) and (2) refer to intervention in sets of behavioural events issued by AEs associated with a same macro-AE. Points (3) and (4) denote intervention in behavioural events issued by a single AE.

B. Intervene in Cognitive Events: The platform should offer mechanisms to intervene in the agents' internal mechanisms, for instance modify the values of program variables, order of method invocation and the agents' beliefs. This may alter the order of invocation and the nature of behavioural events. Point (6) denotes the intervention in AEs associated with a same macro AE, and point (5) in a single AE. In order to provide structured interventions the platform should comply with requirement §2.5D, called cognitive reflectivity.

C. Manage Social Opacity: The problematic of social opacity analyses the organisational conditions under which the control of cognitive information transfer between different social spaces at the same level of abstraction is possible [7], for instance between different multiple societies (see §2.3D). Social opacity is therefore related to organisational borders.

The platform should provide the means to instantiate different topologies of opaque social spaces in a dynamic way. This is useful to simulate agents that have the ability to instantiate and observe given models of other artificial agents and societies, allowing the agents to reason autonomously about the heterogeneity of different models of societies at various levels of observation. Nevertheless, while the observed agents and societies must be visible to the observer agent, the observer agent and societies must be opaque to the observed agents. The platform should provide organisational ingredients and services to instantiate multiple societies and opaque social spaces.

D. Provide Models of Cognitive Reflectivity: Cognitive reflectivity refers to the identification of cognitive structures and internal procedures of agents at run time. The templates of agent architectures (see §2.3A) should provide adequate models of cognitive reflectivity, allowing the user or other system agents to observe and intervene in the simulated agents' cognitive events. Thus, different models of cognitive reflectivity should be provided according to different generic agent architectures.

3 Comparative Analysis of MABS Platforms

We are now in conditions to present the platforms that will be subject to the comparative analysis: CORMAS, Swarm and MadKit. The main purpose of CORMAS and Swarm is to simulate agent-based models of social and biological targets. CORMAS is a domain dependent platform in the area of renewable natural resources. Swarm is a general-purpose platform to simulate complex adaptive systems. MadKit is an organisation-centered platform based on MAS organisations. It is a general-purpose simulation platform, although more oriented to MAS engineering.

The Common-pool Resources and Multi-Agent Systems (CORMAS) platform is being developed by the Centre de Coopération Internationale en Recherche Agronomique pour le Dévelopment (CIRAD), France. The platform supports interactions between individuals and groups sharing renewable natural resources (see [3, 6]). CORMAS works with three types of entities: spatial, passive and social. Spatial entities define a topological support for simulations. They hold natural resources and arbitrate their allocation according to pre-defined protocols based on a metaphor of physical harvest. Passive entities are subdivided in passive objects and messages; and social entities are agents.

Table 3.1. Comparative outline of MABS platforms.

	CORMAS	MadKit	Swarm
Technological Facilities			
Manage Scheduling Techniques	Adopts discrete time simulation	The couple Scheduler-Activator define and manage personalized scheduling techniques	Adopts event-based simulation
Domain Facilities			
Launch Agents	Agents can be launched as objects	Agents can be launched as objects, threads or applets	Agents can be launched as objects or threads
Manage Intentional Failures	Not available	Not available	Not available
Integrate Controlled and Non-Controlled Environments	Not available	Not available	Not available
Development Facilities			
Develop Agent Architectures	Flat architecture	Flat architecture	Flat architecture
Manage Messages	Synchronous and asynchronous modes	Synchronous and asynchronous modes	Synchronous mode
Use Organisational Abstractions	Does not work with roles. It works with agents aggregations, through the Group class	There are many-to-many relation among agents and roles. Each group has its inner characteristics	Does not work with roles and groups
Use Multiple Societies	Not available	Groups do not quite resemble the concept of societies, but can be made alike	Multiple societies are swarms, but must be allocated in hierarchical levels
Use Ontologies	Not available	Not available	Not available
Analysis Facilities			
Observe Behavioural Events	Not formally available	Hook mechanisms and system agents	Not formally available
Observe Cognitive Events	Designer implements methods in SmallTalk	Watcher agents and Probe class	Observer agents and probe interface
Provide Data Analysis	Provides a rich set of tools	Not available	Libraries like simtools and random

The Multi-Agent Development Kit (MadKit) platform is being developed by Jacques Ferber and Olivier Gutknecht of the Laboratoire d'Informatique, Robotique et Micro-Electronique of Montpellier (LIRMM), France. MadKit is based on the 3-tupla Agent-Group-Role (AGR). The platform adopts the principle of agentification of services where all services are modelled using the AGR concepts, except for the services provided by the micro-kernel. Services are defined through roles and delegated to agents allocated in groups (see [10, 16]).

In the Santa Fe Institute, U.S.A., Chris Langton initiated the Swarm project in 1994. Swarm is a multi-agent platform to simulate complex adaptive systems. The main component that organizes agents is a `swarm`, a collection of agents with a schedule of agent activities. Agents interact with each other through discrete events (see [14,19]).

In Table 3.1 we present a comparative overview of CORMAS, MadKit and Swarm. Exploration facilities were not considered since none of the platforms meets those requirements, at least in a formal and structured way. We will present some general principles to guide the development of exploration facilities in section 4.

3.1 Technological Facilities

In general, we found that requirements related with technological facilities are well structured in all platforms.

A. Manage Scheduling Techniques: CORMAS works with discrete time simulation. As stated by [3] this technique was chosen due to its simplicity. Swarm works with event-based simulation. A swarm is composed by a collection of agents with a schedule of events over those agents. Each event is an action that an agent can perform (see [14,19]). MadKit does not define *a priori* any type of scheduling technique. There are two classes related with scheduling in MadKit. The class `Activator` defines a basic scheduling policy and relates this policy to a set of agents. According to [18], the specialization of the class `Activator` permits the customisation of different scheduling techniques for different sets of agents. The class `Scheduler` defines the agents who are responsible for the integration and consistency of these different techniques.

3.2 Domain Facilities

The platforms do not provide a very rich set of domain facilities. This is not very strange since all the platforms are relatively recent. One can expect an improvement on this class of requirements with the use and development of new releases.

A. Launch Agents: Depending on the simulation domain it may be adequate to launch agents as a thread, or as an applet, or as an object. This requirement, determines, for instance, if the platform allows distributed simulation (or easy evolution towards that goal). CORMAS uses a single thread of control in a simulation and its agents are SmallTalk objects. This feature hampers distribution of agents. In MadKit agents can be launched as objects, threads or applets. In Swarm agents can be instantiated as objects in their own threads, allowing the modelling of distributed simulations.

B. Manage Intentional Failures: This requirement is not available in any platform.

C. Integrate Controlled and Non-Controlled Environments: This requirement is not available in any platform.

3.3   Development Facilities

Requirements related to development facilities are well structured in MadKit, since the platform is based on the Aalaadim organisational model [10]. Swarm also adopted an organisation-centered approach, well adapted to model biological systems, but in essence Swarm serves the purpose of agent-centered models. In Swarm, agents can be composed of other swarms in a nested composition, generating organisational structures in hierarchical levels of access and control. CORMAS adopted an agent-centered approach, and its services attend the needs of such modelling.

A. Develop Agent Architectures: CORMAS does not impose restrictions on the agents' internal architectures and the user is fully responsible for such implementation. In MadKit agents are defined as active communicating entities that play roles within groups. Although MadKit does not define *a priori* the agents' internal architectures, it provides templates to help the modelling of reactive and cognitive agents. An agent in Swarm is an entity that is able to generate events that affect other agents and himself. Swarm does not define *a priori* the agents' internal architectures, but provides libraries of agent templates. For instance, the ga and neuro libraries provide models for genetic algorithms and neural networks, respectively.

B. Manage Messages: CORMAS works with message passing and the user can define their own communication language. The class Msg defines a basic syntax with the attributes: sender, receiver and symbol [6]. Distributed communication is not supported in the current version of CORMAS. Both MadKit and Swarm allow local and distributed communication, but in different levels of functionality. Communication in MadKit occurs through asynchronous message passing. The users can define their own agent communication language, and the platform provides various codifications, such as StringMessage, XMLMessage and ActMessage. A MadKit micro kernel handles local message passing between agents. The exchange of messages between different micro-kernels is also possible. In Swarm, agent communication is always synchronous and bounded inside each swarm. Different swarms can run in different machines and processors, but agents located in different swarms cannot communicate with each other. Like CORMAS and MadKit, the user can define their own communication language.

C. Use Organisational Abstractions: CORMAS does not adopt the concept of role. This is understandable since its domain-dependent character does not emphasise the work with cognitive agents and organisation-centered approaches. This also applies to Swarm, since the platform was initially developed according to artificial life principles. A role in MadKit is an abstract representation of an agent function, service or identification within a group. Several agents can play a same role, and a same agent can play several roles. In CORMAS the concept of group represents a composite social entity; entities in different groups can interact with entities in other groups, so as to simulate interactions between different scales and organisational levels. The concept of group is implemented through the class Group and its subclasses (see [6]). In MadKit groups are atomic sets of agent aggregation. Each group has its own inner characteristics, like communication language, ontology, coordination techniques [16]. In Swarm the concept of group is not explicitly defined. The underlying concept of swarm, as a collection of agents, does not quite resemble the concept of group, since swarms in different hierarchical levels are opaque to each other.

D. Use Multiple Societies: The platform CORMAS runs with a single kernel and manages a single society. Considering that communication between different simulations in different kernels is not possible, CORMAS does not work with multiple societies. Conversely, MadKit and Swarm can deal with multiple societies, although in a limited way. In Swarm, each swarm may be viewed as a single society, but the concept of swarm cannot be decoupled from the concept of agent. It is possible to define different swarms allocated in hierarchical levels. However, swarms in higher hierarchical levels are necessarily opaque to swarms in lower levels. A parent swarm can launch and observe agents in swarms of lower levels, and swarms in the same level interact implicitly if they share a same parent swarm. However, a same agent cannot move between different swarms. Since swarms in the same nested level cannot explicitly interact, topologies of multiple societies are necessarily hierarchical. In MadKit the concept of group does not quite resemble the concept of society. This is because the concept of group is created with specific inner organisational characteristics, like the roles an agent is allowed to play or communication links between agents. It is possible to build topologies of multiple societies with groups, but the platform does not provide explicit mechanisms to control levels of observation and visibility between multiple societies (see §2.5.C).

E. Manage Ontologies: This requirement is not available in any platform.

3.4   Analysis Facilities

In CORMAS and Swarm the separation between observation of behavioural and cognitive events is not formally structured, there is not a formal distinction between what is objectively observable in the external environment and what is subjectively represented in the agents' mind. In MadKit this separation is not entirely structured, but seems to be more flexible than in CORMAS and Swarm, partly due to its organisation-centered approach.

A. Observe Behavioural Events: In CORMAS the designer needs to implement methods in SmallTalk to operate the observation of behavioural events, and provides sophisticated tools to observe such events. Swarm decouples the observation actions from execution actions, working with a two level hierarchical architecture. In the first level occurs the observation of the simulation (the Observer Swarm). In the second level occurs the execution of the simulation (the Model Swarm). Probes specified in the Observer Swarm can gather events occurring in the Model Swarm, but the notion of behavioural event is not formally represented in the platform; the developer must implement this kind of observation in order to track such events. MadKit provides two ways for observing behavioural events: (i) the hook mechanisms; and (ii) agentified services managed, for instance, by the `OrganisationTrace` and `MessageTrace` agents. Hook mechanisms are generic subscribe-and-publish schemes that keep the subscriber agent informed about the invocation of kernel operations. The role of `MessageTrace` is to intercept calls of `sendMessage()` at the micro-kernel. The agent `OrganizationalTrace` traces all method invocations related to organisational abstractions (e.g. `jointGroup()`, `requestRole()`, see [16]).

B. Observe Cognitive Events: All platforms provide services to observe internal events. However, such services do not explicitly comply with models of cognitive reflectivity. In CORMAS the designer needs to implement methods in SmallTalk in order to observe the entities' internal attributes. In Swarm, this requirement is implemented through the interface `probe` and the `Observer` agents. This mechanism gives access to the agents' internal methods and variables at run time. The MadKit simulation engine, called synchronous engine, observes cognitive events through the `Watcher` agents and the `Probe` class. The `Watcher` agents are in charge of managing a list of `Probes`.

C. Provide Data Analysis: In CORMAS and Swarm there is a reasonable number of tools that fulfil this requirement. Meanwhile, in the current version of MadKit this requirement is not fulfilled. CORMAS allows the design of graphical charts with time-steps as the x-values and values returned by methods as the y-values. Additionally, two levels of data-recording are available. The fist level tracks information from individual agents and the second from the agency. Swarm offers the `simtools` library to aid the process of data analysis, such as batch swarms that store information in files, generation of graphics and histograms. It also provides a very complete library to manage random number generators.

4   Conclusions

The requirement analysis that we have presented in this paper is a useful reference to define development principles for agent-based simulation platforms. The comparative analysis of CORMAS, MadKit and Swarm validated the requirements specification, which allowed us to characterize both the general structure and global behaviour of MABS platforms. Additionally, it was able to show that there is a reasonable consensus in regard to *technological, domain, development* and *analysis* facilities. Of course, some requirements are more developed in a platform than in others, but in general all platforms satisfied most requirements.

It is important to point out that in CORMAS and Swarm the distinction between behavioural and cognitive events is not completely and formally structured. In MadKit the observation of behavioural events is explicit, but the observation of cognitive events is not structured around models of cognitive reflectivity.

In our opinion, these limitations reflect a tendency in MABS to: (i) delegate in the designer the activities associated with structured data gathering; (ii) overlook the importance of integrating both behavioural and cognitive information to describe emergent phenomena. Indeed, none of these platforms fulfilled all requirements associated with exploration facilities (at least in a formal way), which reinforces our observations. Exploration facilities concern the active exploration of different results and qualitative concepts, which is the effective *raison d'être* of agent-based simulation. Such requirements are useful sources to indicate general principles that should be provided in the next generation of multiagent-based simulation platforms:

- Availability of observation and intervention mechanisms, for both behavioural and cognitive events, according to generic models of agent architectures and cognitive reflectivity; flexible management of observation and intervention windows, with respect to both individual and aggregate events;

- Availability of organisational models that should be able to manage topologies of multiple societies in a dynamic way. These models should be able to provide: (i) agentification of observation and intervention activities; (ii) agent primitives to launch different models of societies; (iii) dynamic creation of topologies of opaque and non-opaque observation spaces, which can be autonomously created by observer agents. This means that the topology of multiple societies in the simulation world can assume an emerging autonomous character from the human designer, as well as its different emergent points for opaque observation of social spaces;

- Availability of different ontologies to assist knowledge sharing, reuse, interoperability, simulation modelling and establishment of ontological commitments between simulation components.

References

1. Anderson J. and Evans M. (1995). A Generic Simulation System for Intelligent Agent Designs. *Applied Artificial Intelligent*, v.9, n.5, pp. 527–562.
2. Booch G, Rumbaugh J., Jacobson I. (1999). *The Unified Modelling Language User Guide*. Addison-Wesley.
3. Bousquet F., Bakam I., Proton H. and Le Page C. (1998). Cormas: Common-Pool Resources and Multi-Agent Systems. *Lecture Notes in Artificial Intelligence*, v. 1416, pp. 826–838.
4. Castelfranchi C. (1998). Simulating with Cognitive Agents: The Importance of Cognitive Emergence. In Proc. First. International Workshop on Multi-Agent Based Simulation (MABS'98), *Lecture Notes in Artificial Intelligence*, v.1534, Berlin: Springer-Verlag, pp. 26–41.
5. Ciancarini P. and Wooldridge M. (eds), Agent-Oriented Software Engineering, *Lecture Notes in Artificial Intelligence*, v. 1957, Berlin: Springer-Verlag, 2001.
6. CORMAS: Common-Pool Resources and Multi-Agent Systems - User Guide, http://cormas.cirad.fr, 2001.
7. David N., Sichman J.S. and Coelho H. (2002). Multiple Society Organisations and Social Opacity: When Agents Play the Role of Observers. In 16th Brazilian Symposium on Artificial Intelligence (SBIA'02), *Lectures Notes in Artificial Intelligence*, v.2507, Berlin: Springer-Verlag, pp.63–73.

8. David N., Sichman J.S and Coelho H. (2002). Towards an Emergence-Driven Software Process for Agent-Based Simulation. In this Volume.

9. Decker K. (1996). Distributed Artificial Intelligence Testbeds. In O'Hare and Jennings, editors, *Foundations of Distributed Artificial Intelligence*, New York: John Willey & Sons, pp. 119–138.

10. Ferber J. and Gutknecht O. (1998). A Meta-Model for the Analysis and Design of Organizations in Multi-Agent Systems, In *Third International Conference on Multi-Agent Systems (ICMAS'98)*, IEEE Computer Society, pp. 128–135.

11. Gasser L. (2000). MAS Infrastructure Definitions, Needs, Prospects. In Infrastructure for Agents, MAS and Scalable MAS, *Lecture Notes in Artificial Intelligence*, v.1887, Berlin: Springer-Verlag, 1–11.

12. Gasser L. and Kakugawa K. (2002). MACE3J: Fast Flexible Distributed Simulation of Large, Large-Grain Multi-Agent System, In *First International Joint Conference on Autonomous Agents and Multi-Agent Systems (AAMAS-2002)*.

13. Gruber T. (1993). Toward Principles for the Design of Ontologies used for Knowledge Sharing. In Nicola Guarino and Roberto Poli, editors, *Formal Ontology in Conceptual Analysis and Knowledge Representation*, Kluwer Academic Publishers.

14. Johnson P. and Lancaster A., *Swarm User Guide*, http://www.santafe.edu/projects/swarm/swarmdocs/userbook/userbook.html, 1996.

15. Lemaitre C. and Excelente B. (1998). Multiagent Organization Approach. In *Proceedings of II Iberoamerican Workshop on DAI and MAS*, Toledo, Spain.

16. MadKit, *Multi-Agent Development Kit*, http://www.madkit.org, 2002.

17. Marietto M.B., David N.C., Sichman J.S. and Coelho H. (2002). Requirements Analysis of Multi-Agent-Based Simulation Platforms. *Technical Report*, University of São Paulo.

18. Michael F., Gutknecht O. and Ferber J. (2001). Generic Simulation Tools Based on MAS Organization, In *Proceedings of Modelling Autonomous Agents in a Multi-Agent World (MAAMAW'01)*.

19. Minar N., Murkhart R., Langton C. and Askenazi M., *The Swarm Simulation System: A Toolkit for Building Multi-Agent Simulations*, http://www.santafe.edu/projects/swarm/overview/overview.html, 1996.

20. Moss S., Gaylard H, Wallis S., and Edmonds B. (1998). SDML: A Multi-Agent Language for Organizational Modelling. *Computational and Mathematical Organization Theory*, v. 4, pp. 43–69.

21. Pfleeger S.L. (1991). Software Engineering. *The Production of Quality*, New York: Macmillan Publishing, 2nd edition.

22. Sichman J.S., Conte R. and Gilbert N. (1998). Multi-Agent Systems and Agent-Based Simulation, *Lecture Notes in Artificial Intelligence*, v.1534, Berlin: Springer–Verlag.

23. SimCog. *Simulation of Cognitive Agents*, http://www.lti.pcs.usp.br/SimCog.

24. Uschold M. and Jasper R. (1999). A Framework for Understanding and Classifying Ontology Applications, In *Proceedings of the IJCAI99 Workshop on Ontologies and Problem-Solving Methods (KRR5)*, Stockholm, Sweden.

25. Vincent R., Horling B. and Lesser V. (2000). An Agent Infrastructure to Build and Evaluate MAS: The Java Agent Framework and Multi-Agent System Simulator. In *Infrastructure for Agents, MAS and Scalable MAS*, Lecture Notes in Artificial Intelligence, v. 1887, Berlin: Springer-Verlag, pp. 102–127.

26. Zambonelli F. Jennings N. and Wooldridge M. (2001). Organisational Rules as an Abstraction for the Analysis and Design of Multi-Agent Systems. In *Int. J. of Software Engineering and Knowledge Engineering*, v. 11, n.3, pp. 303–328.

On the Simulation of Multiagent-Based Regulators for Physiological Processes

Francesco Amigoni and Nicola Gatti

Dipartimento di Elettronica e Informazione
Politecnico di Milano
Piazza Leonardo da Vinci 32, I-20133 Milano, Italy
{amigoni,ngatti}@elet.polimi.it

Abstract. The multiagent approach allows to effectively address and manage the complex regulation of physiological processes. In this paper we argue why multiagent regulating systems need to be simulated in order to assess the properties of interest. In particular, we consider a multiagent regulator of the glucose-insulin metabolism and we show how the effectiveness of its control activity and other salient properties of this system can be derived from simulation.

1   Introduction

Physiological processes represent an extremely complex class of phenomena to study and regulate [1]. This is mainly due to the fact that each physiological process emerges from the interaction of several elements belonging to an intricate network of relationships, where each element can be involved in more processes. In previous papers we have introduced the *anthropic agency* approach in which multiagent systems are employed to regulate physiological processes in an effective and flexible way [2,3].

In this paper we show why such multiagent regulators need to be simulated in order to assess the properties of interests. The main reason is connected to the lacking of any general established formal framework to prove the properties of the multiagent-based control systems; this has the consequence that the effectiveness and the properties of the control activity can be verified only by simulation.

We explicitly remark that our approach to multiagent based simulation is "philosophically" different from that adopted in almost all papers in this volume and in the literature (see, for example, [4]). While these works use agents as more or less precise models of people (even in cases in which the simulation of a society is not addressed [5]), we intend agents as entities that embed partial and specific submodels [6] of a phenomenon. Abstractly, in both approaches the agents are conceived as autonomous heterogeneous entities that take independent decisions. In particular, our approach can be traced back to the work of Marvin Minsky on the "society of mind" [7].

This paper is organized as follows. In Section 2, we characterize the distributed nature of both physiological processes and their regulation systems and

J.S. Sichman, F. Bousquet, P. Davidsson (Eds.): MABS 2002, LNAI 2581, pp. 142–154, 2003.

we motivate the need for simulation. In Section 3, we describe the anthropic agency paradigm to control physiological processes; this architecture is also well-suited to simulate the controllers. In Section 4, we illustrate the particular anthropic agency implementation we developed for the glucose-insulin metabolism and the corresponding simulation results. Finally, Section 5 concludes the paper.

2   The Distributed Nature of Physiological Processes and of Their Regulators

Physiological processes are among the most complex phenomena related to the human being [1]. It is possible to identify several reasons of complexity, including the facts that such processes can be rarely modelled with linear models and that often the interesting physiological parameters involved in these processes and in their relations can be measured only in an intrusive way (by introducing exogenous elements in the human body and thus altering the natural human metabolism) [1] [8]. In this paper we focus on another source of complexity: a physiological process is not isolated from the other ones, but their behaviors are closely related. In fact, a physiological process influences with its activity a number of other physiological processes, each one of them in turn influences other physiological processes, and so on. For instance, the high-value concentration of blood glucose increases the heart beat frequency and this, in turn, increases the blood pressure. Hence, the scenario of the human metabolism comprises a network of physiological elements interconnected by biological transmitters, such as hormones, neurotransmitters, and electric impulses. Usually a part or a subpart of an organ that has a single and specific function is considered as an element of such network. We emphasize also that the behavior of an element is affected by the environment and, at the same time, the element itself affects the environment. In such way, several chain reactions develop in the network when a physiological element responds to the actions of some elements affecting, in turn, other elements in a very complicated way.

We are interested in the regulation of this physiological network. When we regulate each element of the network, namely each physiological element, according to a control model, the result we obtain is a network of physiological process regulators. It would be preferable that the elements of this regulation network had the following properties [9]: autonomy, since each element is related to a specific physiological process; asynchrony, since each element does not need to wait for any signal coming from others before changing its state; concurrency, since the elements act in parallel; pro-activeness, since each element can be thought as independently pursuing an objective; and hiding, since each element does not need to know the details of the internal behavior of the others. These properties lead naturally to the adoption of multiagent systems to control physiological phenomena (by the way, these properties are similar to those required in the well-known agent definition of [10]). The agents embed the control models for the elements of the physiological network. The interactions among the regulating agents mimic the relations among the physiological elements. We have developed a general approach, called *anthropic agency* (described in the next section), to regulate and control physiological processes. Moreover, we have demonstrated the usefulness of this approach by addressing the case of glucose-insulin metabolism (see Section 4). In the system we have developed, we considered three interconnected interesting aspects: the insulin production in relation to meal absorption [11], the effects of physical activity [12], and the effects of stress hormones [13].

The multiagent-based regulator obtained in this way must be simulated to determine its response time, its stability, its limitations, and other properties. As in other control paradigms (e.g., fuzzy control) alternative to the classical control theory based on dynamic systems, simulation is the only way to verify these "external" properties of the regulator (viewed as a black box). This is because a general formal framework for mathematically proving the properties of multiagent control systems is still lacking. The fact that the regulator actually stabilizes the controlled physiological process and the identification of boundaries on response time are two basic information needed to claim that the multiagent regulator is safe and that it is conceivable to apply it to a real patient. Moreover, the simulation activity brings another fundamental contribution to assess the "internal" properties of the regulator. Since, due to their nature, in multiagent regulators coexist different controllers for different subphenomena, it is important to evaluate the interactions between the controlled physiological processes and the corresponding controllers. In particular, it is significant to check by simulation if the insertion of a new controller in the system brings to an incorrect interaction with the other controllers and with the physiological processes (with obvious unpleasant consequences for the patient). In this context, it is fundamental the adoption of a multiagent-based approach (both to develop and to simulate the controllers) to gain the flexibility to easily reconfigure the system to test different configurations of the controllers. This flexibility is not usually exhibited by classical dynamic system models used in control theory. In fact, it is easier to modify the composition of a multiagent system than that of a dynamic system. For example, in a multiagent system it is usually possible to insert a new agent without any modification to the other components, while the insertion of a new set of equations in a dynamic system usually requires to reconsider all the components. This is a consequence of the clear separation, provided by multiagent systems and not by dynamic systems, between the specificity of the components (the agents) and the uniformity of their interaction. Similar considerations hold also for neural networks based control systems.

The main reasons to use multiagent systems to develop a network of different interacting regulators are summarized in what follows.

– The properties that characterize an agent favor the embedding of every kind of regulators (based on dynamic systems, neural networks, fuzzy rules, expert systems, and so on) in the agent itself. The availability of these coursegrained interacting elements advantages the multiagent systems over neural networks and dynamic systems.

- The multiparadigmatic nature of multiagent systems allows for the coexistence of several different heterogeneous regulators as required by the complex physiological phenomena that can be hardly modelled. This is a property that neural networks and other control techniques have not.
- The asynchrony of the agents and the flexibility in modifying the system configuration give to the multiagent systems a clear advantage over the traditional dynamic systems.

Finally, we note that in this paper we employ the multiagent approach *both* to build the physiological regulator and to simulate it. The multiagent regulator is expected to be composed of physical agents, namely of devices acting on the human body, when technology evolution will allow to do it safely and effectively. The simulation system we describe in the following reproduces this regulator by simulating each device with a distinct software agent, according to [14]. Moreover, both the regulation and the corresponding simulation systems are based on the anthropic agency paradigm.

3   Anthropic Agency

Anthropic agency (introduced in [2,3]) is a powerful paradigm that allows to regulate and control physiological phenomena by means of multiagent systems. According to the technological evolution, anthropic agency will support the development of physiological control systems that will be eventually implanted in the human body. The name 'agency' derives from our conception of a multiagent system as a single machine composed of complex components like computers and robots, the agents [15]. The adjective 'anthropic' derives from the Greek *anthropos*, namely man, and evidences the application field of the system. In what follows we briefly overview the anthropic agency paradigm. In the next section, we show the system we implemented as an instance of this general paradigm.

According to the anthropic agency approach, a multiagent regulation system operates in three major steps: knowledge extraction, decision making, and plan generation (see Fig. 1). Each step is performed by a group of agents and the interactions between these groups are mediated by shared memory areas called blackboards [16] usually employed in multiagent systems.

The agents performing the first step are called *extractor agents*. An extractor agent is connected to (a part of) the sensor network from which it acquires the signals that are filtered and processed to generate the values of a set of parameters. The signals represent the available information about the controlled phenomena (e.g., the current glucose level) while the parameters represent the (often non-directly measurable) information needed to determine the control actions (e.g., the variation over two consecutive time instants of the glucose level). Each extractor agent, that in a future perspective will be a physical perceptive device, is currently simulated by a software agent. The parameters values generated by all the extractor agents are stored in a shared memory area called *parameters blackboard*.

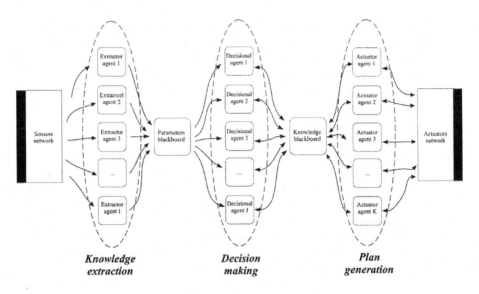

Fig. 1. The general anthropic agency architecture

From the parameters blackboard, the values of the parameters are read by the *decisional agents*, namely by the agents that contribute to the second step: decision making. Each decisional agent is a software agent that embeds the model of the controller of a particular physiological process and that takes its *decisions* about what to do on the basis of its internal specific control model, of the current values of parameters, and of the effects of the past actions performed by the agency. A decision is a pair: a desirable state and a set of weights. The weights measure how much the decisional agent "wants" to reach the proposed state. Hence, each decisional agent takes its autonomous decision about the values it desires for some parameters (e.g., for insulin level). In our implementation, the decision function of a decisional agent is represented as a potential function that gives the "goodness" value of a combination of parameters. The control activity of each decisional agent is thus implemented as a gradient descent algorithm. The control models embedded in the decisional agents are all different, but they may overlap in two ways: the intersection of the input parameters and the intersection of the output proposed decisions could be not null. The decisional agents are not directly connected to each other, but they are all connected to a shared memory area, the *knowledge blackboard*, where they put their decisions. Hence, in general, the anthropic agency approach provides for a society of decisional agents (although they are only three in our implemented system illustrated in the next section), where each agent represents a part of the global controller, namely it is the controller of a single physiological process. Metaphorically, we can consider the decisional agents of this society as representative of medical experts in particular (non-disjoint) domains. By the interactions among the decisional agents, a network of physiological processes is regulated.

THE NEGOTIATION PROCESS

Each decisional agent j repeats these steps for a given parameter p^h:
(1) determines a set of possible target values
$\{x^h_1, x^h_2, .., x^h_{n(j)}\}$ for p^h that minimize the potential $P_j()$ of its partial control function;
(2) selects the proposed target value x^h_j for the parameter p^h, in order to minimize the value
$|x^h_j - x^h_{curr}| * (Cn(p^h_j) + Ca(p^h_j))$ (where $Cn(p^h_j) = |x^h - x^h_j|$ is the negotiation cost);
(3) communicates $p^h_j = x^h_j$ to the knowledge blackboard along with the weight
$(1 + |P_j(x^h_j) - P_j(x^h_{curr})|) * I_j$ (where I_j is the importance of the decisional agent j).

The knowledge blackboard repeats these steps for each p^h:
(1) calculates the weighted average x^h of the proposed values for p^h;
(2) sends x^h to the decisional agents;
(3) every 30s, sends the last calculated x^h to the actuator agents.

The actuator agents calculate, on the basis of the models of actions for p^h, the actuation costs $Ca(p^h_j)$
for reaching x^h_j from x^h_{curr} and send them back to the decisional agents.

Fig. 2. The negotiation mechanism adopted in anthropic agency architecture

The society of decisional agents (when introduced within the human metabolism) is placed above the isomorphic network of physiological elements. Each decisional agent dynamically puts its decisions in the knowledge blackboard, which operates in order to optimize the social welfare by coordinating the negotiation process that involves the decisional agents with their weights, the costs, and the importance of the decisional agents. The costs involved in the negotiation process are three: the *variation cost* expresses how much the desired state is far from the current state; the *actuation cost* expresses how difficult is for the actuator agents to reach the desired state from the current state; and the *negotiation cost* expresses the measure of the difficulty to change a single parameter according to the desires of the other decisional agents. The *importance* of the agents discriminates between the decisional agents that control life functions and those that control less important functions; the importance depends on the current state parameter values, as exemplified in Section 4.

The negotiation process is a cyclic repetition of two phases. In the first one each decisional agent selects its desired state among those that minimize its potential function in order to minimize a combination of the variation, actuation, and negotiation costs. In the second one, the knowledge blackboard calculates the weighted average of the proposed values for each parameter and sends this value back to the decisional agents. Then, the process restarts with the decisional agents that calculate the new negotiation costs and express the new decisions. In addition, after a fixed amount of time (in the implementation described in Section 4, this amount is 30s) the knowledge blackboard communicates the current weighted averages of the negotiated parameters to the actuator agents that send back to the decisional agents the actuation costs. In this way, a unique final decision that maximizes the social welfare is determined. The negotiation process is schematically summarized in Fig. 2, while a more complete description can be found in [3].

The adoption of the knowledge blackboard, which decouples the decisional agents, guarantees the building of a flexible and dynamic system of agents, which composition can be easily modified. Moreover, it acts as a mediator between the decisional agents, which take the decisions, and the actuator agents, which are the executors of the agreed-upon final decisions and that carry out the third step in the anthropic agency approach.

The *actuator agents* determine and perform actions. An action on a parameter is a sequence of operations, namely a plan, to produce a given parameter variation. The plan depends on the entity of the agreed upon parameter variation, on the side effects of the parameter variation, and on the dynamics of already undergoing parameter variations (and of related parameters). The actuator agents perform mutually exclusive actions by operating mutually exclusive physical actuators. The actuator agents embed the models of the actions they can perform; these representations are used to generate the plans that accomplish the final decision of the system and to generate the actuation costs involved in the negotiation process. As for extractor agents, also actuator agents will be, in a future perspective, real physical effector devices, but they are currently simulated by software agents.

We outline that the activities of the agents composing the anthropic agency are all asynchronous.

The advantages of using the multiagent approach in anthropic agency architecture can be divided in two classes: the first one is related to the dynamic flexibility of the system composition, the second one is related to the regulating and simulating activities. As about the first class of properties, the modular architecture of the anthropic agency approach offers the possibility to have a variable and scalable system, in which it is possible to change the composition by adding or removing agents. In such a way, it is possible to control a complex process starting from the control of a single aspect (e.g., a subprocess) and to enrich the controller by adding, step by step, the control of other aspects (by adding the related controllers embedded in the decisional agents) without modifying the already implemented portion of the system.

As regarding the second class of properties, the adoption of the anthropic agency approach guarantees that all the properties listed in the previous section hold. Specifically, in our architecture each decisional agent is autonomous, asynchronous with respect to the other agents, pro-active in pursuing its optimal behavior, concurrent, and the adoption of the knowledge blackboard ensures that each decisional agent is also hidden to the others. Moreover, the modular structure of the anthropic agency allows, as shown in the following section, to simulate and evaluate the interactions among different configurations of decisional agents (i.e., controllers). Finally, we remark that the anthropic agency approach is applicable in situations in which different partial independent control models are available. This is the case of glucose-insulin metabolism discussed in the next section.

4   The Glucose-Insulin Metabolism Regulation

We have implemented the described general anthropic agency architecture to address the regulation of the glucose-insulin metabolism. The physiological processes involved in such metabolism have a Shannon frequency of few minutes and can be appropriately controlled by a multiagent-based control system that reacts in some seconds. Specifically, in our system the agents are set to work with a discretization time of $30s$ (actually, the simulations have been speeded up 6 times). As long as the slow dynamics of the glucose-insulin metabolism are concerned, our system can be considered a real-time system. The human metabolism of glucose-insulin is simulated by a system that implements the model of [11] with modified pancreas secretion parameters to obtain the metabolism of a diabetic patient in order to check the response of the control system. In particular, the control system tries to keep the glucose concentration of a simulated diabetic patient as close as possible to the concentration of a normal person. Our implementation is constituted by an extractor agent, two decisional agents (the implementation of the third one is currently in the testing phase), and an actuator agent; all are implemented in Java. The extractor agent puts in the parameters blackboard the vector $p(t) = (I(t), G(t), \Delta G(t), A(t))$, where $I(t)$ is the current level of insulin (measured in $pmol/l$), $G(t)$ is the current level of glucose (measured in mg/dl), $\Delta G(t)$ is the current variation of the glucose (namely $G(t) - G(t-1)$), and $A(t)$ is the current level of the physical activity (measured in $pmol/l$). The first decisional agent embeds a control model of the glucose metabolism related to food absorption [11]. The model is quite complex since it includes 10 (discretized) differential equations with 8 variables and around 20 parameters. Starting from the equations of this model we devised a decision (potential) function $\mathcal{D}_1((I(t), G(t), \Delta G(t))) = d_1(t)$, where decision $d_1(t)$ is a vector whose elements are the target values of $I(t)$, $G(t)$, and $\Delta G(t)$ and their corresponding weights, as proposed by the first decisional agent. Its goal is to reduce the glucose concentration during food absorption. The second decisional agent embeds a control model of the glucose metabolism related to physical activity. This model (with complexity comparable with that of the first decisional agent) has been derived from [12] and embedded in a decision (potential) function $\mathcal{D}_2((I(t), G(t), A(t))) = d_2(t)$, where decision $d_2(t)$ is a vector whose elements are the target values of $I(t)$, $G(t)$, and $\Delta G(t)$ and their corresponding weights, as proposed by the second decisional agent. Its goal is to keep constant the glucose level by limiting the exogenous insulin introduction when the physical activity is intense. Finally, the actuator agent implements the following actuation function: $\mathcal{A}(\bar{d}(t)) = \Delta I(t)$, where $\bar{d}(t) = (\bar{I}(t), \bar{G}(t), \bar{\Delta G}(t), \bar{A}(t))$ is the agreed-upon decisions vector and $\Delta I(t)$ is the variation of insulin planned according to the following procedure. The actuator agent compares the desired state $\bar{d}(t)$ with the current state (as read from the parameters blackboard, this connection is not shown in Fig. 1) to obtain the required variation for each parameter. The actuator agents embed a functional model of the effects on human metabolism of insulin secretion; in this way it determines the quantity (dose) of insulin to pump on the patient's blood in order to obtain the required variations for each

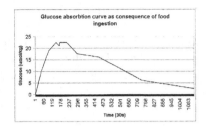 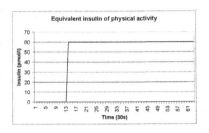

Fig. 3. The curves representing the food absorption (left) and the physical activity (right) used in our experiments

parameter. The insulin concentration is the only quantity that the actuator (a insulin infusion pump, thus $\Delta I(t)$ is always positive) connected to the actuator agent can vary.

We present here a synthetic overview of the most significant results we have obtained from the simulation of the interaction (according to the negotiation mechanism outlined in the previous section) among the two controllers embedded in the decisional agents and the glucose-insulin metabolism of a diabetic patient. Our aim in performing these simulations was to determine the stability, the response time, and, in general, the appropriateness of the implemented system.

In Fig. 4 (top), we report the curves of insulin and glucose we have obtained from a simulated normal person during the absorption of a typical meal represented in Fig. 3 (left). These curves are quite similar to those measured in a real normal person [11]. In Fig. 4 (bottom), we report the curves of insulin and glucose we have obtained from a simulated diabetic person supplied with the anthropic agency during the absorption of the same meal. The graphs show that the result obtained by the adoption of the proposed multiagent regulator are close to the target ones. The high frequency oscillations of insulin in the bottom left graph are due to the asynchrony between the control system and the person simulation system. In such scenario, the decisional agent that controls the meal absorption effects has greater importance (see the discussion in Section 3) than the other one.

In Fig. 5 (top), we report the curves of insulin and glucose we have obtained from a simulated normal person during an intense physical activity session represented in Fig. 3 (right). Also these curves are quite similar to those measured on a real normal person [12]. In Fig. 5 (bottom), we report the curves of insulin and glucose we have obtained from a simulated diabetic person supplied with the anthropic agency during the same physical activity session. The graphs show that the result obtained by the adoption of the proposed multiagent regulator are close to the target ones. In such scenario, the decisional agent that controls the physical activity effects has a greater importance than the other one.

Finally, in Fig. 6, we report the curves of insulin and glucose we have obtained from a simulated diabetic person supplied with the anthropic agency during both the meal absorption and the physical activity session of Fig. 3. Also in this case,

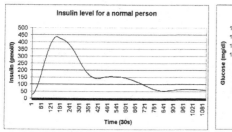

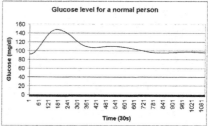

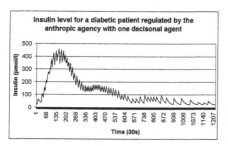

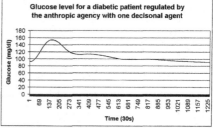

Fig. 4. The insulin and glucose curves of a normal person (top) and of a diabetic patient subject to the regulation activity of the anthropic agency (bottom) when eating according to the absorption curve in Fig. 3 (left)

the results are satisfactory since the curves account for both meal absorption and physical activity.

In general, the simulations we performed, of which we reported here only a part, allowed us to evaluate the response time, the stability, and other properties of our implemented anthropic agency. Let us start from the response time. Even when the machine is heavy loaded, namely when all the agents of the agency are simulated on a single computer, the response time to changes in the state of the simulated patient has always been less than 30s. Since the requirements are on the order of few minutes (see the beginning of this section), such result guarantees that our system based on the anthropic agency approach for the glucose-insulin metabolism regulation reacts correctly. The stability has been proved, initially, for the regulating agency with a single decisional agent (these simulations are not shown here). In addition, it has been proved the stability of the agency with two decisional agents (see for example Fig. 6), demonstrating that the introduction of a new decisional agent in the agency does not corrupt the stability of the system. This is a promising result that envisages the possibility to experimentally prove the stability of our negotiation mechanism also with a larger number of decisional agents. In conclusion, the simulations we have performed (varying the conditions, such as the importance of the decisional agents and the negotiation parameters) have demonstrated that the interaction between the two control models embedded in the decisional agents leads to a stable and quick (with

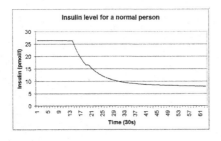
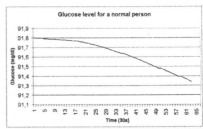
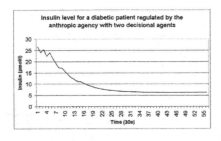
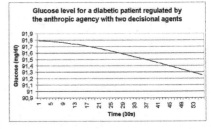

Fig. 5. The insulin and glucose curves of a normal person (top) and of a diabetic patient subject to the regulation activity of the anthropic agency (bottom) when undergoing the physical activity of Fig. 3 (right)

respect to the time dynamics of the glucose-insulin metabolism) regulation of the glucose and insulin levels in a diabetic patient in three different scenarios: meal absorption, physical activity, and their combination.

5   Conclusions

In this paper we have illustrated why an adequate simulation activity is needed for the evaluation of the effects of different controllers on physiological processes. The discussion has been set in the scenario of anthropic agency approach we developed. This approach is expected to produce multiagent regulators that operate on real persons. The simulation is indispensable since, on the one hand, the physiological processes usually are not adequately regulated by classical dynamic systems controllers due to their distributed complexity discussed in Section 2 and, on the other hand, for multiagent-based regulators it is difficult to mathematically prove properties such as those related to stability and response time. As a practical case, we have shown how the simulation can be useful to assess properties for the controllers related to the glucose-insulin metabolism we implemented.

Future work will address the evolution of the glucose-insulin regulator system with the insertion of new controllers (i.e., decisional agents). In this way, we intend to evaluate the scalability of our architecture, especially in relation with

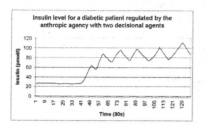
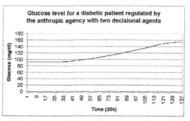

Fig. 6. The insulin and glucose curves of a diabetic patient when absorbing food and undergoing the physical activity according to the curves of Fig. 3, and subject to the regulation activity of the anthropic agency

the centralized communication management provided by the two blackboards. Moreover, we plan to compare, both from a theoretical and from an experimental point of view, our approach to regulation with other control techniques (e.g., those based on dynamic systems). Moreover, we aim to apply the anthropic agency paradigm to new applications, in particular to the regulation of the pacemaker frequency in order to assess the impact on our implementation of a time interval of about $1s$. This new application will allow us to study the relations between the anthropic agency architecture, its negotiation mechanism, and the time intervals required by different controlled processes. Finally, an important issue to address is the qualitative and quantitative evaluation of different alternative ways to decompose a complex physiological phenomenon and the related controller.

Acknowledgements. The authors are glad to thanks the fruitful discussions with Marco Somalvico, the contributions of Marco Dini and Martino Noris, and the valuable comments and suggestions from the three reviewers and the workshop attendees.

References

1. Goldberger, A.L., West, B.J.: Chaos in physiology: health or disease. In Holteon, A., Olsen, L.F., eds.: Chaos in Biological Systems. Plenum Press (1987) 1–5
2. Amigoni, F., Gatti, N., Somalvico, M.: A multiagent interaction paradigm for physiological process control. In: Proceedings of the First International Joint Conference on Autonomous Agents and Multiagent Systems, Part 1, Bologna, Italy (2002) 215–216
3. Amigoni, F., Dini, M., Gatti, N., Somalvico, M.: Anthropic agency: a multi agent system for physiological processes. Artificial Intelligence in Medicine (2003) In press.
4. Moss, S., Davidsson, P., eds.: Multi Agent Based Simulation. Springer Verlag (2000) LNCS series 1979.

5. Davidsson, P.: Multi agent based simulation: Beyond social simulation. In Moss, S., Davidsson, P., eds.: Multi Agent Based Simulation. Springer Verlag (2000) LNCS series 1979.

6. Amigoni, F., Schiaffonati, V., Somalvico, M.: Dynamic agency: Models for creative production and technology applications. In Riva, G., Davide, F., eds.: Communications Through Virtual Technology: Identity, Community, and Technology in Internet Age. IOS Press (2001) 167–192

7. Minsky, M.: The Society of Mind. Simon & Schuster, New York, USA (1985)

8. West, B.J.: Fractal Physiology and Chaos in Medicine. World Scientific (1990)

9. Lee, J.J., Norris, W.D., Fishwick, P.A.: An object-oriented multimodel approach to integrate planning, intelligent control and simulation. In: Proceedings of the Fourth Annual Conference on AI, Simulation, and Planning in High Autonomy Systems. (1993) 267–273

10. Wooldridge, M., Jennings, N.R.: Intelligent agents: Theory and practice. Knowledge Engineering Review **10** (1995) 115–152

11. Cobelli, C., Nucci, G., Prato, S.D.: A physiological simulation model of the glucose-insulin system. In: Proceedings of the First Joint Meeting BMES/EMBS Conference, Atlanta, GA, IEEE Computer Society Press (1999)

12. Rutscher, A., Salzsieder, E., Fischer, U.: Kadis: Model-aided education in type i diabetes, karlsburg diabetes management system. Comput-Methods-Programs-Biomed. **41** (1994) 205–215

13. Waldhausl, W.K., Bratusch-Marrain, P., Komjati, M., Breitenecker, F., Troch, I.: Blood glucose response to stress hormone exposure in healthy man and insulin dependent diabetic patients: Prediction by computer modeling. IEEE Transaction on Biomedical Engineering **39** (1992) 779–790

14. Davidsson, P.: Agent based social simulation: A computer science view. Journal of Artificial Societies and Social Simulation **5** (2002) http://jasss.soc.surrey.ac.uk/5/1/7.html.

15. Amigoni, F., Somalvico, M., Zanisi, D.: A theoretical framework for the conception of agency. International Journal of Intelligent Systems **14** (1999) 449–474

16. Weiss, G.: Multiagent Systems: A modern approach to distributed Artificial Intelligence. The MIT Press, Cambridge, MA, USA (1999)

Multi-agent Patrolling: An Empirical Analysis of Alternative Architectures

Aydano Machado[1], Geber Ramalho[1], Jean-Daniel Zucker[2], and Alexis Drogoul[2]

[1] Centro de Informática (CIn) – Universidade Federal de Pernambuco
Caixa Postal: 7851
50732-970 Recife-PE Brasil
{apm, glr}@cin.ufpe.br

[2] Laboratoire d'Informatique de Paris VI (LIP6) – Université Paris 6
Boîte 169 – 4 Place Jussieu
75252 PARIS CEDEX 05
{Jean-Daniel.Zucker, Alexis.Drogoul}@lip6.fr

Abstract. A group of agents can be used to perform patrolling tasks in a variety of domains ranging from computer network administration to computer wargame simulations. Despite its wide range of potential applications, multi-agent architectures for patrolling have not been studied in depth yet. First state of the art approaches used to deal with related problems cannot be easily adapted to the patrolling task specificity. Second, the existing patrolling-specific approaches are still in preliminary stages. In this paper, we present an original in-depth discussion of multi-agent patrolling task issues, as well as an empirical evaluation of possible solutions. In order to accomplish this study we have proposed different architectures of multi-agent systems, various evaluation criteria, two experimental scenarios, and we have implemented a patrolling simulator. The results show which kind of architecture can patrol an area more adequately according to the circumstances.

1 Introduction

To patrol is literally "the act of walking or travelling around an area, at regular intervals, in order to protect or supervise it" [1]. This task is by nature a multi-agent task and there are a wide variety of problems that may reformulate as particular patrol task. As a concrete example, during the development of the Artificial Intelligent component of an interactive computer wargame, we did face the problem of coordinating a group of units to patrol a given rough terrain in order to detect the presence of "enemies". The quality of the agent architecture used for patrolling may be evaluated using different measures. Informally, a good strategy is one that minimizes the time lag between two passages to the same place and for all places.

Beyond simulators and computer games, performing this patrolling task efficiently can be useful for various application domains where distributed surveillance, inspection or control are requires. For instance, patrolling agents can be used for helping administrators in the surveillance of failures or specific situations in a Intranet [2], for detecting recently modified or new web pages to be indexed by search engines

J.S. Sichman, F. Bousquet, P. Davidsson (Eds.): MABS 2002, LNAI 2581, pp. 155-170, 2003.

[6], for identifying objects or people in dangerous situations that should be rescued by robots [14], etc.

Despite its relevance, the patrolling task has not been seriously studied yet. On one hand, the literature has sound works concerning related studies, such as network mapping [10], the El Farol [4], steering behaviors [3, 5, 13]. However, these studies' characteristics are quite different from the patrolling task, which requires specific solutions. On the other hand, the works devoted precisely to patrolling tasks [9, 11, 12] do not present a systematic evaluation of the possible coordination strategies, agent models, agent society organizations, communication constraints, and so on.

In this paper we present an original in-depth analysis of the patrolling task issues and the possible multi-agent-based solutions. To do this study we followed a methodology. First, we have defined some criteria for evaluating the solutions. Second, we have proposed several multi-agent architectures varying parameters such as agent type (reactive vs. cognitive), agent communication (allowed vs. forbidden), coordination scheme (central and explicit vs. emergent), agent perception (local vs. global), decision-making (random selection vs. goal-oriented selection), etc. Third, we have implemented a dedicated simulator to enable the experimental tests. Fourth, we have tested the different solutions using two scenarios.

The remainder of this paper is organized as follows. Next section defines precisely what we mean by the patrolling tasks. Section 3 shows the main steps we have followed in our study according to the methodology we mentioned early. Section 4 presents the results and the discussion about them. Section 5 draws some conclusions and indicates directions for future work.

2 The Patrolling Task

There are many situations where one needs to protect, rescue, search, detect, oversee or track either something or someone. Computers can already perform these tasks in virtual worlds (such as those of computer games or computer networks) and, probably, in real world in a near future [17]. These tasks can involve some sort of patrolling, which may exhibits slightly different characteristics according to the domain and circumstances. It is then necessary, for our study, to have a more precise definition of patrolling.

In terms of area, the most complex case is the patrolling of continuous terrain, since the search space is large [16]. In these cases, one of the techniques used to change the representation of the terrain is *skeletonization* [15, 16], which consist of replacing the real terrain by a graph (skeleton) representing the possible paths as shown in Fig. 1. Voronoi diagrams, visibility graphs and C-cells can be used to generate such a graph. Once the terrain abstraction is available, the patrolling task is equivalent. A further advantage of adopting such an abstract representation is that the patrolling solutions proposed to it can be applied to different kind of problems, from terrain motion to web navigation.

Given a graph, the patrolling task refers to continuously visiting all the graph nodes so as to minimize the time lag between two visits.

There are some variations in the graph to be patrolled. In some situations, such as a terrain containing mobile obstacles, the graph edges may change. In other situations, priorities may be set to some regions covered by sub-graphs. The edges may have different associated lengths (weights) corresponding to the real distance between the nodes.

In our case study, we have reduced the patrol task to graphs with the following characteristics: static edges (no mobile obstacles in the terrain), unitary edged length (the distance between two connected nodes is one), uniform patrolling (the same priority for all nodes). In other words, given N agents, K nodes, connected by edges with equal weights, the patrolling problem is to achieve a global behavior that minimizes the time lag in which any agent has not visited a node.

3 Methodology

As discussed in the introduction, despite the applicability of multi-agent systems for patrolling tasks, as far as we know, there is no systematic study concerning the subject in the literature. In particular, various questions remain opened, such as: which kind of multi-agent system (MAS) architecture should be chosen by the MAS designer for a given patrolling task? What are the means to evaluate an implemented MAS? To what extent parameters, like size and connectivity, influence the overall MAS performance?

To answer these questions we have adopted a methodology that consists of the following steps: definition of performance measures, proposition of different MAS architectures, definition of some case studies (patrolling scenarios), and the implementation of the simulator to perform the experiments. These steps will be explained in the rest of this session.

3.1 Evaluation Criteria

One of the contributions of our work lies in the choice of evaluation criteria for comparing different MAS architectures, since defining performance measures adapted to the patrolling task is still an open problem in the related works [9, 11, 12]. As discussed next, we have chosen the following evaluation criteria: idleness, worst idleness and exploration time. Other criteria could have been adopted, but the ones we propose are adequate to measure the quality of the solutions.

Considering that a cycle is the time necessary for an agent to go from a node to an adjacent one, we call *instantaneous node idleness* the number of cycles that a node has remained unvisited. This *instantaneous node idleness* is measured at each cycle. The *instantaneous graph idleness* is the average instantaneous idleness of all nodes in a given cycle. Finally, the *graph idleness,* or simply idleness, is the average *instantaneous graph idleness* over n-cycle simulation.

In the same context, another interesting measure is the *worst idleness,* i.e. the biggest value of instantaneous node idleness occurred during the whole simulation.

The last evaluation criterion is, what we call the *exploration time,* which consists of the number of cycles necessary to the agents to visit, at least once, all nodes of the graph. This corresponds intuitively to the notion of exploring an area in order to create its geographic diagram.

These performance measures naturally tend to exhibits better results as the number of agents patrolling the graph grows. However, if the coordination among the agents is not good enough, the improvement caused by the insertion of new agents may be minimized. In order to measure coordination quality, as the number of agents augments, we have decided to measure the individual contribution of the agents, normalizing the three criteria (idleness, worst idleness and exploration time) as stated in equation (1):

$$normalized \_ value = absolute \_ value \times \frac{number \_ of \_ agents}{number \_ of \_ nodes} \tag{1}$$

3.2 Multi-agent Systems to Be Investigated

In order to define the MAS architectures that would be interesting to be evaluated in the patrolling task, we have explored four basic parameters (as displayed in Table 1). Of course, other parameters could have been taken into account, but the idea underlying our choice was to explore the choice of agent architectures described in the literature in a methodological way. This bottom-up and incremental approach to agent design has been shown to be essential for understanding and measuring the impact of these architectures on the dynamics of a collective problem-solving process [19]. The architectures displayed in Table 1 follow this principle. In the same way, we have only considered homogeneous groups of agents (i.e., all the agents share the same architecture), except, of course, the last two ones, which require an explicit coordinator agent

Table 1. Resume of the main features of the chosen agents.

Architecture Name	Basic Type	Communication	Next Node Choice	Coordination Strategy
Random Reactive	reactive	none	locally random	emergent
Conscientious Reactive			locally individual idleness	
Reactive with Flags		flags	locally shared idleness	
Conscientious Cognitive	cognitive	none	globally individual idleness	
Blackboard Cognitive		blackboard	globally shared idleness	
Random Coordinator		messages	globally random	central
Idleness Coordinator			globally shared idleness	

Straightforwardly, the first parameter we have considered is the classical difference between reactive and cognitive agents: whereas reactive agents simply act based on their current perception, cognitive ones may pursue a goal. A further and natural constraint we have imposed is that the field of vision of reactive agents is one-node depth, i.e., a reactive agent only perceives the adjacent nodes. This follows the fact that reactive agents can not, by definition, plan a path to distant nodes. Cognitive agents can perceive a depth d $(d > 1)$ of graph, in this work the agents can perceive the whole graph and use *path-finding* techniques (Floyd-Warshall Algorithm in our case) to reach any goal-node.

An important issue in performing collectively a patrolling task is the communication among the agents. Taking into account the real-word situations agents may face while patrolling, there are roughly three ways for the agents communicate to each other: via *flags*, via *blackboard*, and via *messages*. In the first case, agents leave flags or marks in the environment [7, 8]. These marks are recognized by themselves or by the other agents. In the second case, the information about the environment is stored in a common base (e.g., a command and control center) that can be accessed by all agents. In the last case, agents can communicate with the others directly by exchanging *messages*. In a first moment, the agents can only exchange messages with the coordinator, when it exists. Enabling this kind of communication among all agents would require more complex architectures, including, for instance, negotiation mechanisms for conflict solving, such as the next node choice.

Decision-making is also an important point in generating possible solutions. In other words, the question is to determine how the *next node* will be chosen. Two aspects should be considered: the field of vision, which can be *local* or *global* as discussed earlier; and the choice criteria, which can be random or heuristically based on node idleness. In the node idleness case, there are two variations depending on whether an agent knows about what the other agents have been doing. In the *individual idleness* heuristic, the agent considers only its own visits, whereas in the *shared idleness* heuristic, it takes into account the movement of all agents. Choosing nodes according to the individual idleness is equivalent to follow a gradient, as this technique is used in multi-agent systems [3, 5].

Finally, a key aspect in multi-agent movement coordination is to use a central coordinator, which chooses the goal-node of each (cognitive) agent, or a decentralized one, where coordination emerges from agent interaction.

There are several possible MAS architectures of combining these four parameters. We have studied all of them and then chosen the ones that seemed to be the most appropriated to the task (Cf. Table 1, column 1).

We have also considered another coordination parameter (not shown in Table 1): the *monitoring capability*. While a cognitive agent is following a path to its goal-node, it is useful to monitor whether any other agent is visiting this given node in the meantime in order to reassign another goal. After the first experiments, we have noticed that agents with monitoring capabilities always performed better than the equivalent agents without monitoring. In order to keep the presentation of results graphics more readable, we have just included in this paper the agents capable of monitoring (whenever monitoring is feasible), i.e. Blackboard Cognitive Agent, Random Coordinator and Idleness Coordinator.

3.3 Experiment Scenarios

After reflecting about the influence the environment parameters could have on the system performance, we have realized that more than the number of nodes, it is important to control the graph connectivity, i.e. the number of edges. In this perspective, we have created two different maps (as shown on Fig. 1). Map A has few obstacles and a highly connected graph, representing the fact that it is easy to go to any region. Map B has some bottlenecks, generating a graph with the same number of nodes but with much fewer edges.

Instead of changing the number of nodes, we have equivalently changed the number of agents. We have used populations of 1, 2, 5, 10, 15, and 25 agents in order to keep adequate ratios between the number of nodes (50) and the number of agents.

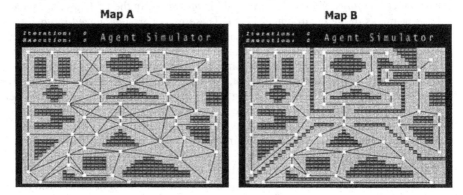

Fig. 1. Maps A and B in our simulator. Black blocks in the maps represent obstacles. The graphs of possible paths are shown. The graph of Map A has 106 edges and 50 nodes, and the graph of Map B, with more bottlenecks, has 69 edges and the same 50 nodes. These figures are also snapshots of the simulator.

3.4 Simulator

In order to accomplish a larger number of experiments, we have developed a dedicated simulator using C++/OpenGL, which is a commonly used development platform in computer games community. This simulator implements the agents defined in Table 1 and emulates the patrolling task recording the data for later analysis.

A map is described in a proprietary format, allowing the researcher to indicate all the characteristics of environment, such as the size of the map, the obstacles, the graph, the agents initial position, the number and kind of MAS architecture to use (according to Table 1), the number of steps to run, etc.

4 Experimental Results and Discussion

For each of the seven MAS architectures of Table 1 (column 1), we have run 360 (2 x 6 x 30) simulations, corresponding to 2 maps (A and B), six different number of agents (1, 2, 5, 10, 15 and 25) and 30 different staring points (i.e., initial positions of the agents). The 30 initial positions are randomly chosen once and then used in testing the different architectures.

Each simulation is composed of 3000 cycles, i.e. the agents change from a node to another 3000 times. At the beginning of simulation, we consider that all instantaneous node idleness is zero, as they had just been visited. Consequently, there is a sort of transitory phase in which the instantaneous graph idleness tends to be low, not corresponding to the reality in a steady-state phase, as shown in Fig. 2. For this reason, the (final) graph idleness is measured only during the stable phase. According to some early experiments, we have noticed that the transitory phase always finishes before the cycle 750 (except for the Random Reactive Agents and the Random coordinator whose behavior may sometimes be highly unstable). The graph idleness is the measured along the remaining 2250 cycles.

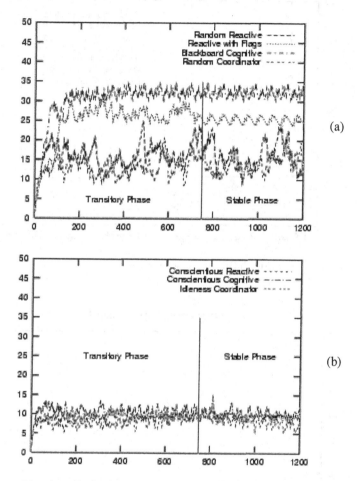

(a)

(b)

Fig. 2. The graphics show the evolution of 5 agents during a simulation (idleness in y-axis and cycles in x axis).

4.1 Results Graphics

In the following graphics, each different line type represents a different MAS architecture and the vertical bars show the standard deviations on the average calculated from the 30 variations of initial position of agents. The graphics are shown in pairs, showing respectively the absolute and normalized performances.

Fig. 3 and Fig. 4 show the graph idleness measures (in y-axis), and the corresponding normalized value, in Map A respectively, as the number of agents grows (x-axis).

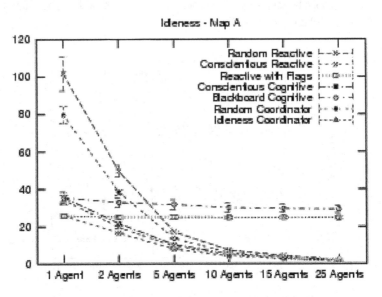

Fig. 3. Graph representing Idleness for Map A.

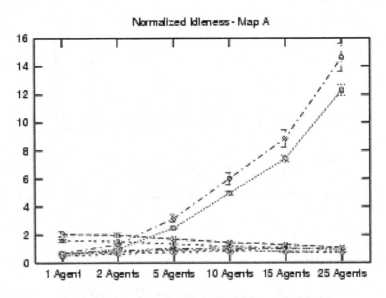

Fig. 4. Graph representing Normalized Idleness for Map A.

Fig. 5 and Fig. 6 show the graph idleness measures (in y-axis), and the corresponding normalized value, in Map B respectively, as the number of agents grows (x-axis).

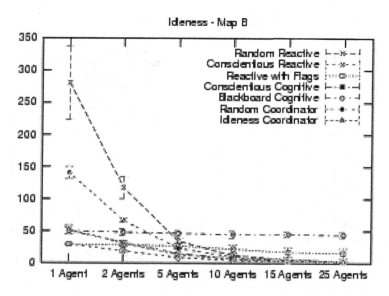

Fig. 5. Graph Idleness for Map B.

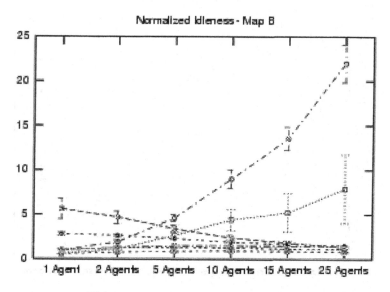

Fig. 6. Graph Normalized Idleness for Map B.

Similarly, Fig. 7 and Fig. 8 present the results of the graph worst idleness. The main difference in this case is that worst idleness is measured over the 3000 cycles, whereas (average) idleness does only consider the stable phase.

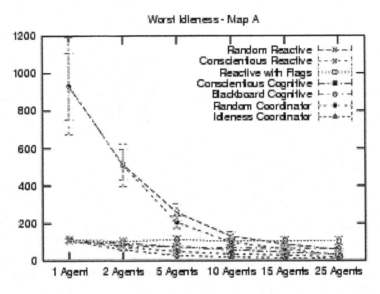

Fig. 7. Graph Worst Idleness in Map A.

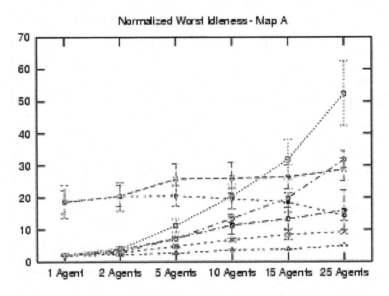

Fig. 8. Graph Normalized Worst Idleness in Map A.

Fig. 9 and Fig. 10 present the results of the graph worst idleness, in Map B, and the corresponding normalized value.

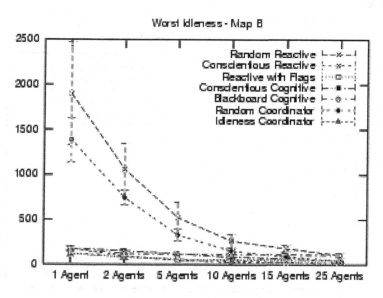

Fig. 9. Graph of Worst Idleness in Map B.

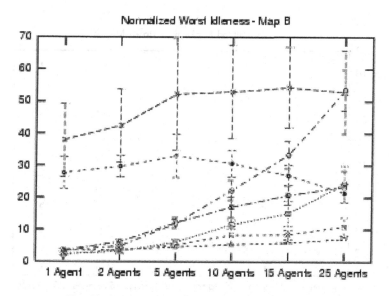

Fig. 10. Graph of Normalized Worst Idleness in Map B.

As opposed to previous graphics, Fig. 11 (resp. Fig. 12) plots the number of cycles (resp. normalized number of cycles) required for a complete exploration of the Map A.

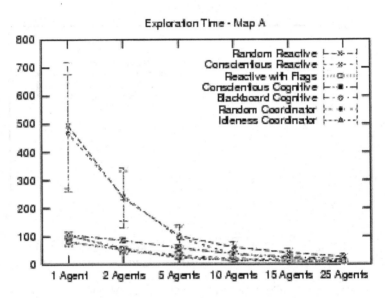

Fig. 11. Graph Exploration Time in Map A.

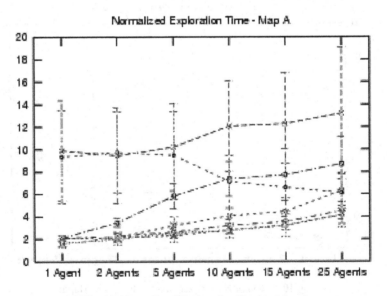

Fig. 12. Normalized Exploration Time in Map A.

As opposed to previous graphics, Fig. 13 (resp. Fig. 14) plots the number of cycles (resp. normalized number of cycles) required for a complete exploration of the Map B.

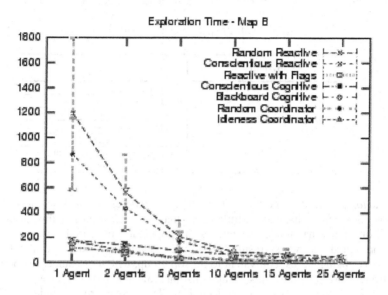

Fig. 13. Graph Exploration Time in Map B.

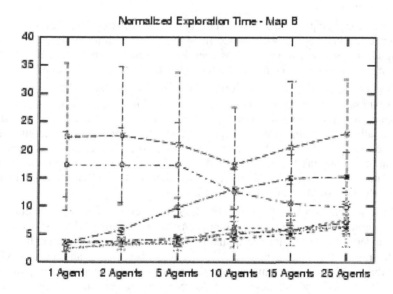

Fig. 14. Normalized Exploration Time in Map B.

4.2. Discussion

From a general perspective, we can see three distinct groups which we call *random*, *"non-coordinated"* and *top group*. Table 2 indicates the composition of each group.

Table 2. MAS acrchitecture groups

Group	Agents
Random Group	Random Reactive Agent
	Random Coordinator
Non-coordinated Group	Reactive Agent with Flags
	Blackboard Cognitive Agent
Top Group	Conscientious Reactive Agent
	Conscientious Cognitive Agent
	Idleness Coordinator

The *top group* obtained the best results in all metrics. The Conscientious Reactive Agent performance has been a little better that the other agents of this group, but this small difference has tended to zero as the population increased. The *random group* has presented the worst results for small populations. These results have been improved, being almost equivalent to the top group, with more numerous populations. A strong characteristic of this group is its unpredictable behavior (there is not exactly a "stable phase"), which is reflected in large standard deviations. The *non-coordinated group* presented an expected behavior: every agent tends to go to the same places at the same moment. Consequently, the groups somehow behave as a single agent.

Concerning Map A vs. Map B. (i.e., graph connectivity) the multi-agent system performance has been always worse in Map B than in Map A, in all experiments, using all metrics. The *top group* has been less affected by the bottlenecks in Map B. The *random group* was the most affected, with truly bad results in Map B.

The *normalized results* are very interesting since they show the individual contribution of each agent in the architecture. Moreover, the normalized results indicate clearly the coordination capability of a given architecture: the best is the coordination, the strongest is the impact of adding new agents to the architecture. For instance, the performance of the non-coordinated group is even worse considering the normalized measured. Regarding the *exploration time*, curiously increasing population does not yield a significant increasing of the individual performance, no matter the kind of MAS architecture used.

Besides identifying the top group of MAS architectures, these experiments show us some preliminary guidelines in designing MAS for patrolling. The first and main step is to understand the application domain constraints and characteristics. It is essential to determine the path graph in terms of number nodes and connectivity, the availability of agent communication, the maximum accepted idleness, the desired average idleness and idleness variation over the cycles, and the necessity of an exploration phase and the maximum time lag for it. Knowing these characteristics, it will be easier to choose the best MAS architecture. For instance, for graphs containing bottlenecks, random approaches are not recommended. If no significant variation on idleness is desired, random approaches should also discard. Moreover, according to the desired idleness, the number of agents can be determined (the ratio one agent for 10 nodes yields enough good results).

5 Conclusions

This work presents a many-fold contribution to the problem of multi-agent patrolling. First, a general characterization of the multi-agent patrolling problem is given, and its wide range of application in a variety of domains is pinpointed. Second, the method proposed for evaluating different MAS architectures for patrolling is generic and meant to be used as a basis for future analysis. Third, different MAS architectures for patrolling are suggested as well as a preliminary typology, according to some coordination parameters (this typology follows the same approach we have been using in other tasks [18]). Finally, this work furnishes some preliminary guidelines for MAS designers interested in patrolling tasks.

The simulator developed for the purpose of this study is available upon request for other researchers interested in experimenting with their own patrolling strategy.

In the future we intend to augment the complexity of the agent and MAS architectures. This includes features such as different path-finding techniques, which instead of searching shortest paths take into account the instantaneous idleness of the nodes in-between the current location and the goal. In the same direction, we plan to use the exact distance between two nodes, instead of a unitary one, in order to use more realistic heuristics for choosing the next node. Finally, explicit communication between agents is another direction of exploration, which would give the opportunity to explore negotiations mechanisms for solving conflicts

References

1. Abate, Frank R.: The Oxford Dictionary and Thesaurus: The Ultimate Language Reference for American Readers. Oxford Univ. Press. 1996
2. Andrade, R. de C., Macedo, H. T., Ramalho, G. L., and Ferraz, C. A. G.: Distributed Mobile Autonomous Agents in Network Management. Proceedings of International Conference on Parallel and Distributed Processing Techniques and Applications, 2001
3. Arkin, Ronald C.: Behavior-Based Robot Navigation for Extended Domains. Adaptive Behaviors. Fall 1992, vol. 1(2):201–225
4. Arthur, W. B.: Inductive Reasoning and Bounded Rationality (The El Farol Problem). American Economic Review (1994) 84: 406–411.
5. Balch, Tucker and Arkin, Ronald C.: Behavior-Based Formation Control for Multi-robot Teams. IEEE Transactions on Robot and Automation (1999) vol. XX
6. Cho J., Garcia-Molina, H.: Synchronizing a database to Improve Freshness. In Proceedings of 2000 ACM International Conference on Management of Data (SIGMOD), May 2000.
7. Dorigo, M. Maniezzo, V. & Coloni, A. The Ant System: optimization by a colony of cooperating agents. IEE Tarns. System, Man and Cybernetics B26(1) (1996). 29–41
8. Ferber, Jacques: Multi-Agent Systems: An Introduction to Distributed Artificial Intelligence. Addison-Wesley (1999) 439–445.
9. Howland, Geoff: A Practical Guide to Building a Complete Game AI: Volume II. http://www.lupinegames.com/articles/prac_ai_2.html, 1999

10. Minar N., Hultman K, and Maes P. Cooperating Mobile Agents for Mapping Networks. In the Proceedings of the First Hungarian National Conference on Agent Based Computing, 1998

11. Pottinger, Dave C.: Coordinated Unit Movement. Game Developer (January 1999) 42–51

12. Pottinger, Dave C.: Implementing Coordinated Unit Movement. Game Developer (February 1999) 48–58

13. Reynolds, C.W.: Steering Behaviors for Autonomous Characters. Presented at Game Developers Conference (1999). http://www.red3d.com/cwr/steer/

14. RoboCup Rescue home page: http://www.r.cs.kobe-u.ac.jp/robocup-rescue/, 2001.

15. Russell, Stuart J. and Norvig, P.: Artificial Intelligence: A Modern Approach. Prentice Hall (1995) 796–808

16. Stout, Brian W.: Smart Moves: Intelligent Path-Finding. Game Developer (October/ November 1996) 28–35

17. Sukthankar, G. and Sycara K.: Team-aware Robotic Demining Agents for Military Simulation. Robotics Institute - Carnegie Mellon University.
    http://www-2.cs.cmu.edu/~softagents/iaai00/iaai00.html, 2000.

18. Zucker, J.-D. and C. Meyer. Apprentissage pour l'anticipation de comportements de joueurs humains dans les jeux à information complète et imparfaite: les "Mind-Reading Machines". Revue d'Intelligence Artificielle 14(3-4). (2000). 313–338

19. Drogoul, A. et A. Collinot. Applying an Agent-Oriented Methodology to the Design of Artificial Organizations: a Case Study in Robotic Soccer. *Journal of Autonomous Agents and Multi-Agent Systems* 1(1): 113–129. 1998

On Multi Agent Based Simulation of Software Development Processes

Tham Wickenberg and Paul Davidsson

Department of Software Engineering and Computer Science,
Blekinge Institute of Technology
Soft Center, 372 25 Ronneby, Sweden
{Tham.Wickenberg,Paul.Davidsson}@bth.se
http://www.ide.bth.se/~pdv

Abstract. The simulation of software development processes is gaining increasing interest within both academia and industry. The reasons for making this kind of simulations range from supporting strategic and operational management of software development projects to process improvement and understanding. Despite the fact that the process of developing software is performed by a set of cooperating individuals, most approaches to simulate this process are using a centralistic activity-based view rather than an individual-based view. It is possible to use both of these approaches for any particular simulation problem, but in most cases one of them is much more suitable than the other, and in many situation only one is practically feasible. In this paper we will investigate the applicability of Multi Agent Based Simulation (MABS) for simulating software development processes. The result is a set of general guidelines concerning when to use MABS as well as three concrete examples where MABS seem particularly promising.

1 Introduction

A software development process (SDP) can be viewed as a set of activities performed by a set of developers. The result of a SDP is a set of artifacts, some of which are produced to support subsequent development activities. The activities and the order in which they will be performed are planned in the early stages of a development project, usually according to some predefined process. Activities can be for example requirements elicitation, architectural analysis, unit test specification, programming, or designing a use case. Most activities take some artifacts as input and produce one or more new or altered artifacts as output. For instance, in the Rational Unified Process model [12], architectural analysis is defined as an activity that takes a use case model, supplementary requirements, a business model and an architecture description as input. The output of the activity is defined as an outlined analysis package, an outlined analysis class and a modified architecture description.

The software development industry has a long track record of failing to meet expectations in terms of cost, quality and schedule. Focus of the community has been turned to the SDP in order to reduce cost and schedule time, increase quality and to allow predictions of these variables during a development effort. Static SDP models have been used with some success to make better predictions, and empirical

J.S. Sichman, F. Bousquet, P. Davidsson (Eds.): MABS 2002, LNAI 2581, pp. 171-180, 2003.

investigations have lead to an improved understanding of how activities affect, and are affected by, the artifacts they manipulate. Less is known however about the effects of combining different activities, and how they relate to the organization in which they are performed. Changing the way in which an organization develops software may lead to significant cost reduction and improvement of quality, but the cost of implementing the changes may be high. One approach to the study and prediction of the dynamics of SDP is simulation. The simulation of software development processes is gaining increasing interest within both academia and industry. An expression of this interest is the annual ProSim (Software Process Simulation Modeling) workshop, which had its first meeting in 1998.

The reasons for simulating SDPs range from supporting strategic and operational management of software development projects to process improvement and understanding. Despite the fact that the process of developing software is performed by a set of cooperating individuals, most approaches to simulate this process are using a centralistic activity-based view rather than an individual-based view. It is likely that it is possible to use both of these approaches for any particular simulation problem, but in most cases one of them is much more suitable than the other, and in many situation only one is practically feasible. In this paper we will investigate the applicability of individual-based simulation, or Multi Agent Based Simulation (MABS) which we also will call this approach, for simulating software development processes.

In the next chapter we will describe the field of SDP simulation and compare current approaches with individual-based approaches. The result is a set of general guidelines concerning when to use MABS for SDP simulation. We conclude by presenting three concrete examples where MABS seem particularly promising.

2   Simulation of Software Development Processes

We will in this section try to give a brief introduction to the problems that SDP simulation currently address and how the scope and abstractions of the simulation model are selected. We will also describe the simulation techniques and approaches that are currently being used, and discuss some of their limitations.

2.1   Why Simulate Software Development Processes?

Software development processes and organizations are complex and it is therefore often hard to predict how changes made to some part of the process or organization will affect other parts and the outcome of the process as a whole. Making changes to the process is often time consuming and generally only one process change can be performed at the time. Moreover, as there is no guarantee that the change imposed on the process is actually an improvement, managers are typically hesitant to experimentation. Simulation is a relatively cost efficient way to allow developers and managers to elaborate with many different configurations of the process, and understand the effects of various policies.

SDP simulation may serve a variety of objectives. It can be used, as a method for gaining better understanding of the development process in general, in these cases, the goal is to achieve some generally applicable knowledge about some part(s) of the SDP. Alternatively, it can be used to better understand a specific project or organization to forecast the outcome as a support for risk management, planning, strategic management or some other decision-making activities.

2.2   What to Simulate?

The scope of the simulation model needs to be large enough to fully address the main questions posed. This often requires an understanding also of the implications of these questions. For instance, a change in an early part of the SDP may cause impact also in later parts of the process, which must be taken into account when assessing the overall project performance. Therefore, the scope may vary from a small part of an SDP, such as requirements elicitation, to covering the complete process. Really large simulation studies may even include long-term software evolution covering several releases of a software product, or long-term organizational development. Thus, the scope may vary in at least three dimensions:

- the time span, which may vary from months to years,
- the entity being developed, which may vary from parts of a product to multiple products, and
- the organizational breadth, which may vary from parts of a team of developers to multiple teams of developers.

The result variables should hold the information needed to answer the key questions of the simulation study. These variables, which are heavily dependent of the key questions, could be of many different types. However, Kellner et al. [8] has listed the most common result variables:

- Effort/cost
- Cycle-time (a.k.a. duration, schedule, time to market, interval)
- Defect level
- Staffing requirements over time
- Staff utilization rate
- Cost / benefit, return on investment, or other economic measures
- Throughput / productivity
- Queue length (backlogs)

When the purpose, scope and result variables have been selected the simulation modeler is confronted with selecting process abstractions and input parameters. The modeler identifies the key elements of the process, which are believed to significantly affect the result variables, and are relevant to the purpose of the model. Examples of such elements are: the key activities and tasks, the primary objects (e.g., code units, designs, and problem reports), and the vital resources (e.g., staff and hardware). Then the relationships between the identified elements need to be described, e.g., activity dependencies, flows of objects among activities, iteration loops, feedback loops, decision points, and other structural interdependencies (e.g., the effort to revise a code unit after an inspection, as a function of the number of defects found during the inspection) [8].

2.3   Current Approaches

Many different simulation techniques have been used to simulate SDPs [8] The most commonly used approaches in recent research are system dynamics (equation based modeling) [13, 6, 1], state based simulations [11, 7] and discrete event simulations [5]. Other techniques that have been used are rule-based languages [3] and Petri-net models [9].

Although many different simulations techniques have been used, all applications we have found so far focus on activities or phases rather than individuals. The SDP is modeled as a set of activities implicitly performed by developers in which some artifacts are produced in support of subsequent activities. Alternatively, the activities have people as input and output, for instance hiring or training staff. [1] What activities, and in which order they are performed is generally specified in a static and 'ideal' process model such as the analysis process shown in Fig. 1. Note that in a static process model activities are related to some 'role', (shown here in the upper left corner of each row), in the SDP, but this relationship is generally not taken into account in the simulation models.

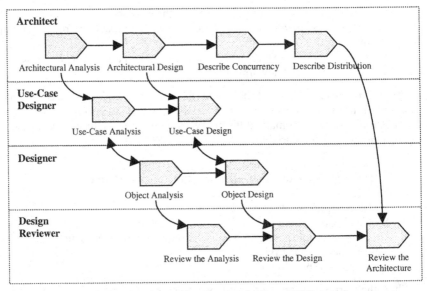

Fig. 1. An example of an activity-based SDP model.

In activity-based approaches, the software developers are described in terms of averages of all individual developers in the organization. For instance, the time taken to complete an activity is usually determined using an average productivity rate of all developers in the organization. Alternatively, the individuals are divided into a number of categories, and the number of individuals in each category is used to describe the state of the organization. One explanatory and somewhat representative example is from a report by Burke [1] where the staff members were categorized as for or against process improvements, and experienced or recently hired respectively. Rather than assigning these characteristics to individuals, the number of individuals belonging to each of the categories were modeled. In effect, the modelers are assuming homogeneity among the individuals, whereas the individuals in actual software development organizations are highly heterogeneous. A result from using system level variables to drive the simulation is that local variations in an organization cannot be predicted or explained. For example, Burke reported that one development team in the organization he modeled was far more efficient and more in favor of process improvement than other teams in the organization, something that could not be explained nor predicted in his model. Parunak et al. [10] have presented several examples where false assumptions of homogeneity in simulation models have lead to problems.

Another problem with activity-based approaches concerns how discrete decisions are modeled. In many SDP simulations, the SDP is modeled as a flow of activities according to a predefined process and decisions are not explicitly modeled at all. Other SDP simulations, such as most System Dynamics simulations, attempt to model management policies. However, these simulations suffer from some of the problems that arise when discrete decision-making is modeled using equation-based simulations, which have been discussed by Parunak et al. [10].

Kellner et al. [8] suggest that the most appropriate simulation modeling technique should be selected based on scope, result variables desired, etc. However, which approach is better suited for a certain situation is a question that has only been scarcely researched. Some guidance is given regarding the dimension of time. Kellner et al. [8] state that continuous time simulations (e.g., System Dynamics) tend to be more convenient for analyses above the detailed process level, whereas discrete event and state-based simulations tend to be more convenient for detailed process analyses. We will here investigate another dimension, namely activity-based vs. individual-based SDP simulation.

2.4   Individual-Based versus Activity-Based SDP Simulation

An alternative view of SDP is that it is performed by a set of individuals that have different characteristics and which interact with each other. These aspects are difficult to capture by more abstract activity-based approaches. An individual-based approach to SDP simulation could focus on individual staff members of a software development organization. The individuals interact either by communication, or by manipulation of artifacts such as design specifications or code units. When the simulation is executed we can observe characteristics of the interactions between the actors, and the effects thereof. The behavior of staff members could be captured on different abstraction levels depending on what aspect of the development is to be understood or predicted. On the very detailed level, we could (in principle) model conversation among developers during their work. At the other end of the scale, we could model the behavior in terms of staff joining/leaving the organization and making software process improvement suggestions. However, we are not limited to modeling people working in an organization, agents may also be useful to model different departments in an organization or even model the interaction between different development firms and their clients, thus allowing for even higher levels of abstraction.

A limitation in the applicability of MABS in the SDP simulation domain comes from the fact that the behavior of the individual developers is sometimes known only in terms of a predefined process, that is the flow of activities that constitutes the SDP. Little would be gained by modeling the system using agents to represent developers if both:

1. The behavior of the developers is defined in a way such that the behavior corresponds one to one with a predefined process.
2. Knowledge about the developers' behavior is limited to collective measures of how they perform during the specific activities.

Under such conditions the output from a simulation would be the same regardless of whether a centralistic or an individualistic approach were used. When two different simulation models produce the same output, the appropriate choice is the model that is more convenient to create. An activity-based model may be a better choice if individual behavior is known only in terms of a predetermined flow of activities in a predefined process because its representation is analogue to how the process is understood.

Modeling the individuals in the development organization may allow us to make better predictions if we have some knowledge about the performance of the individual developers. More accurate predictions could be made if statistics about individual behavior was collected either during development, or using some diagnostics method such as the Personal Software Process [4].

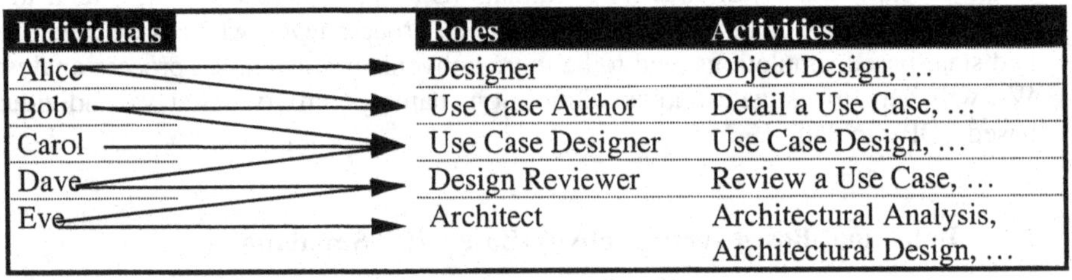

Individuals	Roles	Activities
Alice	Designer	Object Design, ...
Bob	Use Case Author	Detail a Use Case, ...
Carol	Use Case Designer	Use Case Design, ...
Dave	Design Reviewer	Review a Use Case, ...
Eve	Architect	Architectural Analysis, Architectural Design, ...

Fig. 2. An example of a set individuals and their roles and activities.

Another important advantage of individual-based SDP simulation is the ability to model behavior that does not exactly correspond to a predefined flow of activities. Although such a predefined flow of activities exists in most SDP models it is unlikely that the individuals always act accordingly. Sometimes behaviors that are difficult to include in the SDP model significantly affect the performance of an organization. An individual-based approach would allow us to model a predefined flow of activities together with initiatives and decisions made by individuals. When individuals in an organization make decisions they do so based on some personal or organizational goals and information or knowledge that is available to them. Furthermore, information that decisions are based on is often locally rather than globally available. An individual-based approach provides a convenient way to include this aspect of decisions made in an organization by using internalization to model what information is known by an individual at a given time. It also provides a natural way to model how an individual acquires information, e.g., by interacting with other individuals or with the local environment. The activity-based approach, on the other hand, lacks several means necessary to address these issues.

When focus is on the activity rather than the individual there is no natural way to represent information that is local to the individual, therefore the modeler is forced to view information either as globally available or restricted to activities. Most activity-based SDP simulation with a large organizational and time spans use equation-based models [8]. Discrete decisions and step-by-step processes are hard and sometimes even impossible to describe using equation-based models, they are also restricted in how they can represent physical space and interaction space [10]. The use of equation-based models therefore makes it harder to address issues of how decisions made by individuals with locally available information affect the performance of an SDP. Also, because of the difficulty in capturing step-by-step processes and discrete decisions, individual based modeling is preferable when management policies or other step-by-step behavior needs to be translated back into an organization [10].

3   MABS for SDP Simulation

In this chapter we will begin by giving some general guidelines of when to apply MABS for SDP simulation. We will then give some concrete examples of possible applications.

3.1   General Guidelines

The theoretical arguments presented so far seem to support the hypothesis that MABS can become an important complementary tool to the simulation techniques that are currently being used in SDP simulation. We have found that MABS is likely to be a more appropriate tool for SDP simulation than activity-based simulation techniques when:

1. The outcome of the SDP under study is determined by discrete decisions made by individuals interacting with each other and their environment.
2. There is a high degree of locality either in terms of characteristics of the environment, the individuals' characteristics, or of the availability of information.
3. We want to simulate a specific organization or project where the characteristics of the individual software developers are known.
4. We want to study the sensitivity of the SDP to individual characteristics, e.g., measure the impact of changes in behavior of individuals.
5. Management policies and other descriptions of individual behavior needs to be captured in the model or translated back into an organization.

Activity-based simulation is a more natural choice when the behavior of the individuals is known only in terms of a predefined flow of activities and it is reasonable to assume that the defined process is followed. Other important assumptions are that localization of information and characteristics of individuals do not significantly affect the outcome of the process.

Note that the applicability of an individual based approach is not limited to a certain organizational scope. Rather, the scope of the simulation affects which abstraction level the individuals are conveniently selected, and on which abstraction level the behavior of the individuals are most conveniently modeled.

3.2   Example 1: Comparing Extreme Programming and Feature Driven Development

When a new software development method is proposed there is often some debate over the benefits of this new approach. One possible gain from modeling individuals in the development process is that it may allow us to address cognitive and social aspects of software development. As an example of where modeling cognitive aspects of different activities could help improve our understanding of how a specific practice affects the rest of the process, we will study the concept of code ownership. We will compare Extreme Programming (XP), and Feature Driven Development (FDD). In XP collective ownership is practiced, i.e. any programmer is allowed to alter any piece of code (unit) when needed. In FDD, on the other hand, ownership of a unit is bestowed on a specific developer.

The advocates of XP sometimes argue that if a programmer 'A' needs to make changes to a certain unit of code, and the only person allowed to make those changes is programmer 'B', then 'A' will be unproductive while waiting for 'B' to finish what he is currently doing before and then make the changes. Another argument against unit ownership is that it creates a problem when a programmer leaves the development team or is absent for some other reason. Changes made to the unit now have to be made by a programmer that is unfamiliar with it, which leads to increased cost and pressed schedule. Advocates of FDD argue in favor of unit ownership. One argument is that because the owner of a unit is well familiarized with the unit, it will take less time for him to make changes to it. In order to understand which is the better choice of the two approaches, we need to know at least three things:

1. How the efficiency in making changes relates to familiarity with the unit, and how quickly a developer can familiarize with a unit.
2. How often programmers are absent, and how often they leave the development team.
3. How often a developer will depend on changes in a unit owned by someone else.

The first and second of these variables depend on the individual developers, whereas the third factor depends on other aspects of the process and organization as well as the dependencies among different units. By modeling the processes in sufficient detail, so that understanding can be reached on how other elements of the process affect how often collisions of this sort happen, and by modeling the effects of familiarity and learning, we can test under which conditions one practice is preferable to another, and thereby better understand the risks and potential benefits involved with using the two practices.

3.3   Example 2: Formation of Groups with Joint Mental Attitudes

The attitude of staff members may significantly affect the performance of an organization. One example is how attitudes towards improvement of the SDP affect the rate at which suggestions are made on how the process can be improved. Staff members that do not approve of changes in the process may leave the organization if the process changes too often and frequent process improvement may attract persons that are in favor of process improvements. It is possible to study the dynamic consequences of such aspects using an activity-based approach, for example Burke

[1] created a system dynamics model of a large software organization to study the long-term effects of Software Process Improvement (SPI) activities. We believe that an activity-based approach is preferable to an individual based approach to this type of problem for several reasons

One problem with an activity-based approach to this domain is that it uses collective measures of the staff members' characteristics. After interviewing experts in the organization Burke concluded that the staff members influenced each other's attitudes toward SPI. It was said that staff members where for or against process SPI or alternatively they had no opinion. Staff members that had no opinion were said to go along with the group of for/against SPI that where in majority. In effect, every staff member influenced all other staff members in the organization, and when the number of for exceeds the number of against SPI, all staff member without a preference changed their behavior simultaneously.

The natural way to model the same problem using an individual-based approach would be to model the staff members as influencing only staff members they communicate and interact with. It is also likely that a department or project with many employees in favor of process improvements would implement SPIs more frequently and therefore attract more employees in favor of SPI, thus creating local variation within the organization. It is most likely that this would affect the outcome of the simulation but it is difficult to predict its implications on the dynamics of the organization without implementing and executing the simulation model.

3.4 Example 3: Understanding Requirements Elicitation and Negotiation

Some interest in the SDP simulation community has been shown towards how simulation models can incorporate social aspects of software development. In particular, social aspects of requirements engineering has been addressed first by Christie et al. [2] and then revisited by Stallinger and Grunbach [13]. The authors of both articles use system dynamics to model the actors' characteristics, such as technical ability, ability to influence others and openness to influence from others. In [2] the system dynamics model was combined with a discrete event based technique for modeling activities in the process, but the authors report problems because of the different notions of time.

Individual based approaches using MABS afford more convenient creation and are likely to lead to less complicated models than activity-based or hybrid approaches when applied to this kind of problem where social, process-oriented and organizational aspects are modeled. This is partly because the problems of combining the different notions of time can be avoided, but more importantly because of representational advantages. MABS allows for a natural way to describe both communication between individuals, individual characteristics, and the discrete decisions made during the negotiations. Although these conclusions are only supported by experience from other application domains, we find them encouraging and well worth investigating further.

4 Conclusions and Future Work

We have suggested that MABS could be an important complement to the existing activity-based approaches to SDP simulation. Some general guidelines for choosing between these approaches have been provided, as well as three concrete examples where MABS seems more appropriate than an activity-based approach. It is our intention that the guidelines and their motivations presented here should provide a framework for future investigations into the field.

References

1. Burke S.: Radical Improvements Require Radical Actions: Simulating a High Maturity Software Organization. Technical Report, *CMU/SEI-96-TR-024 ESC-TR-96-024*, Carnegie Mellon University, Pittsburgh, Pennsylvania US 1997.
2. Christie A.M. and Staley J.M.: Organizational and Social Simulation of a Software Requirements Development Process. *Proceedings of the Software Process Simulation Modeling Workshop (ProSim 99)*, Silver Falls, Oregon, 1999.
3. Drappa A. and Ludewig J.: Quantitative Modeling for the Interactive Simulation of Software Projects. *Proceedings of the Software Process Simulation Modeling Workshop (ProSim 98)*, Silver Falls, OR, 1998.
4. Humphrey W.S.: The Personal Software Process. Technical Report CMU/SEI-2000-TR-022 ESC-TR-2000-022, Carnegie Mellon University, Pittsburgh, Pennsylvania US 2000.
5. Höst M., Regnell B., Lindesvärd J., and Nedstam J.: Exploring Bottlenecks in Market-Driven Requirements Management Processes with Discrete Event Simulation. *Proceedings of the Software Process Simulation Modeling Workshop (ProSim 2000)*, London, 2000.
6. Kahen G, Lehman M.M., Ramil J.F., and Werinck P.: Dynamic Modelling in the Investigation of Policies for E-type Software Evolution. *Proceedings of the Software Process Simulation Modeling Workshop (ProSim 2000)*, London, 2000.
7. Kellner M.I.: Software Process Modeling Support for Management Planning and Control. *Proceedings of the First International Conference on the Software Process*, IEEE Computer Society Press, Los Alamitos, California, pp. 8–28, 1991.
8. Kellner I., Madachy R., and Raffo D.M.: Software Process Modeling and Simulation: Why, What, How. *Journal of Systems and Software*, Vol. 46, No. 2/3, 1999.
9. Kusumoto., S., Mizuno O., Kikuno O., Hirayama Y., Takagi Y., and Sakamoto O.: A New Software Project Simulator Based on Generalized Stochastic Petri-net. *Proceedings of the 19th International Conference on Software Engineering (ICSE-19)*, IEEE Computer Society Press, California, pp. 293–302, 1997.
10. Parunak V.D., Savit R., and Riolo R.: Agent-Based Modeling vs. Equation-Based Modeling: A Case Study and Users Guide. *Proceedings of Multi-Agent Systems and Agent-Based Simulation (MABS'98)*, Lecture Notes of Artificial Intelligence Vol. 1534, Springer Verlag, Berlin Germany, 1998.
11. Raffo D.M. and Kellner M.I.: Analysing Process Improvements Using the Process Tradeoff Analysis Method. *Proceedings of the Software Process Simulation Modeling Workshop (ProSim 2000)*, London, 2000
12. Jacobson I., Booch G., and Rumbaugh J.: *The Unified Software Development Process.* Addison Wesley Longman, Inc. Reading MA, 1999
13. Stallinger F. and Grunbacher P.: System Dynamics Modeling and Simulation of Collaborative Requirements Engineering. *Proceedings of the Software Process Simulation Modeling Workshop (ProSim 2000)*, London, 2000.

A Simulation of the Market for Offenses in Multiagent Systems: Is Zero Crime Rates Attainable?

Pinata Winoto

Department of Computer Science, University of Saskatchewan
Saskatoon, Saskatchewan, SK S7N5A9, CANADA
piw410@mail.usask.ca

Abstract. The equilibrium of the market for offenses is studied by means of a multi-agent based simulation. The results show more detailed properties of the market's equilibrium compared to the theoretical results derived by Fender [8]. Some preliminary results are described.

1 Introduction

In the context of criminology, crimes can be grouped as economically driven crimes and non-economically driven crimes. Economically driven crimes (or *economic crime* for short) are primarily driven by financial gains and presumably follow the utilitarian concept, i.e., they are controlled by manipulating their pains (punishments) and gains (rewards). Generally, if there are victims left by a crime, it is called a predatory crime. In the human society, crime is a complex phenomenon. In the agent society, crime is less complex due to specific agent's intention/purpose. For instances, violating committed contract or colluding in an auction (committed by bidding agents), sending misleading information (committed by advertising agents), entering restricted area (committed by searching agents), killing a mobile agent or blocking a network channel, etc. The context of this paper is on the study of malicious-open agent society, which is characterized by economic and predatory crimes. The model used is based on the economic model of 'human' crime, which assumes that all criminals follow rational choice behavior. This model may fit well in agent society, especially if agents are pre-programmed to maximize their expected rewards.[1] Therefore, one of the potential applications of this study is to seek optimal policies in governing malicious agents created by human, as shown in the following example.

Example. Suppose there is an open electronic marketplace where software agents may join to sell/buy items (e.g. used PCs, books, etc.) via bargaining. Assume that a bargaining is always initiated by sellers (selling agents) who are looking for buyers (buying agents). In order to facilitate bargaining, the authority (e-market designer) allows an agent to negotiate with multiple agents (e.g. up to 5 other agents) at the same time, so that the agent may find a deal in a shorter time. However, a nasty buyer may replicate itself into 5 identical agents who negotiate with the same seller in an attempt to prevent its rivals (other buyers) from joining the negotiation, so that it has higher opportunity to get the item with lower price (i.e. an unfair competition). Realizing this situation, the authority will prevent any agent from replicating itself in a ne

---

[1] Agents may adopt random/mixed strategies, which violate the rational choice theory.

J.S. Sichman, F. Bousquet, P. Davidsson (Eds.): MABS 2002, LNAI 2581, pp. 181-193, 2003.

gotiation. For instance, by tracing the identity of all agents (owners' name or IP address) and punishing the offender if detected. However, the above action requires additional cost/investment, which can be collected from buyers (e.g. in terms of an additional maintenance fee). If the investment is high, then both the maintenance fee and the chance to detect an offender are high. But higher maintenance fee will reduce the gain made from a transaction. Conversely, if the maintenance fee is low, which follows by a lower chance to detect an offense, then the number of offenses will increase, which reduces the expected gain from the transaction due to unfair competition. ∎

Motivated by this kind of situation, the crime-prevention instruments in a multi-agent system (MAS) become our main research focus, e.g. what is the best policy to reduce the offense rate in MAS, and more generally, what is the appropriate theory of controlling the criminal behavior in MAS. A recent work by Fender [8] shows the existence of multiple equilibria (in terms of crime rate) in the market for offense, whose final equilibrium depends on several factors, such as initial crime rate, law enforcement and its productivity, punishment and reward from the crime, the distribution of the legal income (income inequality), and number of agents (potential victims and potential offenders) in the society. Some assumptions are applied in the model, such as, legal incomes follow uniform distribution, there is only one type of crime in the society, the punishment and reward from the crime are constant, the decision made by a criminal is based on von Neumann-Morgenstern expected utility, etc. And some comparative static results are derived to show the importance of each factor in affecting the final equilibrium. Moreover, the results also show the existence of stable equilibria (e.g. high and low crime rate equilibria); any crime rate will drive the society into either the highest or the lowest crime rate equilibrium. Intuitively, given a high level of the law enforcement and a low level of the crime rate, the probability to convict a crime is high; therefore any additional crime can easily be deterred. Conversely, given the same level of the law enforcement and a high level of the crime rate, the probability to convict a crime is low; therefore any additional crime is difficult to be deterred. However, the results only apply to the long-term phenomena of a large society, where the distribution of agents' properties is smooth and does not change over time, and all information is available to all agents (agents can learn and predict everything correctly). When these assumptions are relaxed, i.e. the distribution is not smooth and changes over time and agents do not have perfect foresight, the final equilibrium may not be exactly the same. An open MAS, such as in our previous example, is one of the examples. It may consist of hundreds or thousands of agents whose income is derived from an independent and identical distribution, they may enter or exit the system at anytime, and they may not gather all information correctly. The simulation described in this paper tries to simulate these situations. Using similar model, we have shown the deviations of the theoretical result in the presence of imperfect foresight [24]. In this paper, agents are assumed to have perfect foresight and the effect of the number of agents to the society's equilibrium is studied. The results show a significant deviation from the theoretical result, especially when the initial crime rate is very low. A deviation towards the lowest crime rate equilibrium is significant when the size of society is very small and the initial crime rate is low. Before we describe the simulation design, we will discuss the theoretical framework of the simulated society.

2 The Economic Theory of Crime

The first study of crime, by means of modern economic analysis, is the seminal work by Gary Becker [3]. Most of the current works by economists still follows genuine Beckerian methods, or mix it with other methods, such as game theory and information processing, e.g. [13, 19]. But all of them aim to minimize the social cost of crime based on economic principles. Some basic theoretical frameworks in criminal studies are:

- **Micro-level:** The decision of a person to participate in an illegitimate activity (crime) depends on:
  1. *The expected gain from that illegitimate activity.* There are three major factors affecting the expected gain, i.e.,
     - Net return from an illegitimate activity, U_1, which equals to the return from the illegitimate activity minus its direct costs.
     - Perceived probability of conviction, p_c.
     - Net return if convicted, U_2, which equals to U_1 minus punishment.

     It is commonly assumed that an offender behaves as if to maximize his expected utility, e.g. [3, 7, 8, 19]. Formally, the combination of those factors could be represented by the von Neumann-Morgenstern Expected Utility:

     $$EU_{crime} = (1 - p_c)\, U_1 + p_c U_2$$

  2. *Certain gain(s) from legitimate activities, U_{legal}.*
  3. *Taste (or distaste) and preference for crimes, U_{taste}* – "a combination of moral values, proclivity for violence, and preference for risk" [7].

  Generally, a person will commit crime if $EU_{crime} > U_{legal} + U_{taste}$. The right hand side constitutes the minimum value (threshold) for a person to enter the illegitimate market. If the value is big, then there might exist a group of people who never commit crime regardless of the penalty or conviction rate. The number of them will increase when EU_{crime} decreases.

- **Macro-level (Ehrlich [7]):** The market for offenses.
  1. The **Supply side** is determined by the distribution of "taste of crime", U_{taste}, or "legal income", U_{legal}, in the population. Where, higher expected return from crime causes higher participations in crime (the upward sloping of supply curve, see Fig. 1).
  2. The **Demand side** is determined by the tolerance toward crime, which is inversely related to the demand for self-protection and public-protection (investment in law enforcement sector). Higher crime rate induces higher self-protection and public-protection, which causes lower expected return from crime (downward sloping of demand curve, see Fig. 1).

- **Some innovations made:**
  Many innovations of the classical economic model of crime have been made. Among them:
  1. *Dynamic model:* Many recent studies have begun to explore dynamic deterrence models, e.g. [5, 12, 18]. The reason is that static models cannot

accommodate many phenomena including recidivism, discount factor of future punishment, accumulation of criminal skills, etc. Some modifications include:

- Using multiple-period rather than one-period framework. In a one-period model, each person has only an opportunity to choose whether or not to commit crime. In a multiple-period model, each person has many opportunities to choose from. This model can accommodate the study of recidivism [12].
- Adding the discount factor for future consumption and future punishment [5, 12].

2. **Information process and social interactions:** Sah [19] adds the Bayesian inference techniques into his model. The inference is used to model how potential offenders predict the probability of conviction from the information given by other people (cohorts, relatives, etc.). Under this model, Sah shows how different crime rates might occur under the same economic fundamentals.

3. **Experimental Economics:** Up to now, there is only one experiment (with human subjects) has been reported on a non-predatory crime, i.e. bribery [1]. The results show a significant effect of penalty to reduce crime. Another equation-based simulation was conducted by İmrohoroğlu *et al* [11] which shows the effect of income redistribution and investment in the law enforcement sector to crime control.

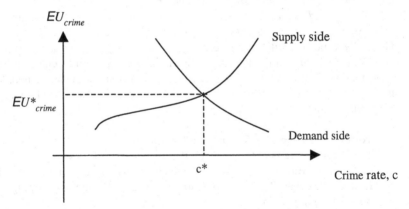

Fig. 1. The market for offenses (from Ehrlich [7])

While many literatures in economics have shown the existence of (theoretical) multiple equilibria in the crime market, e.g. [8, 11, 19], no experiments have been done to study their properties.

2.1 Underlying Equilibrium Theory

Through mathematical derivations, Fender [8] has shown that in the long run, there may exist multiple equilbria in the market for offenses (either stable or unstable equilibria). The underlying intuitions of the existence of the multiple equilbria are:

1. If the investment in law enforcement sector is constant and the crime rate is high and increases, then the conviction rate decreases (due to the diminishing marginal productivity of the investment in law enforcement sector). Thus, an illegitimate activity becomes more attractive and the number of criminals increases (high crime rate).
2. If the investment in law enforcement sector is constant and the crime rate is very low, then any marginal crime could be detected easily (stable low crime rate).

The basic assumptions are:

1. The economy consists of a population of n heterogeneous agents.
2. $(n-m)$ agents never commit crime (honest citizens).
3. The remainder, m, are potential offenders.
4. Honest citizens always work and receive w_h.
5. Potential offenders receive w_p from legitimate work; w_p is generated from a uniform distribution [$w_h - \alpha$, $w_h + \alpha$].
6. If a potential offender succeeds in his crime, his payoff is u_s.
7. But if he fails, he will be punished so that he will obtain u_f, which equals to u_s minus penalty.
8. Denote the number of criminals as C, then the number of non-criminals (workers) is $n-C$, and the number of crime per non-criminal is $C/(n-C)$.
9. Only law-abiding agents are potential victims. If the average loss from crime is l, then expected loss of each law-abiding agent is $lC/(n-C)$.
10. The government collects tax for their law enforcement expenditure E from all workers; the tax (in $) is equally distributed to all agents no matter how much they earn from work, which equals to $E/(n-C)$
11. Every potential offender follows von Neumann – Morgenstern Expected Utility, so that he will commit crime iff

$$pu_2 + (1-p)u_1 - w_h + (lC+E)/(n-C) > 0 \tag{1}$$

From those assumptions Fender derives the relationships between conviction rate p and the number of criminals C (EC locus):

$$p = \left[\frac{1}{u_s - u_f}\right]\left[u_s - 2\alpha\frac{C}{m} - w_h + \alpha + \frac{lC+E}{n-C}\right] \tag{2}$$

where p is bounded to [0, 1].

Another relationship between p and C (PP locus) can be derived from the relationship between the expenditure of law enforcement and the conviction rate as follows:

$$p = \min\left[1, \frac{G(E)}{C}\right] \tag{3}$$

The following graph (Fig. 2) is based on the following parameters: $n = 2000$, $m = 1000$, $E = \$100000$, $u_s = \$2000$, $u_f = \$500$, $\alpha = \$1000$, $w_h = \$2000$, $l = \$2000$, and $G(E) = E^{0.4}$.

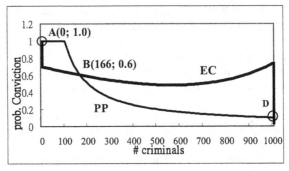

Fig. 2. Theoretical multiple equilibria in EC and PP locus

Fender believes that points A (0% crime rate) and D (100% crime rate) are both stable equilbria (see Fig. 2). He also believes that point B is an unstable equilibrium. A deviation from B to higher crime rate and/or low conviction rate (low probability of conviction) will drag the system to high crime equilibrium (D). However, the dynamic of the system is unknown. The simulations in this paper will test his conjectures for various initial conviction rates and number of agents.

3 A Simulation of the Market for Offenses

3.1 General Model

In addition to the assumptions made in [8], the following assumptions are added into the simulation:

A1. The society follows a 10-generations overlapping model.
All agents live for *10*-period of time, and during each period, a new generation will be born while the oldest die.

A2. The parameters used in the simulation are those shown in Fig. 2, except the number of agents.

A3. The society consists of half honest citizens (potential victims) and half potential offenders.
We choose 50:50 for the purpose of testing only. Some modifications may be more realistic and interesting, such as a non-dichotomous approach (e.g. different degree of honesty), or a dynamic approach (e.g. regret or learn from experience). However, these modifications do not conform to Fender's model.

A4. The society runs for 100 periods.

3.2 Interactions

Fig. 3 shows the interaction among three types of agents: potential offenders, honest citizens and the government. The simulation process follows the following algorithm:

Step1.   Initialize the agents' wage; generate it randomly from uniform distribution.

Step2.   For period = 1 to 100, repeat step3 until step4.

Step3.   All potential offenders make decisions on whether or not to commit crime. If a potential offender succeeds, he will get some money from his victim ($2000). If he fails, he will be punished (receive $500).

Step4.   The oldest generation dies, and a new generation are born. Update the social parameters, e.g., crime rate, conviction rate, number of criminals, etc.

All agents are interacted to produce a time series data, e.g. crime rate, conviction rate, etc.

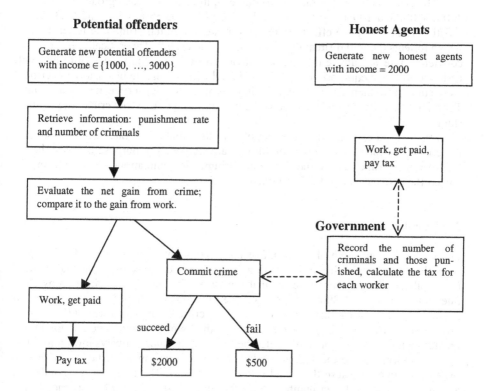

Fig. 3. The process of the simulation with three type of agents: potential offender, honest citizen, and government

3.3 Experiments

Due to the introduction of new generation in each period (which change the distribution of all agent's properties), the final equilibrium may not be the same as what is expected in theoretical analysis. Remember that, one important factor differentiating the simulation result and the analytical result is the random distribution of the agent's properties, i.e., the correctness of 'generated' distribution values from a specific random generator increases as the number of sampling increases. In other words, the correctness of the theoretical analysis relies on the correctness of the distribution value in the real world. If the number of agents in the real world is small, then the correctness of the theoretical analysis will be low. Therefore, from the real world's perspective, the result of a simulation will be better in predicting real world outcomes.

In the first experiment, five groups of treatments are conducted, each with approximately 10 different initial conviction rates. The difference between those five groups is the agents' population, i.e., 1000, 2000, 4000, 8000, and 10000. Moreover, every combination runs for 100 times, hence totally 5000 trials are conducted. The theoretical unstable equilibrium for each groups are calculated using numerical methods. The critical conviction rates of unstable equilibrium for each group (1000, 2000, 4000, 8000, and 10000 agents) are 56.18%, 60.23%, 63.35%, 65%, and 65.33%, respectively. To study the effect of conviction rate, the initial crime rate is set to zero, which reflects the initial situation of the society (no crime). Theoretically, if the initial conviction rate lies above the critical conviction rate, then the final equilibrium will be low crime rate equilibrium. And if the initial conviction rate lies below the critical conviction rate, then the final equilibrium *may* go to high crime rate equilibrium. Therefore, the investigated variable is the probability to attain low crime rate equilibrium.

In the second experiment, the effect of various initial crime rates with various initial conviction rates on the final equilibrium are studied. The purpose is to see the effect of initial crime rate on the final equilibrium. The simulations are written in MS Visual Basic 6 and run on PC PentiumIII-600MHz.

3.4 Results

Fig. 4 and 5 show some of the result of the experiments. The horizontal axis represents the initial probability of conviction, and the vertical axis represents the fraction (probability) of zero crime rate in final outcomes. In Fig. 4, the critical conviction rates for each group (C2000, C4000, etc.) are shown as the shaped points (square, triangle, etc.). It is shown that the right side of the critical points is always (100%) zero crime rates, while the left side varies. It means that, when the initial conviction rate is greater than the critical conviction rate, the final equilibrium is always low (zero). The result conforms to the theoretical result that the equilibrium is unstable to one side (low crime rate), because the initial crime rate is zero. The effect of the number of agents is significant: lower number of agents causes higher chance to drag the society into low crime rate equilibrium, which is shown as the length of horizontal curve in 100% probability to zero crime equilibrium. Currently, there is no explanation toward this phenomenon. However, when the population is high, the correctness of unstable equilibrium is high too (a steep transition from the high crime rate to the low crime rate).

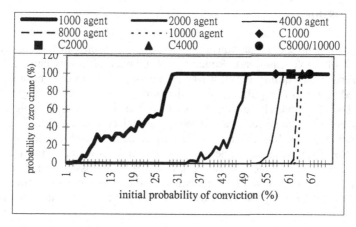

Fig. 4. The probability to attain zero crime rate stable equilibrium for various agent population and initial probability of conviction

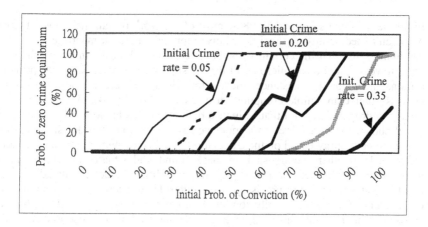

Fig. 5. The probability to attain zero crime rate stable equilibrium for various initial crime rate and initial probability of conviction

Fig. 5 shows the relationships between the probability to attain low crime rate in the various initial crime rate situations and various initial probabilities of conviction. One important result shown in Fig. 5 is that raising the initial probability of conviction cannot always successfully bring the society into zero crime rate equilibrium. For instance, when the initial crime rate is greater than 0.35, a certainty conviction rate in the initial simulation cannot drag the society into zero crime equilibrium. Intuitively, a high initial crime rate will reduce the expected income from legitimate work. Even in the presence of absolute punishment, the net income after being punished ($500 in our simulation) is still higher than the expected income if work legally (income minus expected loss being victimized minus tax); thus attract more potential offender to commit crime.

4 Discussion

It is shown from the simulation that the number of agents in the society affects the property of stable equilibria. Reducing the number of agents can help the society reach zero crime equilibrium. But when the expected return from crime is higher than expected return from legitimate work, the zero crime equilibrium may not be reached at all. Therefore, merely raising the probability of conviction (making investment in the law enforcement sector) may not bring the society into zero crime rate equilibrium as shown in Fig. 5. Many other factors may be helpful, such as increase punishment, reduce the return from the crime, raise the return from work, reduce income inequality, etc. Two issues related to our work that will be discussed further are the stand of rational choice theory in the simulation and the implication of multiagent-based simulation in the study of real world criminal behavior in both human society and MAS.

4.1 Rational Choice Theory: Is It Appropriate?

From the late 1960s until mid 1980s, most of the work on rational choice theory are based on expected-utility principle. Many empirical studies at macro level fit the theory in the sense that the certainty and severity of punishment can deter crime [6, 21, 25]. However, studies at micro level do not support the expected-utility principle in criminal behavior. For instance, most criminals use different kinds of information process other than simple computation of expected utility [4], and most crimes are related to drug and alcohol that influence their rational behavior [10]. Since 1986, rational choice theory evolves to a more general theory, i.e. the decisions to commit crime are not merely based on the calculation of expected punishment and reward, but influenced by other factors such as background and situational factors, previous learning and experience, etc [4]. Hence, rational choice model can be adopted to explain various crimes more precisely at the micro level, such as understanding white-collar crimes (tax evasion, collusion, etc.), organized crimes, professional thefts, etc. However, the rational choice model still cannot explain non-economically driven crimes (e.g. vandalism, aggravated assault, offenses against children, etc.). Recent studies show a tendency to integrate rational choice theory with other theories such as control balance theory [20], strain theory [2], developmental theory [15, 22], etc. into a general theory of crime. The motivation of it comes from the fact that most crimes are the results of complex process influenced by various factors described in those theories [16]. For example, rational choice model cannot be applied to high-moral people, who have high self-control to not to commit crime, but to low-moral people [14] (recall that Ehrlich [7] used the term taste and preferences of crime in his macro model).

Despite the development of rational choice theory in describing economically driven crimes, the classical model (e.g. based on the expected-utility function in equation 1) could still be used in the simulation at a macro level, i.e. by simplifying the complex decision-making process at a micro level (e.g. projecting various complex cognitive processes in humans or algorithms in agents into simple expected-utility formulae). The reason is that the complex processes can be seen as a black box with inputs/outputs according to the model being studied. For instance, intoxicated people can be represented by lowering their perceived probability of conviction, high-moral people can be represented by rising their taste of crime, learning or experience in crime can be represented by both lowering the perceived probability of conviction and rising the perceived net return from the crime, etc. Shrinking the complex decision-making processes into a set of simple formulae may not affect the simulation's output if the decision-making process can be treated as an indivisible process. However, if there is a complex interaction among agents during the process, e.g. potential victims can influence potential offenders' attitude toward crime either by persuasion or threat, then the simple expected-utility formulae are inadequate. Similarly, if the simulation purpose is to study the decision-making processes by criminals, such as the effect of self-control or psychopharmacological agents, then expected-utility formulae are inadequate. In this case, a more complex algorithm must be adopted in simulating the decision-making processes.

4.2 Multiagent-Based Simulation of the Market for Offenses: Is It Useful?

Simulating malicious behavior by means of a multiagent-based simulation is relatively new. At this stage, our studies only showed some differences between mathematical analysis and simulation-based analysis at the macro level. However, it must be acknowledged that the model used in our simulation does not completely reflect the real world situation. Some deficiencies of the model are:

- It uses dichotomous model of the taste of crime, i.e. an agent is either a potential offender or an honest citizen. Though this assumption may be true in MAS, i.e. agent are pre-programmed to be either malicious or not, it does not reflect the situation in human society. In fact, no real world data about the distribution of the taste of crime is available. The results of empirical studies, i.e. by interviewing subjects about their attitude in facing certain criminal scenario such as in [17], can only be applied in a very specific case and represent a specific group of people (e.g. students). The validity of this methodology (interviewing certain group of people about their moral belief) is very weak [23].
- The investment in law enforcement sector and its productivity do not change over time, which is not true in both MAS and human society.
- Agents do not learn over time, or acquire skills/confidence, or change their perceived probability of conviction. Again, this is not true in the real world, but may be true in a MAS in which all agents adopt simple algorithms or do not have enough opportunity to learn.
- The number of agents is constant over time and their lifespan are the same, which are not true in either MAS or human society. This assumption may be true in an open MAS in which the number and lifespan of participants is restricted and the demand to use the system is excessively high.
- The net return and punishment from crime and the income of honest citizens are constant, while the income of potential offenders follows a uniform distribution. These assumptions, which facilitate the mathematical derivation in [8], are not true in both MAS and human society. In fact, no exact income distribution is known in the real world, even if it can be approximated by log normal distribution.

- All agents have perfect foresight. This assumption may be fulfilled only in the perfect information situation, e.g. the authority announces the probability of conviction every day or potential offenders receive complete information from all other offenders. Again, this assumption may not be true in either MAS or human society. In [24], we have relaxed this assumption and showed that a high level of imperfect foresight may eliminate the low-crime-rate equilibrium.

Despite the weaknesses of the model used in the simulation, the simulation results described in this paper and also in [24] have shown the conditions to attain zero crime rate equilibrium that is substantially different from those in theoretical analysis. For instance, reducing the number of agents inside a society and lowering the initial crime rate have positive effects in deterring crime, which may be considered by a MAS's authority. Reducing the number of agents can be attained easily by restricted the agents to enter the system. And screening the first group of agents who enter the system can lower the initial crime rate. However, these actions must be taken carefully due to various assumptions explained above. At last, our simulation has shown the advantages of multiagent-based-simulation-based approach on the study of criminal behavior. The main difficulties in the study of criminal behavior are the ethical issue in conducting experiment with human subjects and the scalable issue in conducting a large-scale experiment. Obviously, multiagent-based simulation is a promising solution to overcome both of them.

5 Concluding Remarks and Future Directions

In this paper, we proposed the study of the market for offenses by means of multiagent-based simulation. We modified Fender's model to fit our simulation and derived some results based on it. The simulation results showed that the number of agents and initial crime rate in the society significantly affects the property of stable equilibria. Under certain condition, merely raising the probability of conviction (making investment in the law enforcement sector) may not bring the society into zero crime rate equilibrium. The results may be applied in a MAS if specific conditions, as discussed previously, are satisfied. We also introduced the economic theory of crime, which focuses on the rational choice model. Then, we discussed the appropriateness of adopting rational choice model in multiagent-based simulation. At last, some weaknesses of our approach are pointed out. With these weaknesses, we can derive some promising future developments as follows:

- Incorporating learning capability, such as agents can learn from other agents or from past experience (e.g. regret).
- Adopting more realistic distribution functions, such as log normal distribution function for agents' income, or various distribution functions to represent agents' *taste (or distaste) for crimes* as mentioned in [7].
- Introducing self-protection of potential victims.
- Introducing various types of crime with various returns and punishments.

Acknowledgements. This work is funded through a research assistantship from the Canadian Natural Sciences and Engineering Research Council. The author would like to thank Tiffany Y. Tang, Paul J. Brewer, Julita Vassileva and three anonymous reviewers for their comments and help.

References

1. Abbink, K., Irlenbusch, B., Renner, E.: An Experimental Bribery Game. SFB Discussion Paper B-459 (1999). (http://www.wiwi.uni-bonn.de/sfb/papers/B400-463.html)
2. Agnew, R.: Foundation for a General Strain Theory of Crime and Delinquency. Criminology, 30 (1992) 47–88.
3. Becker, G. S.: Crime and Punishment: An Economic Approach. Journal of Political Economy, 76 (1968) 169–217.
4. Cornish, D. B., Clarke, R. V. (eds.): The Reasoning Criminal: Rational Choice Perspectives on Offending. Springer-Verlag, (1986).
5. Davis, M.: Time and Punishment: An Intertemporal Model of Crime. Journal of Political Economy, 96 (1988) 383–90.
6. Ehrlich, I.: Participation in Illegitimate Activities: A Theoretical and Empirical Investigation. Journal of Political Economy, 81 (1973) 521–567.
7. Ehrlich, I.: Crime, Punishment, and the Market for Offenses. The Journal of Economic Perspectives, 10(1) (1996) 43–67.
8. Fender, J.: A General Equilibrium Model of Crime and Punishment. Journal of Economic Behavior & Organization, 39 (1999) 437–453.
9. Glaeser, E., Sacerdote, B., Scheinkman, J.: Crime and Social Interactions. Quarterly Journal of Economics, 111 (1996) 507–48.
10. Greenfeld, L. A.: Alcohol and Crime. Technical Report, US Dept. of Justice/BCJ NCJ 168632 (1998).
11. Imrohoroğlu, A., Merlo, A., Rupert, P.: On the Political Economy of Income Redistribution and Crime. Federal Reserve Bank of Minneapolis Research Department Staff Report 216 (1996).
12. Leung, S. F.: Dynamic Deterrence Theory. Economica, 62 (1995) 65–87.
13. Marjit, S., Shi, H.: On Controlling Crime with Corrupt Officials. Journal of Economic Behavior & Organization, 34 (1998) 163–72.
14. Patternoster, R., Simpson, S.: Sanction Threats and Appeals to Morality: Testing a Rational Choice Model of Corporate Crime. Law and Society Review, 30 (1996) 378–399.
15. Patterson, G., Yoerger, K.: Developmental Models for Delinquent Behavior. In Hodgins, S (ed.), Crime and Mental Disorder. Sage Publications, (1993).
16. Piquero, A. R., Tibbetts, S. G. (eds.): Rational Choice and Criminal Behavior: Recent Research and Future Challenges. Routledge, (2002).
17. Piquero, A. R., Hickman, M.: The Rational Choice Implications of Control Balance Theory. In Piquero, A. R., Tibbetts, S. G. (eds.): Rational Choice and Criminal Behavior: Recent Research and Future Challenges. Routledge, (2002) 85–107.
18. Polinsky, A. M., Rubinfeld, D.: A Model of Optimal Fines for Repeat Offenders. Journal of Public Economics, 46 (1991) 291–306.
19. Sah, R. K.: Social Osmosis and Patterns of Crime. The Journal of Political Economy, 99(6) (1991) 1272–1295.
20. Tittle, C. R.: Control Balance: Toward a General Theory of Deviance. Westview, (1995).
21. Trumbull, W. N.: Estimations of the Economic Model of Crime Using Aggregate and Individual Level Data. Southern Economic Journal, 56 (1989) 423–439.
22. Vila, B.: A General Paradigm for Understanding Criminal Behavior: Extending Evolutionary Ecological Theory. Criminology, 32 (1994) 311–360.
23. William, K. R., Hawkins, R.: Perceptual Research on General Deterrence: A Critical Review. Law and Society Review, 20 (1986) 545–572.
24. Winoto, P.: A Multi-Agent Based Simulation of the Market for Offenses. AAAI-02 Workshop on Multi-Agent Modeling and Simulation of Economic Systems, Edmonton, Canada, Technical Report WS-02-10, AAAI Press (2002) 66–71.
25. Witte, A. D.: Estimating the Economic Model of Crime with Individual Data. Quarterly Journal of Economics, 94 (1980) 57–84.

Author Index

Lecture Notes in Artificial Intelligence (LNAI)

Lecture Notes in Computer Science